GOD AND HUMAN SUFFERING

Louvain Theological and Pastoral Monographs is a publishing venture whose purpose is to provide those involved in pastoral ministry throughout the world with studies inspired by Louvain's long tradition of theological excellence within the Roman Catholic Tradition. The volumes selected for publication in the series are expected to express some of today's finest reflection on current theology and pastoral practice.

LOUVAIN THEOLOGICAL & PASTORAL MONOGRAPHS

——————————————— 3 ———————————————

GOD AND HUMAN SUFFERING

edited by
Jan Lambrecht
and Raymond F. Collins

PEETERS PRESS
LOUVAIN

ISBN 90-6831-210-3
D. 1990/0602/5

TABLE OF CONTENTS

FOREWORD

This publication is to a great extent the translation of the Dutch-language collection of essays, *Hoelang nog en waarom toch? God, mens en lijden* edited by Jan Lambrecht and published by Acco, Louvain/Amersfoort in 1988. On 28 and 29 October of 1987 the Faculty of Theology of the Catholic University of Leuven held a conference on suffering and Christian faith. More than a year earlier the Faculty Board had chosen the topic and indicated the procedure. The aim was to reflect on the sense and non-sense of suffering and to ask how suffering in this world influences our speaking about God. Where is God when humans suffer? How does Christian faith deal with suffering, with a suffering person? What does faith mean for us as we suffer?

The Board opted for an interdisciplinary *colloquium*. It was decided that no other faculties of the university would directly participate in our discussion. The six disciplines and departments of the Faculty of Theology were to be involved: bible, systematics, moral theology, church history, pastoral theology and liturgy. We also decided not to invite "outside experts." During these two days the professors and assistents of our own faculty would listen to one other; they would put forth their ideas and by force of their own arguments defend or reject specific theses. The publication of the discussion papers was planned from the outset. It was also decided that the conference should be prepared by the departmental meetings to be held during the 1986-1987 academic year — which happened in a quite satisfactory way. The introductory papers, however, that were presented were the personal responsibility of each of the speakers themselves; they did not necessarily represent the common opinion of the whole department.

The two days of the *colloquium* were organized as follows. Each day three introductions of about one hour were given, the first day by Jos Luyten, Joseph Selling and Cor Traets, the second by Jan Lambrecht, Georges De Schrijver and Kristiaan Depoortere. The papers were followed by an extended and lively discussion. On the first day there was also a public lecture, intended mainly for the students of the English program of the Faculty by Professor Frank De Graeve on "Suffering and Salvation: A Buddhist View." At the end of the second day and again on the following week, Johannes Van Bavel delivered two open conferences for the general university public. There were very well attended.

The present volume somewhat differs from the Dutch original. As in the Dutch book, the text of the public lecture by Frank De Graeve, not ready for publication, is absent. On the other hand, we asked Robrecht Michiels to treat the suffering of Jesus, a topic which had not been explicitly treated during the *colloquium*. With the exception of Mark Steen and Johan Vanhoutte, assistants in the department of systematic theology who are preparing doctoral dissertations on suffering, all contributors are professors of the Faculty. The bibliography at the end of the volume and the bibliographical references present in the other chapters have been shortened and adapted to the English speaking world.

The choice, method and style of each author have, as much as possible, remained unchanged. This provides the volume with its many-sidedness as well as its limitation. The same theme is studied by different disciplines, in a very different way. Profound reflection is to be found in this book. Scripture and tradition are treated. Current theological opinions are presented and discussed; much attention is devoted to men and women of today. Speculation is not severed from pastoral application. Yet, the chosen approach — human suffering and God — always controls and limits the content. Although these written texts do not do justice to the occasional heated arguments that erupted during the conference, it is hoped that through its manifold ideas the reader will be urged to critical reflection and a personal opinion.

With the double question of "how long" and "why" the prophet Habakkuk directs his complaint to God (Hab 1:2-3).

These and similar questions often introduce the Old Testament's individual lamentations. In calamity and illness, in war and persecution, and throughout the ages suffering believers have called out to their God, complaining, rebellious, and puzzled: how much longer and why must I suffer?

Jan Lambrecht and Raymond Collins
Louvain, All Saints, 1989

ABBREVIATIONS

In addition to the standard abbreviations of the English language and those in common use for the books of the Bible, the following abbreviations appear in this volume:

ANET	J.B. Pritchard, ed., *Ancient Near Eastern Texts Relating to the Old Testament*, 3rd. ed.: Princeton, NJ, 1969.
ASTI	*Annual of the Swedish Theological Institute*
BETL	Bibliotheca ephemeridum theologicarum lovaniensium
CBQ	*Catholic Biblical Quarterly*
EncJud	*Encyclopedia Judaica*
EvT	*Evangelische Theologie*
HTR	*Harvard Theological Review*
ICC	International Critical Commentary
ICEL	International Commission on English in the Liturgy
JBL	*Journal of Biblical Literature*
JES	*Journal of Ecumenical Studies*
JR	*Journal of Religion*
JSOTSup	Journal for the Study of the Old Testament, Supplement Series
LTK	*Lexikon für Theologie und Kirche*
OBO	Orbis biblicus et orientalis
OTL	Old Testament Library
PL	Patrologia latina
QD	Quaestiones disputatae
RB	*Revue biblique*
RTL	*Revue théologique de Louvain*
TLZ	*Theologische Literaturzeitung*
TOB	Traduction oecuménique de la Bible
TQ	*Theologische Quartalschrift*
TWAT	G.J. Botterweck and J. Ringgren, eds., *Theologisches Wörterbuch zum Alten Testament*
USQR	*Union Seminary Quarterly Review*
VTSup	Vetus Testamentum, Supplements
WMANT	Wissenschaftliche Monographien zum Alten und Neuen Testament
WUNT	Wissenschaftliche Untersuchungen zum Neuen Testament
ZAW	*Zeitschrift für die alttestamentliche Wissenschaft*
ZTK	*Zeitschrift für Theologie und Kirche*

PERSPECTIVES ON HUMAN SUFFERING IN THE OLD TESTAMENT

Jos Luyten

A Complex and Evolving "Theological" Perspective on Suffering

While several theologies of the Old Testament have seen the light of day since the 1930's,[1] none offers an independent and systematic treatment of suffering in the Old Testament. This topic has, however, been the subject of several more recent studies. Three of them deserve mention here: an article by Ernst Kutsch, "Von Grund und Sinn des Leidens nach dem Alten Testament" (1974);[2] a lecture by Otto Kaiser (1983), "Von der Gerechtigkeit Gottes nach dem Alten Testament";[3] and an article by Horst Dietrich Preuss, "Die Frage nach dem Leid des Menschen – ein Versuch biblischer Theologie"(1987).[4]

Among these authors the biblical theological approach dominates. Preuss, in his striving for a "common biblical theology," goes so far as to propose an "Overview of the Testaments from the perspective of the theme of human suffering," which for him

---

1. See, especially, the works of W. Eichrodt, L. Köhler, Th.C. Vriezen, G. von Rad; cf. H.G. Reventlow, *Hauptprobleme der alttestamentlichen Theologie im 20. Jahrhundert* (Ertrage der Forschung, 173) Darmstadt, 1982.

2. This article appeared in H. Schultze (ed.), *Der leidende Mensch*, Neukirchen-Vluyn, 1974, pp. 73-84; reprinted in E. Kutsch, *Kleine Schriften zum Alten Testament*, Berlin, 1986, pp. 336-347.

3. This lecture first appeared in print in O. Kaiser, *Der Mensch unter dem Schicksal. Studien zur Geschichte, Theologie und Gegenwartsbedeutung der Weisheit*, Berlin, 1985, pp. 154-181.

4. In, *Altes Testament und Christliche Verkündigung*, A.H.J. Gunneweg *Festschrift*, Stuttgart, 1987, pp. 52-80. On page 54, note 6, the author gives a selection of the most important publications between 1926 and 1983 dealing with the theme of "suffering."

means, in large measure, to place the Old Testament under the criticism of the New. Our attention will be exclusively directed to Old Testamental images of suffering which, apart from any explicitly biblical theological evaluation, are to be examined especially in their diversity of form and, to a degree, in their origin and development as well.

In the preface to his work titled, *Suffering as Divine Discipline in the Old Testament and Post-biblical Judaism* (1955), James A. Sanders postulates that there are eight answers to the problem of suffering in the Old Testament: "Briefly, sufferings are retributive, disciplinary, revelational, probational, illusory (or transitory), mysterious (only God has Wisdom), eschatological, or meaningless." As is evident from the title he limits his research to just one of those "eight solutions." If one were to take into account all possible variations on those basic positions, the list provided by Sanders could be lengthened considerably.

On the other hand, the reactions to suffering and the reflections offered by the Old Testament might be reduced to three fundamental tendencies: suffering is punishment for sin, suffering is absurd, and suffering is a source of renewal. In the texts to be considered these three fundamental tendencies not only run parallel with each other, they are also intertwined. A few brief remarks might prove useful as an introduction to these three biblical perspectives on suffering.

As the study of Josef Scharbert, *Der Schmerz im Alten Testament*[5], has shown, biblical Hebrew has many terms denoting many different forms of pain and sorrow. It does not possess, however, one term carrying the same wide field of meaning as does our word "suffering."[6] Furthermore, in Hebrew the same terms are often used to express concepts which may be very different for us. For example, the hiphil of the verb *yakah* may mean, depending on the context, "reprimand," "punish,"

---

5. **BBB**, 8, Hanstein, 1953.

6. The biblical term most closely approaching this breadth of meaning is probably *mak'ob,* as it is used in Exod 3:7; Isa 53:3-4; Lam 1:12,18; Ecc 1:18; 2:23. It appears only sixteen times (cf. the article *"k'b" TWAT*, 4, 8-13).

"discipline," "mediate," or "do justice." [7] This polyvalence makes it sometimes difficult to determine precisely which form of suffering is meant in a specific text.

Where the Old Testament speaks about suffering, it deals primarily with concrete or incidental suffering, with extraordinary and brutal disturbances in the life of an individual or community — such as serious illness, sterility, untimely death or the consequences of war, pestilence, famine, and other disasters. The curse-lists of Leviticus 26 and Deuteronomy 28 are pertinent illustrations of this perspective. No or little distinction is made among different forms of suffering. All attention is directed to the subject of suffering: it is the whole human being who suffers. [8]

Divinity is the Prime Mover, the *Urheber*, of suffering. This outlook belongs to the dynamistic worldview of the Ancient Near East in general. Because of biblical monotheism this is true of Yahweh, the God of Israel, to an even greater degree. It is peculiar to the Old Testament that intermediate agencies such as demons, angels, spirits of the dead, personifications of divine attributes and impersonal or magical powers such as magic, curses, or fate are rarely mentioned. When viewed in the total biblical perspective, they fulfill only a very secondary role. On this point it is of course possible to object that in ancient Israel there was a wide gap between the beliefs of the faithful elite and those shared by the rest of the population. [9] Isa 45:7 nonetheless may be viewed as representative of the entire Old Testament: "I am Yahweh, and there is no other who forms the light and creates darkness, who brings prosperity and creates disaster."

---

7. Cf. *TWAT*, 3, 620-628.
8. Cf. Preuss, *Die Frage*, pp. 54-57.
9. Cf. R. Albertz, *Persönliche Frömmigkeit und offizielle Religion. Religionsinterner Pluralismus in Israel und Babylon*. Calwer theologische Monogrien, A, 19, Stuttgart, 1978.

Suffering as Punishment for Sin

Collective Retribution

That suffering is punishment for sin and guilt is clearly the
perspective which dominates the Old Testament from beginning
to end. It is to be found in narrative texts and prophetic oracles,
in psalms and wisdom literature. Because of their contemporary
context the law texts can also be seen from this perspective. In the
beginning of the Decalogue as an introduction to the law corpus
of the Pentateuch, it is said: "I, Yahweh your God, am a jealous
God, punishing the children for the sin of the fathers to the third
and fourth generation." (Exod 20:5)
The curse-list which brings to a close the entire collection of laws
in Deuteronomy 28 begins in verse 15 with the warning: "However, if you do not obey Yahweh your God and do not carefully
follow all his commands and decrees I am giving you today, all
these curses will come upon you and overtake you" (Deut 28:15).

This general rule is commonly expressed in speaking about
God's wrath which is ignited against the individual or the
community and is expressed in all sorts of calamity.[10] Deploying
both old and new material, K. van der Toorn[11] has once again
clearly demonstrated that in the Ancient Near East in general the
gods are viewed as guarantors of law and order on the one hand,
and that, on the other, all manner of disasters, calamities and
illnesses are ascribed to the wrath of the gods. In Israel this image
of a causal connection between suffering and divine punishment
has its own application and evolution.

10. Some typical examples are found in Deut 29:19; 32:21-22; Jer 15:13-14;
Ezek 24:14; Isa 65:5; and Ezra 9:14.
11. *Sin and Sanction in Israel and Mesopotamia. A Comparative Study* (Studia
Semitica Neerlandica, 22), Assen, 1985, especially chapters three and four. The
root *'np* — a term used in connection with divine wrath — also appears on the
stele of King Mesa (cf. 2 Kgs 3:4) of about 840: "When Omri was King of Israel,
he humbled Moab many years, for Chemosh was angry at his land" (cf. *ANET*,
1955[2], 321).

The prophets from the eighth to the sixth century, identified by means of their threats and exhortations, particular sins which especially offended Yahweh, the Holy One of Israel. These specifically concerned the various forms of social injustice (Isa 1:15; Jer 5:26-28; Amos 5:7,10-12; Mic 3:1-3), the stubborn and shortsighted foreign politics of the court (Isa 30:1-5; 31:1-3; Jer 2:35-37; Ezek 16:26; Hos 5:13), and the syncretistic worship[12] which so provoked the wrath of Yahweh. In consequence, "the Day of Yahweh" actually becomes a day of darkness (Amos 5:18), the land dries up (Hos 4:3), and hostile armies overwhelm the country, destroy the cities, and decimate the population or carry the people into captivity (Isa 5:25-30; Jer 4:5-31; Ezek 21:23-32).[13]

One must not forget the fact that the fall of the Northern Kingdom with the conquest and destruction of Samaria by the Assyrians in 722, the destruction of Jerusalem and its temple by the Babylonians in 587, and the Babylonian exile have all been particularly determinative for the biblical presentation of Israel's history. It is especially after its total downfall as an independent state and nation — thus during and after the exile — that Israel began to portray its whole history as one of sin and punishment.

Despite the complexity of the texts and all the possible layers to be found in them, this narrative pattern dominates the deuteronomistic history (Joshua to 2 Kings). This is also the notion

12. What is in the first place under consideration here is the exclusive adoration of Yahweh as the God of Israel, and not the criticism of the cultus or the fertility religion as such. "In fact, the main purpose of prophetic activity in Israel was to demonstrate convincingly that Yahwism was *the* fertility religion," concludes H.M. Barstad, *The Religious Polemics of Amos. Studies in the Preaching of Am 2:7B-8; 4:1-13; 5:1-27; 6:4-7; 8:14* (VTSup, 34) Leiden, 1984, p. 10 (a footnote refers to Jer 14:22; Hos 2:8-9; Am 4:6ff.). Cf. in this connection B. Lang, "Zur Entstehung des biblisches Monotheismus," *TQ* 166 (1986) 135-142, including an extended bibliography.

13. Cf. J. Blenkinsopp, *A History of Prophecy in Israel*, Philadelphia, 1983, pp. 80-137: III. The Period of Assyrian Expansion, and pp. 138-176: The End of National Independence; see also O. Kaiser, *op. cit.*, who finds Hos 4:1-2 to be: "die eindrucksvollste, die Vergehen gegen Jahwe und den Nächsten zusammenfassende Anklage."

that we find as a set pattern in several texts in which Israel's history is evoked and summed up: the prophetic "Geschichts-reden" of Ezekiel 16, 20, and 23, the history lesson of Psalm 78, the national confession of Psalm 106, the penitential prayers of Ezra 9:3-15; Neh 9:6-37; Dan 9:4-19; Bar 1:15-3:8, and the so-called expanded or broken requisitory of Deuteronomy 32:1-43. Israel eventually placed not only the period stretching from the settlement of the land until the Babylonian exile but also the whole of its prehistory under the sign of sin and punishment.

The backward glance which Israel casts at its past from the viewpoint of its experience of national downfall and exile is clearly evident in the Pentateuch, the deuteronomistic history, and other texts. This interpretation seems to be dominated by the tendency to project the scheme of a history of sin and punishment ever farther back into the past, on the one hand, and, on the other, to ever more radicalize the notion of solidarity in sin and the interconnection of sin and punishment. When we survey Israel's history from end to beginning, employing the Fall of Jerusalem in 587 as a watershed, we are confronted with an historical review consisting of a series of steps:

— that Yahweh allowed Judah to fall "because of the sin of Manasseh" (2 Kgs 24:3; Jer 15:4);

— that the Northern Kingdom fell primarily because of those kings of Israel (2 Kgs 17:8) who persisted in "the sins of Jeroboam;"[14]

— that the division of the Davidic Kingdom is blamed on Solomon, who in his old age let himself be tempted into the service of other gods (1 Kgs 11:3-13,29-36). Yet here also the punishment takes place only after the death of the criminal;

— that the kingship of Saul ends with a severe defeat for the Israelites and the death of their king on Mount Gilboa (2 Sam

---

14. See 1 Kgs 12:28-33; 15:26,34; 16:13,19,26; 21:22,53; 2 Kgs 3:3; 10:31; 13:2,6,11; 14:24; 15:9,18,24; 17:21-22; see also 2 Kgs 18:11-12; cf. E.T. Mullen, "The Sins of Jeroboam: A Redactional Assessment," *CBQ* 49 (1987) 212-231.

31) because he had disobeyed Yahweh and his prophet (1 Sam
13:7b-14 and 15:8-29);[15]
— that in the time of the Judges, after the death of Joshua and
following the death of every judge thereafter, the Israelites
become progressively apostate, break the covenant with Yahweh,
and time and again are punished by lengthy years of oppression
at the hands of the Moabites, Canaanites, Midianites, Ammonites
and Philistines (Judg 2:10-3:6; 3:7ff.; 4:1ff.; 6:1ff.; 10:6ff.;
13:1ff.);[16]
— that during the wilderness journey the entire community
repeatedly tests Yahweh, grumbles, rebels, apostasizes, and is
each time immediately and severely punished (Exod 32:1-35;
Num 11:1,10,33-34; 14:1-4,22-23,26-37; 16:1-35; 21:4-6; 25:1-9).
Sins, such as the worship of the Golden Calf (Exod 32), and
punishments, such as the forty-years of wandering (Num 14:33;
Deut 2:14), function as prototypes of later sins and punishments.[17]

In speaking of the *nations*, it also becomes apparent that in the
prophetic oracles the pattern of suffering as punishment for sin
holds true not only with regard to Israel's immediate neighbors
(Amos 1:3-2:3; Isa 15-17; 23; Jer 47-49; Ezek 25-28) but also in
regard to the superpowers: Egypt, Assyria, and Babylonia (Isa
13-14; 18-19; 21; Jer 25:15-38; 46; 50-51; Ezek 29-32). When
surveying these last texts there is a notable tendency to systematize

15. Cf. F. Foresti, *The Rejection of Saul in the Perspective of the Deuteronomistic School. A Study of 1 Sm 15 and Related Texts* (Studia Theologica —
Teresianum, 5) Rome, 1984.
16. Cf. A.D.H. Mayes, *Judges* (Old Testament Guides, 3), Sheffield, 1985, who
distinguishes between the literary context of the individual "deliverer stories," with
their ever-recurrent scheme of sin-punishment-deliverance, and the deuteronomistic redaction of Judges — especially manifest in chapters 2:11-3:6, and 10:6-16
— which modifies the cyclic presentation of history "by describing history in linear
terms as a time of increasing sin (Judg 2:19)" (pp. 33-34).
17. Cf. J.Vermeylen, "L'affaire du veau d'or (Ex 32-34): une clé pour la
'question deutéronomiste'?," *ZAW* 97 (1985) pp. 1-23, according to whom the
first of the five different redactions of Exodus 32-34 already originated during the
aftermath of the Fall of Jerusalem of which it attempts an explanation.

and radicalize the principle of collective retribution in relation to
both the past and the future:

— the autochthons are so wicked that they must be exterminated
(Exod 23:23-33; 34:11-17; Deut 7:1-5; Jos 3:10; 24:12,18 etc.).
Every act of stubborness on Pharaoh's part is punished with a
special plague which each time afflicts the entire nation of Egypt
(Exod 7-12);

— on the other hand, the punishment of the nations in the end
times becomes not only a cosmic judgment but also an unmea-
sured slaughter on which occasion Yahweh himself brandishes
the sword with such fury that his clothes are entirely spattered
with blood (Isa 24; 34; 63:1-6; Ezek 38-39; Joel 4; Zech 14).

Individual Retribution

Since ancient times, within and without Israel, in connection with
the infraction of laws, the breaking of contracts and treaties, as
well as in relation to individual illness and adversity, a picture of
individual retribution is drawn in which it is understood to be
both immanent, as "the relation of cause and effect," and transcendent, as divine retribution.[18] In Israel, the idea of *suffering as
punishment for individual guilt* developed especially in post-exilic
times, the time in which the Law became the charter of the
faithful community and in which, next to the prophets and
Levites, the sages and the scribes became ever more the spiritual
educators of the nation.

Even though the "we have sinned together with our fathers"
(Ps 106:6; cf. Lev 26:40; Dan 9:16) will remain a typical Jewish
confession,[19] the emphasis on and the increasing systematization
of the doctrine of individual retribution have also been the result

18. Cf. K. van der Toorn, *op. cit.*, pp. 40-55: 3. The Divine Custodians.
Immanent and Transcendant Foundations of the Moral Order.

19. Compare J. Scharbert, "Unsere Sünden und die Sünden unserer Väter,"
BZ 2 (1958) pp. 14-26.

of a reaction against an interpretation of suffering which gave the generations after 587 the bitter feeling that they were doomed to continue atoning for the sins of all their predecessors: "Our fathers sinned and are no more, and we bear their punishment" (Lam 5:7), or again, "The fathers have eaten sour grapes, and the children's teeth are set on edge" (Jer 31:29; cf. Ezek 18:2).

Not only Lamentations 5, Jer 31:29-30, and Ezekiel 18 and 33 but also a variety of other texts, ranging from one word to an entire pericope, bear witness to this reaction. These latter seem to be built into their contemporary context as correctives. We may cite as examples: Ezek 9:4; 20:35-38; Gen 18:22b-33; Exod 20:5 and Deut 5:9 ("... of them that hate me"; cf. Exod 34:7; Num 14:18).[20]

Even though the Chronicler concurs with the interpretation proposed in the deuteronomistic history — namely, that the fall of Israel was ultimately a punishment for its infidelity to Yahweh since the Hebrew people settled in the country right up until the destruction of their chief city and temple (1 Chr 2:7; 5:25-26; 9:1; 2 Chr 29:6-9; 30:6-9; 36:14-16) — he fundamentally shifts the perspective. He does this especially by adopting the standard of individual retribution for his revision of the history of the Davidic monarchy. We read of numerous kings who aptly illustrate the principle: a king who suffers from a foot disease, such as that which afflicted Asah (compare 2 Chr 16:12 with 1 Kgs 15:23); one who contracts leprosy, Uzziah (compare 2 Chr 26:16-21 with 2 Kgs 15:5); and others like Amaziah who fell victim to conspiracy (compare 2 Chr 25:20,27 with 2 Kgs 14:19) or like Josiah who was slain in battle at Megiddo (cf. 2 Chr 35:20-23 with 2 Kgs 23:29). In every instance the Chronicler indicates the trans-

20. In connection with Gen 18, C. Westermann, in *Genesis*. BKAT, I/2, 1981, p. 348, speaks of "die Frage nach Jahwes Geschichtshandeln," which could have only arisen in Israel after the year 587; in connection with the addition to Exod 20:5 and Deut 5:9, A.D.H. Mayes, in his *Deuteronomy*. NCB, 1981, p. 167, states: "The additional phrase ... apparently derives from the deuteronomic compiler of the decalogue."

gressions by which these royal figures have brought down guilt upon themselves and have thus merited such miserable fates. Parallels in 1 and 2 Kings, however, communicate nothing of the kind to us in this regard.[21]

Suffering is most extensively and emphatically interpreted as punishment for individual sin in the poetic dialogue of the book of Job. Eliphaz, Bildad and Zophar appeal to their own experience (15:17), to tradition (8:8-10; 15:18-19), and even to special illumination (4:12-16) in order to postulate their foremost theses: "Those who plow evil and sow trouble reap the same" (4:8); "All his days the wicked suffers torment" (15:20); "Calamity is hungry for him... it eats away parts of his skin" (18:12a,13a); "An unfanned fire will devour him" (20:23). The misery and suffering of Job clearly prove that God is accusing and punishing him, not because of his piety but because of his boundless guilt (15:4-6; 22:4-11).

In spite of the protests advanced by Job himself and those of the Ecclesiast, to which we will later return, the doctrine upheld by Job's friends remains the dominating conviction in the more recent proto- and deuterocanonical works such as Esther, Judith, Tobit, 1 and 2 Maccabees and Sirach. Says Sirach, referring exclusively to a this-worldly retribution: "And had there been but one stiffnecked man, it were a wonder had he gone unpunished; each receives his reward according to his deeds" (16:11a,14b).

21. According to G.von Rad, *Theologie des Alten Testaments*, I, Munich, 1962[4], the author of the deuteronomistic history still honors an "altertümlich anmutendes Kollektivdenken" (p. 357), while the Chronicler seeks to show "dass das Gericht oder Heil Jahwes noch immer jede Generation ganz individuell erreicht hat" (p. 361). W. Johnstone, "Guilt and Atonement: The Theme of 1 and 2 Chronicles," in the W. McKane *Festschrift*. JSOTSup, 42, Sheffield, 1986, takes a somewhat different view: "If one were to be bold, one would say that, as the 'Deuteronomistic History' from Deuteronomy to 2 Kings constitutes an aggadic midrash on the levitical doctrine of the blessing and curse of the covenant, so Chronicles constitutes an aggadic midrash on the complementary levitical (including priestly) doctrine of guilt and atonement" (p. 125).

Universal Sinfulness and Existential Suffering

In the primeval history (Gen 1-11) the cosmos is pictured as a crescending symphony of light, movement, life, and beauty. The harmony and solidarity of all creation, between man and woman and between God and the world, gradually emerges from the initial chaos only to subsequently return to chaos in ever-increasing outbursts of human disobedience, violence, immorality, and pride. Myths, legends and genealogies, all of which are largely borrowed from neighboring nations and autochthons, are intertwined and shaped into a new history of humankind which, possibly in different stages, reflect Israel's view of its own history.[22]

The image of suffering as punishment for sin is further radicalized at this point. Apart from the almost complete annihilation of the human race through the flood, the results of sin signify in the main the ever-widening gap between God and humanity as well as the growing alienation among human beings themselves. The primeval history especially underscores the universal and existential character of the intimate connection between suffering and sin. All persons are sinful and the entire existence of humankind is marked by sinfulness and suffering.

These ideas, poignantly illustrated in the story of the Fall (Gen 3:16-19) and in the Flood-story (Gen 6:5, 8:21), are also expressed, albeit more fragmentarily, in a dozen other texts. Thus, in the book of Job it is stated both by Job and his friends, as many as four times, that no mortal being, no one born of a

22. In recent studies, not only the primeval history in its entirety but also its so-called "Yahwistic" level are increasingly viewed as relatively late compositions (cf. the studies of H.H. Schmid, F.V. Winnett, J. Van Seters, M. Rose, H.C. Schmitt). A clearly delimited thesis of the origin and meaning of the entire primeval history is offered by Susan Niditch, *Chaos to Cosmos. Studies in Biblical Patterns of Creation*, Chico, CA, 1984. We quote here only briefly: "The very collecting, preserving, and ordering of the creation myths of Israel is part of the process of self-definition after the exile and an expression of the nationalism which follows the defeat of the Babylonians. Genesis 1-11 exemplifies the renewed interest in Israel's ancient myths one finds in other sixth century B.C. works such as Zechariah 1-8. The way in which the myths are combined in Genesis 1-11 traces a depressing pattern of increasing evil" (p. 66).

woman, can be just before God (4:17; 14:4; 15:14; 25:4; cf. 1
Kgs 8:46; Jer 17:9; Ps 51:7; 130:3; 143:2; Prov 20:9; Ecc 7:29).
All these statements, both in their formulation and with regard to
the context from which they proceed, remain ambiguous in
intent. They may point to a radicalizing of human sinfulness and
the nexus of its dreadful results. They may also have in view a
deeper relativization of guilt and deserved punishment insofar as
the individual human being is concerned.

Suffering is Absurd

Voices of Protest in the Ancient Near East

Alongside the many texts from the Ancient Near East in which
the gods are pictured as guarantors of justice and avengers of
evil, there is also a number of passages which place the responsibility for disorder, including all the evil and suffering in the
world, partially or entirely with the gods. Thus, in the *The
Admonition of Ipu-wer*, a prophetic writing which is said to have
originated in the turbulent period of transition between the Old
and Middle Egyptian Kingdoms, it is bitterly complained that all
the trials and diseases which trouble human beings result from
the fact that divinity has created humanity with an evil disposi-
tion and permits it to continue to exist. [23]

In the *Lamentation Over the Destruction of Sumer and Ur*, the
four leading deities − An, Enlil, Enki, and Ninhursag − plot,
without the slightest religious or moral motivation, to destroy all
the cities of Sumer as well as the capital city Ur with its palace

23. Cf. J.B. Pritchard, ed., *Ancient Near Eastern Texts Relating to the Old
Testament. ANET*, Princeton, NJ, 1969[3], pp. 441-444; J. Assmann, *Ägypten.
Theologie und Frömmigkeit einer frühen Hochkultur*. Urban-Taschenbücher, 366,
Stuttgart, 1984, p. 201.

and temple, and deliver their inhabitants over to the barbaric Gutians and Elamites.[24] According to the *Atrahasis-epic* the heavy labor of agriculture and irrigation was initially to be performed by the lower Igigu gods. When after forty years they rebel and organize a general strike, the greater gods — Enlil, Anum, and Enki — decide to create humans and force them to do this heavy labor. Because he is disturbed by the noise of these humans during his sleep, Enlil tries three times to annihilate humanity by way of pest, famine, and, finally, by a great flood.[25]

In the *Babylonian Theodicy*, a wisdom dialogue from the Cassite period, a man heavily afflicted by suffering asserts in a discussion with his orthodox companion that the godless flourish while the pious wither away and that the divine triad — the deities Narru, Zulummar and the goddess Mami — which formed humans out of clay made them liars and unreliable from the very beginning, with the result that the rich in the land reap nothing but success while the poor are oppressed to death.[26]

Dissonant Voices in Israel

Parallel with the line of thought in the above-mentioned texts from Israel's surroudings, one may discern throughout the Old Testament a second antithetical tendency which alleges that the suffering of humankind is undeserved, meaningless, and absurd.

This discordant theme resounds in what Gunkel calls "The Reproach of God" found in the individual and collective lamentations in which Yahweh is asked why he hides himself in times of need (Ps 10:1) and how long his wrath will burn against

24. *ANET*, pp. 611-619; in A. Falkenstein — W. von Soden, *Sumerische und Akkadische Hymnen und Gebete*, Zurich, 1953, the lamentation spoken of is still wrongly presented as two separate complaint songs: "Ibbisin-Klage" (no. 37, pp. 189-192) and "Klage um die Zerstörung von Ur" (no. 38, pp. 192-213).

25. *ANET*, pp. 104-106 and 512-514; K.R. Veenhof, "Het Atrachasis-epos," *Phoenix* XVI (1970) 390-396.

26. *ANET*, pp. 601-604; W. Beyerlin, *Religionsgeschichtliches Textbuch zum Alten Testament*, Göttingen, 1975, pp. 157-160.

his people (Ps 79:5). He is reproached for having delivered his people into the hands of the enemy like cattle for slaughter and disperses them among foreign nations even though they have not forgotten him and have not broken his covenant (Ps 44:12-18). He is equally charged that his terrors and fits of anger are like floodwaters overwhelming an already sick and dying person (Ps 88:16-18).

Wails of protestation ascend from the Lamentations when the people cry out that Yahweh has humiliated Zion, that he has mercilessly destroyed the dwelling of Jacob, that he killed those most dear to Zion as if they were enemies, and that he has destroyed his own temple. Children and the elderly, girls and boys, all lie in the dust, murdered on the day of his pitiless wrath.

The lamentations of the prophets also strike this dissonant chord, and in particular the so-called "confessions" of Jeremiah, the called-one who feels himself betrayed and overpowered by a God who has given him nothing to announce but misfortune. The prophet leads a dejected and lonely life, cursing the day on which he was born (Jer 15:17-18; 20:7,14-18).[27]

These gloomy and bitter complaints are nevertheless — and this, by the way, goes for most texts from the Ancient Near East — usually subdued, relativized and even contradicted by the context. A lone exception is Psalm 88, a bitter complaint from beginning to end. The conclusion of Psalm 39 is also unique in this regard: "Look away from me, that I may rejoice again, before I depart and am no more."

Such utterances in the prophetic oracles are even repeatedly put in the mouth of the people and forthwith reproved as irreverent and unrighteous: "Why do you say, O Jacob, and complain, O Israel, 'My way is hidden from Yahweh; my cause is disregarded by my God'?" (Isa 40:27), or, again, "You have wearied Yahweh

27. Cf. Jer 45:3; Isa 48:4a; 1 Kgs 19:4; Num 11:11-15. Cf. James L. Crenshaw, *A Whirlpool of Torment.* Overtures to Biblical Theology, 12, Philadelphia, 1984: Ch. 2. Seduction and Rape: The Confessions of Jeremiah (pp. 31-56). See also H. Mottu, *Les "confessions" de Jérémie: une protestation contre la souffrance.* Le Monde de la Bible, Geneva, 1985.

with your words. 'How have I wearied him?,' you ask. By saying, 'All who do evil are good in the eyes of Yahweh, and he is pleased with them,' or 'Where is the God of justice?'" (Mal 2:17).[28]

As described above, such national lamentations are retrojected into Israel's past and radicalized. Several texts may be cited as examples of this reinterpretation, in particular the story of the wanderings in the desert, thus, "And he called the place Massah and Meribah, because the Israelites quarreled, and because they tested Yahweh, saying: 'Is Yahweh among us or not?'" (Exod 17:7), and "You grumbled in your tents and said: 'Yahweh hates us, so he brought us out of Egypt to deliver us into the hands of the Amorites to destroy us'" (Deut 1:27).[29] Disregarding the rare exceptions, all the laments mentioned up till now undoubtedly have the catastrophe of 587 looming in the near or distant historical consciousness.

The protest against suffering that is experienced as undeserved and meaningless reaches its climax in the *speeches* of Job. These extend over some seventeen chapters of the book and give expression to two types of protestation that appear partly in an alternating and partly in an ascending line in the development of the text. The first type generally assumes the forms of curse, complaint, or death wish. These forms are dictated by the brief and sorrowful existence of the human being, but they are also motivated by Job's own physical decline, psychological confusion, and social alienation (3:3-26; 6:5-20; 7:1-11; 9:25-28; 10:18-22; 14:1-2: 17:1-2,13-16; 19:13-20; 30:1-31). On the other hand, there are Job's declarations of innocence and his accusations against a God who relentlessly cross-examines him in the manner of a Grand Inquisitor; who leaps on him as would a beast of prey; who harasses him with troops and weapons; who takes no heed whatsoever of Job's pleas for justice; who, finally, allows the wicked to flourish even as the innocent fade away (6:4; 7:12-20; 9:16-24; 10:2-17; 13:23-28; 16:7-14; 19:7-12; 21:7-16; 23:8-14; 31:1-40).

28. Cf. Jer 13:22; Isa 49:14; Ezek 9:9b; 33:10; Mal 1:2.
29. Cf. Exod 15:24; 16:2; Num 14:1-4; 16:2-3,12-14.

From the times of the oldest rabbinic attempts at interpretation of the work which bears his name, Job has been a controversial figure.[30] Even in the most recent studies and commentaries opinions vary widely as to the origin, the literary unity, the background and especially the message and meaning of the book.[31] One conclusion can certainly be drawn with regard to the figure of the rebellious Job: age-old doubts and objections with regard to the existence and the execution of the generally recognized divine judicial order in the world are amplified and verbalized in an intensified manner. These expressions arise out of the experience of both individual and collective suffering; the doubts and objections raised are those which, if not flowing from the heart of the author himself, are at the very least those entertained by the public for whom or against whom he wrote.

The absurdity of human suffering is also proclaimed in the book of Ecclesiastes, albeit in fewer words and with far less passion yet ultimately in a more direct and fundamental way. The existence of God is not denied, but, it is stated, "God is in heaven and you are on earth" (5:1). There is no communication between human beings and God. God most certainly holds the fate of every human being in his hands, yet his work remains unfathomable from beginning to end (3:11; 8:17; 11:5). Indeed, the best a human can do is eat, drink and revel in his youth, enjoying life with the woman of his heart's desire, and taking advantage of the opportunities he now receives from God (2:24; 3:12-13,22;

30. Cf. Judith R. Baskin, *Pharaoh's Counsellor's Job, Jethro, and Balaam in Rabbinic and Patristic Tradition.* Brown Judaic Studies, 47, Chico, CA, 1983: One: Job. The Righteous Gentile (pp. 7-43).

31. Compare, for example, N.C. Habel, *The Book of Job.* OTL, London, 1985, for whom the book of Job in its entirety is a splendidly structured dramatic composition of one brilliant author, with works such as V. Maag, *Hiob. Wandlung und Verarbeitung des Problems in Novelle, Dialogdichtung und Spätfassungen.* FRLANT, 128, Göttingen, 1982, and J. Vermeylen, *Job, ses amis et son Dieu. La légende de Job et ses relectures postexiliques,* Leiden, 1986. For these last authors, the present book, excepting the preexistence of an old prosaic story, is the result of at least three consecutive redactions each of which had their own communitarian background. The literary constructions proposed by Maag and Vermeylen nevertheless differ at numerous points.

5:17-19; 8:15; 9:7-10; 11:9-10). Life, however, makes no distinction between the righteous and the unrighteous, between oppressors and the oppressed, between the wise and the foolish (3:16; 4:1-4; 5:7; 7:15; 8:10-12; 9:2-3,13-16; 10:5-7). Moreover, everything is a game of time and chance for the human being (9:11). All of existence is desolation and full of frustration, misery, and bitterness (5:16). Even property and riches, all the productivity and creativity which people exhibit, their quest for knowledge and wisdom, all are ultimately vain and striving after wind (1:2-3; 1:13-18; 2:1-23; 7:23-28) because one and the same fate awaits all (2:14; 3:19; 9:2). All mortal beings go to one and the same place (6:6), and in this netherworld there will be no further thinking and doing, no knowledge and wisdom (9:10). Through his use of *hebel* (breath, air, insignificance) as a leitmotiv the Preacher has forged a technical idiom which we might render as "senseless" or "absurd."[32]

While the words of the rebellious and retracting Job remain ambiguous, it is clear that the Preacher has absolutized the image of absurd suffering − it refers ultimately to the whole of human life − and canonized it as well.[33]

The Absurd in Prelude to and Subsequent Readings of the Biblical Texts

It is also quite possible to classify many Old Testaments texts under the rubric of absurd suffering. These testify to the sense-

32. Cf. M.V. Fox, "The Meaning of 'hebel' for Qohelet," *JBL* 105 (1986) 409-427.

33. The epilogue (12:12-14), which in fact constitutes a warning against the radical statements of the Preacher, has — together with the fictional attribution of the book to Solomon — undoubtedly contributed to the official recognition of Ecclesiastes as holy scripture. In any case the history of the interpretation of Ecclesiastes, like that of the book of Job, is very complex, and Jews and Christians have from the start gone their own ways in this matter. Cf. S. Holm-Nielsen, *The Book of Ecclesiastes and the Interpretation of it in Jewish and Christian Theology. ASTI*, 10, 1976, pp. 38-95.

lessness of suffering even though in the text itself such an evaluation is neither stated nor suggested. One may, for example, with
James L. Crenshaw,[34] read Genesis 22 as a "monstrous test." A
God who in Jer 19:5 condemns the Kings of Judah for building
sacrificial high places in order to immolate their children as
offerings to Baal — sacrifices which Yahweh, had neither ordered
nor ever wished to hear of — orders Abraham to slay and
immolate his only son on his behalf.

According to W. Lee Humphreys,[35] an ancient story in 1
Samuel — in which Saul appears as a tragic hero, in the sense of
a Gilgamesh or of an Oedipus — is subsequently transformed in
prophetic and royalist circles respectively in such a way that Saul
is changed from a tragic hero into a criminal. The tragic and the
absurd element in the downfall of Saul is then present on the level
of the ancient story in which the hero Saul clashes with "a savage
god" and his inexorable prophet. Taking Humphries' cue with
regard to this metamorphosis, Saul's downfall is transformed into
a punishment for his disobedience towards Yahweh and his
jealousy of David. Whatever may be the prehistory of the text,
something absurd remains in the actual story regarding the fate
which Saul meets, especially if one compares his transgressions
and the retribution meted out to him with those of David.

The oppression of absurd suffering suggested in the above-
mentioned sense is also intimated by the many texts in which the
idea of suffering as punishment for sin is demonstrated *ad absur-
dum*. We note but several examples: some prophetic threats (Jer
15:1-9 and Ezek 24:9-14, for instance); the curses of Deuteronomy 28; the stories of the plagues of Egypt in which an entire
nation is beaten senseless ten times over because of the obstinacy
of one man; the image of Yahweh which pictures him ordering
the annihilation of entire populations (Deut 7:1-2; Jos 10:40;

34. *A Whirlpool of Torment*, pp. 9-29.
35. *The Tragic Vision and the Hebrew Tradition*. Overtures to Biblical Theology, 18, Philadelphia, 1987: Ch. 1. The Tragedy of King Saul (pp. 23-42); Ch. 3.
From Tragic Hero to Villain (pp. 43-66).

24:18); Yahweh's approval of the massacre led by Jehu against the house of Ahab and the worshippers of Baal (2 Kgs 10:30); the violent slaughter which Yahweh will execute in the days to come (Jer 46:10; Isa 34:7ff.; Ezek 39:18ff.) These are but a few of the texts which make the notion of merited suffering appear absurd in view of the overreaction, overkill, and sadism in the description of the punishments allotted.

Finally, one could in this context also point to the manifold instances of suffering mentioned or implied throughout the Old Testament which receive no clarification whatsoever, and sometimes not even the slightest attention: the grief of Rizpah, who for months stands vigil over the dead bodies of her sons (2 Sam 21:10); the anguish of the foreign women who are sent away with their children by their Israelite husbands at the command of Ezra (10:44); the suffering and the fate of all those who were innocently murdered, from Abel — whose name *Hebel* is in itself highly suggestive — to Zechariah, the son of Jehoiada, who at Joash's order was stoned in the courtyard of Yahweh's temple (2 Chr 24:20-22).

Suffering as a Source of New Life

However negatively suffering is usually experienced and interpreted, there is to be detected throughout the Old Testament yet another tendency which views suffering as a prelude to renewal, even as a source of new and richer life. This tendency takes on different forms.

Suffering as Discipline and Purification

According to the wise and very ancient counsel of Jesus Sirach,

"An unbroken horse turns out stubborn, and an unchecked son
grows headstrong" (30:8). This doctrine is prefigured not only in
the different collections of the book of Proverbs.[36] But also in the
wisdom teaching of different periods of Egyptian history.[37]
Nevertheless, in Israel, it is once again the experience of national
downfall and exile which evokes an interpretation of suffering as
an instrument in the hands of Yahweh for the purpose of
disciplining, purifying, and educating his people.

Ezek 22:20-22 evokes the image of the purification process
effectuated in the smelting furnace. Whereas this passage treats of
purification in a principally negative manner, in the context of the
coming punishment and destruction of Jerusalem[38], the same
metaphor takes on a positive dimension in Isa 48:9-10: "For my
own name's sake I defer my wrath; for the sake of my praise I
restrain it for you, that I may not cut you off. Behold, I have
refined you, though not like silver;[39] I have tried you in the
furnace of affliction."[40]

This interpretation is also projected onto Israel's past and
especially the period of the wilderness wanderings. According to
Deuteronomy 8 Yahweh led the Israelites "through that vast and
dreadful desert" (v. 15) for forty years to discipline them "as a
man disciplines his son" (v. 5), and to "humble" them and to
"test" them, "so that in the end it might go well with them"
(vv. 2,16). The era of oppression in Egypt also obtains the
character of purification when it is pictured as a stay in the
smelting furnace (Deut 4:20; 1 Kgs 8:51; Jer 11:4).

In the younger Yahwistic or "theologized" wisdom[41] – to

36. Cf. Prov 13:24; 18:18; 22:15; 23:13-14; 26:3; 29:17, 19.

37. Cf. N. Shupak, "The 'Sitz im Leben' of the Book of Proverbs in the Light
of a Comparison of Biblical and Egyptian Wisdom Literature," *RB* 94 (1987) 98-
119, especially pp. 107-111.

38. Cf. Isa 1:25; Jer 6:27-30; 9:6.

39. The line is probably best emended as "... purified as silver" (cf. J.L.
Mackenzie, *Second Isaiah*. AB, 20, 1968, p. 94.

40. Cf. Ps 66:10-12.

41. W. McKane, *Proverbs. A New Approach*. OTL, 1970, distinguishes three
types of material in the book of Proverbs as well as in the section Prov 1-9. The

which Deuteronomy 8 is related — this concept is applied to the suffering of the individual: "My son, do not despise Yahweh's discipline and do not resent his rebuke, because Yahweh disciplines those he loves, as a father the son he delights in" (Prov 3:11-12).

Eliphaz, Job's first partner in the poetic dialogue, takes up the same line of argument found in the passage just quoted. In the first of his speeches he states: "Blessed is the man whom God corrects; so do not despise the discipline of the Almighty" (5:17). It is, however, Job's fourth friend Elihu who gives the most sophisticated description of purification through suffering. The process is initiated with a drawn-out illness, takes a turn with the intervention of an angelic mediator, and further progresses by way of healing, prayer, confession, and thanksgiving (Job 33:14-33; cf. 36:8-15).[42]

In the story of the sacrifice of Isaac (Gen 22) and in the narrative framework of the book of Job (Job 1-2; 42:7-17), the aspect of "trial"[43] does not serve to bring the sinner to conversion and correction but rather to make public the disinterested piety, faith, and confidence of the righteous.[44]

These two aspects of suffering as purification and trial — as a means to correct and bring about the conversion of the sinner

third and youngest type (class C) to which belong Prov 3:1-12, contains statements which are a Yahwistic reinterpretation of ancient profane wisdom. "The instruction has been brought into the fold of Yahwistic piety and retains no recognizable contact with its primary educational Sitz" (p. 8). *TWAT*, 3, 626 also mentions Prov 3:12 in connection with this *Theologisierung* as applied to wisdom.

42. Cf. J.F. Ross, "Job 33:14-33: The Phenomenology of Lament," *JBL* 94 (1975) 38-46; and N.C. Habel, *op. cit.*, pp. 462ff.

43. The specific term *nissah* is employed only in Gen 22:1.

44. Cf. E. Blum, *Die Komposition der Vätergeschichte*. WMANT, 57, Neukirchen-Vluyn, 1984, pp. 320-331. Blum sees Genesis 22 as a rather recent *kontextunabhängige Einzelüberlieferung* in which Abraham is presented as "einer, der bei allem Gehorsam im Vertrauen auf das zukünftige Handeln Gottes die Ablehnung des Sohnesopfers durch Gott als Erwartung vorwegnimmt" (pp. 327-328). T. Veijola, "Das Opfer des Abraham — Paradigma des Glaubens aus dem nachexilischen Zeitalter," *ZTK* 85 (1988) 130-164, interprets Genesis 22 along the same lines and prefers a date in the fifth century B.C.

and as a seal on the piety of the righteous — live on in the
apocalyptic and in the more recent deuterocanonical and apocry-
phal didactic and narrative literature.

Zech 13:9 speaks of a third of the inhabitants of the land who
"on that day," in the messianic time, will be left in the land to be
purified as silver and gold in the fire so as to prepare a new
people of God. According to Dan 11:35, "some of the wise will
stumble, so that they may be refined, purified, and made spotless
until the time of the end."[45]

Sirach further warns: "My son, if you aspire to be a servant of
the Lord, prepare yourself for testing; for gold is assayed by fire,
and the Lord proves men in the furnace of humiliation" (2:1-5).[46]
In the so-called "Praise of the Fathers" (Sir 44-50), the author
points to Abraham who was found faithful through trial (44:20).
Judith (8:26) and Mattathias (1 Macc 2:52) also cite the fidelity
of Abraham during his time of testing.[47]

Finally we may mention how in the Talmud the suffering of
someone who is not aware of having committed any sin receives
the beautiful appelation *yissûrîn sjel 'ahabah*, "chastisement out
of love." This view is suggested with an appeal to Prov 3:12.[48]

45. Cf. Dan 12:10.
46. Cf. Sir 4:17; 33:1.
47. The depiction of suffering as purification and trial is practically the only
rational explanation, other than the theme of suffering as punishment, which was
still advanced in later Judaism. In this sense it is especially the picture of the Job
provided by the framework story which survives into late Judaism and early
Christianity, witness Sir 49:9; Tob 2:12 Vg (where the trial of Tobit is explicitly
compared with the testing undergone by "Job the saint."); the Testament of Job (a
Greek midrash on Job LXX from the first century A.D.) and Jas 5:11. Cf. N.N.
Glatzer, "The God of Job and the God of Abraham," *Bulletin of the Institute of
Jewish Studies* 2 (1974) 41-57.
48. Cf. *b. Berachot* 5a. The idea that God would send *yissûrîn sjel 'ahabah*
upon the righteous in order to reward him in the hereafter is rejected by
Maimonides in his *Moreh nevukîm* ("Guide for the Confused") because, in his
view, all suffering is punishment on account of previous sin (cf. "Maimonides," in
EncJud, 11, 754-781, especially c. 774.)

Vicarious Suffering

As surprising as "a shoot rising from the dry ground" (Isa 53:2) is the fourth song of the "Servant of Yahweh" (Isa 52:13-53:12) offering a perspective of suffering that is unique in the Old Testament. The servant's story had not been heard by kings and nations (52:15); it was incredible even for his own people (53:1). Indeed, the latter viewed this "man of sorrows" as one "smitten of God" (53:2-4a). But finally they had to recognize the truth he represented: "Surely, he took up our infirmities and carried our sorrows... he was pierced for our transgressions, he was crushed by our iniquities; on him fell the punishment that brought us peace... Yahweh has laid on him, the guilt of us all" (53:4*-6*).

Whoever is meant by "servant" − an unknown prophet, a prince of the royal house, an exilic or post-exilic group of the faithful, or deutero-Isaiah himself − it is sure that the idea of vicarious suffering, of suffering and death which bring salvation and redemption to others, is emphatically confirmed.[49]

Although the fourth song is very original, it forms the junction and terminus of many different roads of thought concerning the problem of suffering. It combines the presentation of suffering as curse and punishment for sin with those of the absurd suffering of the innocent and of suffering as the trial of the righteous. Its terms and motifs have their background and multiple parallels not only in the three preceeding "Ebed Yahweh" songs and in the remainder of Isaiah 40-55,[50] in the oracles describing the "sentinel" role

---

49. "So ist Jes 53 der einzige alttestamentliche Beleg für stellvertretendes Sühneleiden" (E. Kutsch, *op. cit.*, p. 342); cf. E. Haag, "Die Botschaft vom Gottesknecht," in N. Lohfink, ed., *Gewalt und Gewaltlosigkeit im Alten Testament.* QD, 96, Freiburg, 1983, pp. 159-213, especially 206-210.

50. While E. Haag, *op. cit.*, pp.160-177, seeks to reconstruct a "Grundschicht" of the four Ebed Yahweh songs comprising eight strophes (of which Isa 53:1-10a would form the last three), O.H. Steck, "Aspekte des Gottesknechts in Deuterojesajas 'Ebed-Jahwe-Liedern,'" *ZAW* 96 (1984) 372-390, recognizes only the original unity of the first three songs. In "Aspekte des Gottesknechts in Jes 52:13-53:12," *ZAW* 97 (1985) 36-58, the author describes similarities and differ-

played by Ezekiel (3:16-21 and 33:1-9) or recounting how Ezekiel embraces Judah's guilt in a symbolic act (Ezek 4:4-8),[51] but also in numerous cultic texts on the transfer of "all the wickedness and rebellion of the Israelites" to the head of the goat "for Azazel" (Lev 16:20-22,26); the typical Israelitic rite of the sprinkling of blood (Lev 16:14-15,18-19; 17:11); the high priest who bears the guilt of the Israelites (Exod 28:38; cf. Zach 3:1-7); the rituals accomplished by the priests responsible for making atonement (Lev 4:20,25-26,30-31; 16:32-33; 1 Chr 6:34; 2 Chr 29:24); and collective confession, self-chastisement and humiliation on the day of atonement and other penitential occasions (Lev 16; Neh 9; Joel 2:12-17; Zech 8:19). All of these texts are characteristic of Jewish piety of exilic and post-exilic times.[52]

The person of the Suffering Servant is further prepared and foreshadowed through the figure of Joseph whose trials are ultimately used by God to bring about the salvation of an entire nation (Gen 50:20);[53] by the figure of the persecuted and magnanimous David who twice spares Saul's life (1 Sam 24 and 26), who allows the curse of Shimei to come over him (2 Sam 16:10-12), and who requests that the punishing hand of God oppress him rather than the people (2 Sam 24:17);[54] by the figure of the Psalmist who is persecuted in spite of his prayers and acts of penance and his zeal for his God (Ps 35:13-14; 69:8,10-12; 109:4,24); and especially through the figure of the suffering prophetic mediator, of whom Jeremiah and Moses are the foremost exponents. Not only the "confessions" but also the biogra-

ences of the fourth song in relation to the three others. He concludes that this fourth song has been composed by another author at a later date.

51. Cf. W. Zimmerli, *Zur Vorgeschichte von Jesaja LIII*. VTSup, 17, 1969, pp. 236-244.

52. Cf. K. Koch, "Sühne und Sündenvergebung um die Wende von der exilischen zur nachexilischen Zeit," *EvT* 26 (1966) 217-239; and R. Rendtorff, *Studien zur Geschichte des Opfers im Alten Israel*. WMANT, 24, 1967.

53. Cf. "*miṣrayim*," *TWAT*, 4, 1106-1107, where the connection with the fertility motif and the possible influence of the Osiris myth on the history of Joseph are pointed out.

54. Cf. A. Schenker, *Die Mächtigen im Schmelzofen des Mitleids; eine Interpretation von 2 Sam 24*. OBO, 42, 1982.

phical sections of the book of Jeremiah (especially ch. 37-44) offer
the prophet's passion narrative. Moses repeatedly stood in the
breach for his people (Ps 106:23) and begged Yahweh[55] to blot
him from his book if there were to be no forgiveness for his
people (Exod 32:32).[56]

More distant prefigurations of the suffering and death of the
Servant in Isaiah 53 are to be found in the mythical stories
depicting dying gods such as Dumuzi in Mesopotamia, Osiris in
Egypt, and Baal in Ugarit. The latter, after having reached the
summit of power through the construction of a magnificent
temple, descends submissively into the mouth of the god of the
underworld with the vow: "Hail, O divine Môt! I am your
servant, yes, yours forever" (UT 67:II:11-12).[57]

Apart from the emphatic and unique reinterpretation which the
figure of the Suffering Servant obtains in the New Testament, the
theme is not without sequel in the Old Testament. The reference
to the "pierced one" in Zech 12:10 in all likelihood already
witnesses to that fact. This is surely the case in the description of
the persecuted, and finally executed, "sages" of Daniel 11-12
(especially 12:3) as well as of the "righteous ones" from Wisdom
2-5 who during their lives were despised and oppressed. The motif
of vicarious suffering resounds explicitly in the words of the
Jewish martyr in 2 Macc 7:37-38, in order to subsequently
become a primary motif in 4 Maccabees. (especially 6:28-29;
17:20-22; 18:4), a rhetorical, philosophical treatise of the first/
second century A.D. dealing with the Jewish martyrs of the
Maccabean period.

55. Cf. N. Ittmann, *Die Konfessionen Jeremias: Ihre Bedeutung für die Verkündigung des Propheten.* WMANT, 54, 1981; P.D. Miller, "'Moses my Servant.' The Deuteronomic Portrait of Moses," *Int* 41 (1987) 245-255.
56. Cf. Num 14:11-23; 34:9-10; Deut 9:6,19.

Growth and Renewal Through Suffering

Suffering may be transformed into a source of growth, renewal, and deepening of faith in that it can lead to greater solidarity with one's fellow human beings and harmony with nature, to greater freedom, peace and openness to the transcendent. Nowhere in the Old Testament, however, are such beneficial values of suffering for the afflicted individual directly and explicitly stated. Nevertheless, taking into account the polyvalence and "deep level structure" of narratives, songs and oracles, one may also discover this purely positive evaluation in many texts.

This is most clearly the case when one considers the structure of the individual lamentation psalms: in the sudden transitions from lamentation and accusation, or from prayer and cursing to the *tôdah*, thanksgiving and praise. Psalm 22 offers a particularly beautiful example in this regard. After a vivid description of the most bitter physical and psychological misery the Psalm abruptly explodes in an appeal to the entire community, to all the poor and God-seeking, to all nations and to all ends of the earth to share in the happiness and joy, in the thanksgiving and jubilation of one who has just previously portrayed himself as "a worm, a no-man, the scorn of man, and despised by the people" (v. 7).

The same may be said of the present structure of the prophetic books where doom oracles and visions of downfall and destruction, not only in the major pronouncements but also in the smaller units, alternate time and again with the perspective of return from exile and dispersion, of social and political restauration, of renewed fertility and welfare, or of national and sometimes even international peace and reconciliation. This is also true of the final redaction of Lamentations where suddenly, after waves of gloomy and bitter complaints, the tone changes to confidence in the third song with: "therefore I have hope" (3:21).[58]

57. J.C.L. Gibson, *Canaanite Myths and Legends*, Edinburgh, 1978, p. 69.

58. Cf. J. Renkema, *"Misschien is er hoop…"* De theologische vooronderstellingen van het boek Klaagliederen, Kampen, 1983; cf. also B. Johnson, "Form and Message in Lamentations," *ZAW* 97 (1985) 58-73, for whom the answer to the

Even in the interpretation of the primeval history there is room for a positive reading of suffering. This history is not only one of sin and punishment but also a beginning of cultural history, in which, not only after the flood narrative but in various other passages as well, the sign of the rainbow is built in.

This is the case, moreover, for the macro-structure of the book of Job, where, after a futile exchange with his friends and following all Job's complaints and protestations, God himself appears, answers Job, proves him to be ultimately right over and against his friends, and restores his previous beatitude in even greater abundance.

The idea of renewal and growth through suffering lies encapsulated in the Old Testament in the image of Yahweh as the one who daily recreates and renews (Ps 104:30); who will accomplish new and hidden things (Isa 48:6): a new Jerusalem, new heavens and a new earth (Isa 54:11-14; 60:1-22; 65:17); who takes delight in a broken and contrite heart and puts a new heart into and pours out a new spirit upon men and women (Ps 51:12-13,19; Ezek 11:19-20; 36:26-27; cf. Jer 31:31-34; 32:39; Joel 3:1-2).

The renewal of the human being through suffering is perhaps most strikingly illustrated by the paradoxical image of a God who himself grows and changes, indeed, becomes more human through the very sufferings with which he afflicts humankind. It is rather because he begot Israel as a father (Deut 32:18a) and gave birth to her as a mother (Deut 32:18b), because he loved Israel as a husband his wife (Jer 2:2), because he cared for his people as a bird for its young (Deut 32:11), and as a farmer lovingly tends his vineyard (Isa 5:1-7), that his wrath is fired up against the nation and that he brings down terrible calamities upon the people which has deserted, insulted and grieved him (Deut 32:15-25). Having observed the misery and suffering of his people, however, his heart is changed towards them (Hos 11:8), he repents of the evil which he has inflicted upon his own (Jer 42:10), and he vows

---

problem which dominates Lamentations is offered in the pericope 3:21-42, exactly in the middle of both the third chapter and of the entire book.

to modify his behavior: "In a surge of anger I hid my face from you for a moment... as I swore that the waters of Noah would never again cover the earth, so now I have sworn not to be angry with you, and I will never rebuke you again" (Isa 54:8*,9*).[59] Once again Yahweh recommences his love affair with the city and the nation which are no longer called "deserted" and "desolate," but "well-beloved" and "spouse" (Isa 62:4).

Suffering as a Pledge of Eternal Life

The presentation of suffering as a pledge of resurrection or of a purely spiritual survival after death is clearly recognized in the Old Testament's apocalyptic texts (Isa 26:19; Dan 12:1-4), in 2 Maccabees 7, 12, and throughout the book of Wisdom.

The righteous who have led many others into righteousness (Dan 12:3),[60] who have been temporarily purified and tested through persecution and even martyrdom (Dan 11:35; 2Mac 7:36; Wis 3:1-6),[61] even though they now sleep in the dust, will awake to live eternally (Isa 26:19; Dan 12:2; 2Mac 7:9,14). It is they who will shine like stars in the firmament (Dan 12:3) and will receive their reward with the Lord (2Mac 12:45; Wis 2:22; 5:15-16).[62]

Various approaches developed by the Old Testament in its struggle with the problem of suffering are not only combined but are also transformed at this level. The view of individual retribution as a correction of the interpretation of Israel's national catastrophes in terms of collective punishment is here radicalized and extended into the world to come. Even that suffering which leads to death is also pictured as a passing purification and trial. With the Ecclesiast it is implicitly taken for granted that suffering

59. Cf. Gen 8:21; Ezek 39:29.
60. Cf. Isa 53:11.
61. Cf. Isa 26:16-17.
62. Cf. Isa 53:12.

and even life would be absurd were death to have the last word
(Wis 2:1-5). But here death is conquered (Isa 25:8); out of the
chaos of suffering God creates utterly new life and an eternal
relationship between himself and humanity.

The breakthrough of the belief in immortality in Israel is
usually connected with the persecution and martyrdom of many
law-abiding Jews and teachers during the reign of Antiochus the
Fourth (175-164). Apart from the greater antiquity of Isa
26:19,[63] there are, in and outside of the Old Testament,[64]
indications that this belief already existed in Israel and does not
just coincidentally appear "at the edges" of the Old Testament.
Especially the utterances of confidence in some Psalms (23;
49:16; 73:25-26; cf. 22:30-31) suggest that the doctrine of resurrection was long an ingredient of Israel's piety, at the very least in
the form of dormant buds. In any case one may not, given the
diversity and evolution of the perspectives on suffering considered
thus far, state that Isa 26:19 and Dan 12:1-4 form erratic blocks
within the Old Testament.[65]

63. That is, if it indeed belongs to the original Isaian Apocalypse (Isa 24-27).

64. Cf. O. Kaiser, "Die Zukunft der Toten nach den Zeugnissen der alttesta-
mentlich-frühjüdischen Religion," in O. Kaiser, *Der Mensch unter dem Schicksal*,
Berlin, 1985, pp. 182-195 (from a lecture given in 1976), in which reference is made
(pp. 192-193) to fragments of the Aramean book of Henoch, whose prehistory
may date as far back as the fourth/fifth century B.C., which express the expectation of "eine Auferstehung der Geister der Seelen der Toten". L.J. Greenspoon,
"The Origin of the Idea of Resurrection," in the F.M. Cross *Festschrift*, Winona
Lake, IN, 1981, pp. 247-321, even asserts that "a concept of bodily resurrection is
expressed in Biblical material ranging in date of composition from the ninth to the
second centuries B.C.E." (p. 319). See also H. Rouillard and J. Tropper, "Vom
kanaanäischen Ahnenkult zur Zauberei: Eine Auslegungsgeschichte zu den
hebräischen Begriffen 'wb und yd'ny," *Ugarit Forschungen* 19 (1987) 235-254.

65. Cf. G. F. Hasel, "Resurrection in the Theology of the Old Testament
Apocalyptic," *ZAW* 92 (1980) 267-283, who concludes his study of Isa 26:19 and
Dan 12:1-4, in the context of apocalyptic: "Seen in proper perspective the
resurrection does not function at the periphery of OT apocalyptic but is a
principal element of the apocalyptic theology of the Hebrew Bible" (p. 284).

Conclusion

In conclusion, we can highlight a few elements which clearly emerge from this descriptive survey of the basic approaches to suffering explored by the Old Testament.

The national catastrophes formed a watershed in the religious experience of ancient Israel. The Fall of Jerusalem in 587 and the Babylonian Captivity especially represent the "Big Bang" which catalysed the peculiar and intense Old Testament reflection on the theme of suffering.

The contents of the book of Job are consequently not to be written off as a discussion of a "theological side issue."[66] The work is every bit a point of convergence and a forum for the diverse Old Testament perspectives on suffering. One may even detect in some passages an embryonic presence of the perspective of vicarious suffering (42:7-9) and of the interpretation of suffering as a pledge of eternal life (14:13-17; 16:18-17:1; 19:21-27).[67]

The texts of the Old Testament which touch upon the suffering and sorry fate of human beings laboriously and gradually disclose the image of a God who — even though He is the First and the Last (Isa 41:4; 44:6; 48:12) and is enthroned above the celestial sea (Ps 29:10; 104:3) — is so engrossed with the history of humankind that he grows with his creation, groaning as a woman in labor (Isa 42:14) on account of this his unfinished symphony. They give way to the belief that God suffers with his people and also with those who do not themselves know why and for what purpose they suffer.[68]*

66. G. von Rad, *Theologie des Alten Testaments*, 1, p. 430.

67. N. C. Habel, *op. cit.*, refers in his commentary on these texts to "a dream of post-mortem litigation." Job expresses the wish, and gradually the firm hope as well, that even if his protestations fall on deaf ears during his own lifetime, his case will be taken up by God himself in truth and in justice after his death, even though Job will then no longer be present.

68. "The attempt to offer a theodicy threatens to become blasphemous unless it takes into account divine pathos" (J.L. Crenshaw, *Whirlpool*, p. 115). In connection with the suffering of God Crenshaw refers to K. Miskotte, *When the Gods are Silent*, New York, 1967, p. 392. Now he might also refer to T. E. Fretheim, *The Suffering of God*. Overtures to Biblical Theology, 14, Philadelphia, 1984.

* Translated from the Dutch by Peter Crossman.

JESUS AND SUFFERING - THE SUFFERING OF JESUS

Robrecht Michiels

Every and any reflection on suffering and death must begin by doing justice to actual human experience. Not all suffering is meaningless. Suffering can be an opportunity for maturation, an occasion to direct one's life to the essential. Is it not the case that, precisely in difficult circumstances, persons often grow in strength and greatness as well as in understanding and solicitude for others? Nevertheless, the suffering which one most often encounters is deadening, barbaric, and meaningless. The world is awash in a sea of suffering. If any have the right to speak, it is those who suffer — the poor, the oppressed, those facing death. Job, Jesus, Romero, and many others have availed themselves of this right. In Jesus' case, Gethsemane and Golgotha were the principal occasions for its exercise. Those who have spoken have also often given voice to peoples whose own voice has been silenced, even murdered, peoples whose names have been eradicated.

In the midst of all this, the concrete experience of human suffering continues to call for a response, continues to raise the issue of its meaningfulness or, alternately, its meaninglessness. There have been attempts to find a *solution* to the *problem* of suffering and death. The very word "problem" indicates a predicament that calls for some solution; once solved the problem ceases to be, or, at least, ceases to be a real "problem" for me. Viewed in this fashion, that is, as a "problem," suffering and death are, both theoretically and practically speaking, insoluble.[1] All the sciences,

1. Cf. E. Schillebeeckx, "The Mystery of Injustice and the Mystery of Mercy," *Stauros Bulletin* 3 (1975) 3-31.

the positive no less than the human, theology no less than philosophy, ultimately stand perplexed and speechless before the problem of natural, personal, interpersonal and structurally related suffering in this world. Our own factual, necessary, and practical endeavors to banish suffering and death from the world likewise provide no effective guarantee or hope that our earthly suffering, and our inevitable death will ever be overcome. Our victories over suffering and death are, indeed, always only partial: the whole person — physical, psychological, existential, and social — is never healed. Neither are our victories universal: they are not enjoyed by all the inhabitants of our world. Moreover, they are always only provisional: we are continuously stopped short by our finitude, by death. Suffering can never be kept at a distance: I am always involved in it, I share in it, either personally or insofar as I have a share in the lives of others.

So it is that suffering is always a *question*, and even a *mystery*, precisely because I am involved. Even more, the history of the suffering of humankind is always the history of *my* suffering. A question calls for an *answer*, and a mystery calls for meaning, or for an *interpretation*.

Jesus and Suffering

To seek to do justice to the human experience of suffering and death is to raise the question of its meaningfulness or meaninglessness. Just as there have been attempts to solve the problem of suffering and death, so have there been attempts to interpret or give meaning to the mystery of suffering and death. Let us reflect on biblical attempts in this regard.

In the Old Testament, as Jos Luyten has indicated in the foregoing essay, there are three contexts of meaning or three fundamantal tendencies in the interpretation of suffering. These three exist alongside, and interpenetrate, one another. First, suffering and death are viewed as a *punishment for sin*. Consider, for example, the narrative of the origins of humanity (Gen 1-11), which posits a causal connection between human suffering and death and God's retribution. Israel interpreted those disasters which befell the nation in 722 and 587 in the same fashion, perceiving in the events a connection between sin and punishment. From a second perspective, suffering and death are *absurd and meaningless*, pure negativity even. This view is reflected in many psalms of lamentation. In the Book of Job, especially, it reaches a pathetic climax. Therein, there is a reaction to the proposition of a definite relationship between sin and suffering. Finally, suffering is regarded as a means of *purification towards the good*, as a trial or pedagogical device. Subsequent to the events, Israel interprets the disasters which befall it in this fashion. Occasionally, there is talk, in this regard, of substitutional or vicarious suffering or of redemptive death, that is, suffering and death for others. We find this approach reflected in the four songs of the Suffering Servant of Yahweh (Isa 40-55, especially Isa 53). Suffering and death are also viewed as a source of new and richer life, as pledge of immortality and resurrection, of continued personal existence beyond death. One thinks, in this regard, of certain psalms, but especially of 2 Maccabees and the Book of Wisdom.

Looking to the New Testament, to the story of Jesus' life and passion, we see that Jesus is opposed to the view, indeed, he dismisses the view that suffering and death are a *divine punishment*, that, in other words, suffering and guilt are always related. On the contrary, Jesus sought out the sick and needy, reintegrated them into society, laid his hands on them, touched them, and healed them. Never did he attach any moral label to the sick, or require of them some moral recompense. He related to them in an atmosphere of total goodness, devoid of prejudices or preconditions. Most importantly, however, Jesus offered no explanation, religious or otherwise, for sickness and suffering. Instead, he called people to solidarity with the suffering and to the performance of deeds of hope. Were it the case that suffering and guilt stood in relationship to one another, then humankind would have suffering in its power, merely by the maintenance of its own innocence.[2]

A second feature of the New Testament vision is the notion that suffering can serve as a means of *purification*, that it can be of service to humanity and its world, that, indeed, suffering and death are ultimately a *way to life*: the whole life, suffering and death of Jesus of Nazareth point in this direction.

A third element of the New Testament vision must, however, also be borne in mind: not every instance of suffering serves to purify or encourage growth. Why would Jesus have otherwise so opposed himself to all suffering and death? There are forms of suffering which are meaningful, but that meaning must come from without, from beyond the actual suffering itself. There is certainly suffering which is of service to life and community, but there is especially that suffering which leaves us speechless. As such, the great mystery of suffering and death is meaningless. More even, it is *absurd*, pure negativity. One possible meaning which it might receive comes from God, in Jesus' cross. A little later on, we shall call this the final or ultimate meaning.

The Suffering of Jesus

A study of the Gospel passion narratives[3] readily brings to light the way in which Jesus, from within a primarily existential and social critical interpretive context, experienced his own suffering and death. This raises the problem of how Jesus' own experience of his suffering and the Pauline preaching of the reconciliatory

2. This is the view expressed by T. J. Van Bavel in his contribution to this book. Suffering is only a punishment for sin, in the sense that humanity can punish itself, that humanity can, indeed, cause itself untold misery.

3. See my *Binnen het jaar: Het lijden en de dood van Jezus*, Averbode, 1983; and *De eeuwigheid in ons hart: Een theologie van het sterven*, Kapellen, 1985. Both of these works contain extensive bibliographies.

See also the special issues of *Collationes: Vlaams Tijdschrift voor Theologie en Pastoraal* 11 (1981) 5-21, 22-49 (F. Lefevre on Mark); 14 (1984) 161-190 (J. Lambrecht on Matthew); and 191-210 (R. Michiels on Luke).

character thereof can be viewed from a single perspective. Many dogmatic theologians simply ignore this problem. They certainly ignore the way in which exegetes and historians speak about it. Nevertheless, there is a need for the transition to be made from the redemptive significance of Jesus' suffering to human suffering in general. The cross of Jesus is not simply a *chiffre* for this suffering alone; its *ephapax* character (Rom 6:10; Heb 7:27; 9:12; 10:10) is probably richer in content. Indeed, it must be if Jesus' suffering is related to our sin. But how precisely are we to make clear that *this* suffering is possessed of a redemptive power and a substitutional function? This particular problem urgently needs to be readdressed. [4]

Historical Setting

Access to the history of Jesus' suffering and death can only be achieved by a diachronic or tradition historical reading of the texts, one which seeks to distinguish tradition from redaction in the oldest, that is, the Marcan, passion narrative. By applying this literary- and historical-critical method, a number of exegetes have sought to reconstruct the original passion tradition. One may not expect unanimity among them as to the contours of this reconstruction. They do, however, agree that older and younger traditions are interwoven, and that, by means of this process, all sorts of additions have been made.

On the basis of this tradition historical approach, exegetes have concluded to a diachronic structure which consists of two large segments: Mark 14:1-42 (up to the arrest of Jesus), and 14:43-15:39/47 (from the arrest onwards). It is to the second segment that exegetes look for the original passion tradition, the actual account of Jesus' suffering, an account possessed of its own

4. Cf. H.-E. Mertens, "Jezus de Golgotha-situatie meester geworden: Oude vragen omtrent de soteriologie opnieuw gesteld," in *Tijdschrift voor Theologie* 29 (1989) 131-147.

theme, namely, Jesus' pains and sorrows. This original narrative is concerned with the following four points: Jesus is arrested at the instigation of the Jewish leaders (14:43, 45-46), is brought before the high priest (14:53), is sent forth from there to Pilate (15:1), and is tried, sentenced, and executed by the latter (15:2-39). Moreover, many exegetes look to the Golgotha scene, namely, the story of Jesus' carrying of the cross, his crucifixion and death (15:20b-32, 34a,37) as the oldest, the most primitive element of the narrative, the core, as it were.

A distinction is made, therefore, between the basic text, the pre-Marcan tradition, and Marcan redaction. This means that passages in the basis text of Mark 15:1-39 were supplemented by the early Christian or pre-Marcan tradition. These passages represent christological interpretations of Jesus' suffering and death: 15:24b, 29a, 34b, 35-36 on the basis of Ps 22:19; 22:8; 22:2 and 69:22; 15:33 on the basis of the motif of darkness; and finally, 15:38 on the basis of the motif of the temple. At the same time, one can discern redactional additions that derive from Mark himself. These are concerned with translations and clarifications (15:16, 22, 34), with the progress of the narrative or the chronological ordering of events (15:1a, 25, 33), and the christological interpretation of Jesus' suffering and death (15:31-32, 39). Historical facticity immediately called forth an interpretation of this historical Jesus event, and a "faithful" or christological interpretation of the same was present from the outset. We shall return to this.

The original passion tradition in Mark does answer the three following historical questions: how and why did Jesus die, and who is historically responsible for this death? Historical data beyond dispute are: that Jesus died a violent death by Roman crucifixion, a death also which involved great moral suffering; that the Sanhedrin conducted a hearing and issued a condemnation; that Pilate, the Roman governor, brought charges and passed sentence; that, moreover, Jesus was condemned for claiming to be "King of the Jews," such that political and religious motifs are intermingled; that historical responsibility for his death is shared by the then ruling Roman and Jewish authorities. And, most importantly, the redemptive significance of Jesus' death is to be found in the redemptive significance of his whole life.

Why was Jesus Condemned?

A full treatment of all these questions is beyond the scope of this article. We limit ourselves to the issue of Jesus' condemnation. Jesus' real or alleged (that is, attributed to him by others) claim to be the "King of the Jews" appears as the historical reason for his execution. Here, however, one discerns the beginning of a great misunderstanding. Jesus was king in a religious sense, that is to say, not through the exercise of power or the power of weapons and violence, but in complete service of others, and, moreover, with an eye to the coming of God's redemptive rule and kingdom. The Romans could not, of course, understand the precise scope of this title (15:2, 12, 17). For them, it was territorially and politically colored: it signified that Jesus desired to be king of the land peopled by the Jews. Pilate accordingly interpreted the title in a political sense, as if Jesus were the opponent of the Roman emperor and would incite the populace against him. As King of the Jews, Jesus could be regarded in precisely the same fashion as the freedom fighters or Zealots, and this allowed Pilate to condemn him on the basis of supposed Zealot sympathies. Pilate was, however, quick to realize that Jesus could not be tried simply as another murderer or Zealot. Indeed, he even sought to free him (see the episode of Barabbas, or the paschal amnesty). Finally, though, Pilate condemns Jesus on the basis of a faulty understanding, or even a complete misunderstanding, of the royal title.

In the case of the Jews, however, it must have been the religious significance and interpretation of this title which dominated: in their eyes, Jesus deserved death because he was perceived as having thoroughly defied the authority of the religious establishment, and therefore as having allegedly claimed to be

Messiah-King (14:61-64). They, too, however, would seem to
have misunderstood the full scope of such a royal title. This
understanding could only result from a more profound insight, in
faith, into the peculiar or characteristic exercise of Jesus' authority and power. This consisted in the fact that Jesus' mission
would not be accomplished according to Jewish expectations, but
in accordance with the will of God, that is, through complete
servitude even unto death itself. Jesus was, then, condemned
because of his complete fidelity to his God-given prophetic mission, his unshakeable and constant confidence in his Father who
had sent him. In view of the fact Jesus remained silent regarding
the charges brought against him (14:61a), the Sanhendrin could
not arrive at a unanimous decision in his case. Therefore, Jesus
was handed over to the Roman governor, Pilate who sentenced
him to death (15:15b).

Consequently, we can say that in the final analysis, Jesus was
executed because he lived one way and not another. The ultimate
reason for his condemnation and execution must be sought in his
life itself: the story of Jesus' passion is, as it were, the story of his
life. The redemptive significance of his suffering and death are to
be found in the redemptive significance of his whole life. The
former is, so to speak, an extension of his primary concern, the
preaching — and praxis — of God's Kingdom. Jesus was executed because of the message and praxis manifest in his life, and
this messsage and praxis were, in many respects, truly revolutionary. His teaching and activity in fact prompted a complete
reordering of things. His condemnation was the result of this life
and activity. Jesus turned against the existent, established order
whenever this represented to him religious and social disorder. He
always gave priority to the person, to each and every person,
including the lawless, and especially the poor, the overlooked and
the defenseless, or those excluded from the Jewish religion and
Jewish society. Jesus always reached out to the insignificant, and,
from them, to others: salvation was for the poor and from the
poor. In this way, Jesus disposed of all taboos, privileges, and
monopolies, and demanded that all reevaluate their perceptions

and patterns of behavior. In this way, too, however, he earned the wrath of all those external and internal parties who controlled his nation at that time.

In the final analysis, then, Jesus did not fit into any schema or category, any religious or political group. He was without either system or ideology. He served the cause of God and humanity, and, for him, these two coincided. However, this whole approach soon proved fatal for him: Jesus had become an impossible man, socially no less than religiously, one who could not be situated anywhere. In both respects, social and religious, his life was so revolutionary that it must be brought to a violent end, within the year according to the Synoptics (or a couple of years according to John). The whole of that life, up to the hour of death which was preceded by the Last Supper — a paschal, farewell, and memorial meal — had been an offer of divine salvation. It was this fact which allowed Jesus to understand and withstand his death as also his final and ultimate service to God's cause and the cause of humanity. For this reason, critical-historical exegesis, too, can speak of this death as the most intensely characteristic salvific deed and the most intensely characteristic salvific word of the historical, pre-paschal Jesus himself: his death on the crosss is the last station, the termination of his path through life and to Golgotha. In this way, Jesus' love, unto death, redeems us. His life, suffering, death and resurrection must be seen as a unit, as God's liberating deed in Jesus Christ, on behalf of humanity, a deed that reaches beyond death. Therefore, every christological consideration will address two central questions: who was/is Jesus for God, and who was/is Jesus for humanity?

Christological Interpretation

We are, then, already on the road to the christological interpretation of Jesus' suffering and death. The Gospel passion narratives are not intended simply to report the facts. On the contrary, they view these facts and events from a faith perspective, to proclaim their significance for faith. In that instant, Jesus' suffering and death acquire a value in themselves.

This is true in the first place of the oldest passion narrative, that of Mark. The evangelist interprets the historical data. Mark's passion narrative, indeed, his whole Gospel, must be seen as the confession and proclamation of Jesus as Christ and Son of God. This means that an early Christian or pre-Marcan interpretation of Jesus' suffering and death was inserted into the oldest layer or foundational layer of the Gospel, and that these, along with Mark's own (or redactional) interpretation of the events, were then later woven into a whole.

The very first interpretation sees Jesus' death in the light of Psalm 22 (15, 24b, 29a, 34b, 35-36), that is, Jesus' cry to God in the hour of his death. This psalm, in which a just man (according to Old Testament norms) cries to God for justice, occurs four times in the Golgotha scene. This is some indication of the importance of this psalm in the early Christian interpretation of Jesus' death on the cross: the one crucified is not simply a lonely mortal who weeps and shouts in his last hour; his death cries are suffused with the psalm-prayers of centuries and with a prophetic protest against suffering and death. The original passion tradition reported simply (but realistically) that "Jesus cried with a loud voice" (15:34a), that he "uttered a loud cry, and breathed his last" (15:37). This cry was filled in by the first Christian tradition and/or the redactors of the Gospel. So it is that we are presented with three different interpretations of Jesus' death, in accordance with the three versions of Jesus' last words. There is a threefold religious-literary filling in of Jesus' death cry: Mark 15:34b — compare Matt 27:46b; Luke 23:46b and John 19:30b.

According to Mark (and Matthew), Jesus died with the words, "My God, my God, why have you forsaken me?" In this way, the evangelist, as interpreter of the oldest tradition, explains Jesus death cry with the aid of the second verse of Psalm 22, a psalm which is, in fact, a psalm of trust, trust in God. There are, however, two facets to this psalm: abandonment by God and humanity (vv. 2-22), and faith and trust, even praise and thanksgiving for liberation from the most extreme suffering and the greatest need (vv. 23-32). The early Christian tradition had, indeed, the whole psalm in mind where the event of Golgotha was concerned. This means that Jesus' death was understood in terms of the prayer and protest of the just man of the Old Testament — the person who enjoys God's favor. In his address to God, such a one at once gives voice to both his misery and suffering and his confidence in, and certainty of, God's dominion and triumph. The crucified Jesus is this just man. On Golgotha, in his emptiness and need, he turns to God, who, he is certain, is even here, present for him. In this moment the connection between Jesus' life and death which we mentioned above becomes abundantly clear: the story of Jesus' suffering is the story of his life. For that reason, Psalm 22, though it is not an historical word of Jesus at his death, is, nevertheless, an authentic interpretation of his suffering and death, completely coincident with his life and activities. I mean by this, that the attempt to understand the Crucified in the light of his life, the life that brought him to the cross, is the most obvious approach. Therefore, we must repeat with the early Christian tradition that Jesus suffers and dies as the Just One — a theme, incidentally, which is applicable not only to the cross (15:34), but is also articulated in Jesus' prayer of agony in Gethsemane (14:32-42; see v. 36). In the Garden, no less than on the cross, the person who weeps and cries out is the one who expects everything — absolutely everything — from God. Jesus' prayer in Gethsemane and his psalm prayer on Golgotha are a confrontational encounter with God. By means of this confrontation, Jesus comes to the fundamental discovery that God will not keep him *from* suffering and death, but that God will keep him *in* this suffering and this death. For that reason it is said that Jesus died to his God. His life ended as it began and as it progressed: with an open question to God. "God, my God, why have you forsaken me?" means that the crucified Jesus cried loudly to God in his life, suffering and death. God answered him by raising him from the dead and glorifying him. Jesus' resurrection means that God has answered the open question, — the question addressed to God, the question about God — with which Jesus lived and died. In the resurrection, the conversation, the relation or communion, between Jesus and his God is resumed. Hence, the resurrection of Jesus by God represents the ratification and fulfillment of his life and death, and Jesus' life and death become the index, the key to the meaning of, of his resurrection.

Resurrection faith is therefore the experience and articulation of our faith in ourselves and in our deepest longings, and expectations for the future, of our faith, too, in God who will triumph over the "last enemy," and of our faith in Jesus, who, as the risen Just One, will bless us with his Spirit. In this fashion, one achieves a coherent theology and christology of the resurrection, an approach which seems to be almost completely present in this pre-Marcan interpretation of Jesus' suffering and death. This latter tradition interpreted Jesus' death as the death of the Just One, who opens for himself and for others the way to the definitive salvific reign of God over all. Such a life, one lived in service to humanity, and in surrender to God — surrender unto death — such a life and such a death, in which one calls unto God, cannot be in vain. On the contrary, God will respond by raising this person and all such people from the dead. God is therefore present *in* the suffering of Jesus and of every human person; he does not abandon his just servants, but sets his answer forth in their resurrection. The resurrection is not, then, so much an escape as a way out of suffering.

This foundational interpretation of Jesus' death on the cross was augmented, in the early Christian tradition, by two others which attained prominence. On the one hand, there was an understanding of Jesus' death as God's judgment upon the world — reflected in the apocalyptic darkness motif at around the hour of Jesus' death (15:33); on the other hand, the relativizing of the Jewish religion and/or Jewish society — reflected in the, likewise apocalyptic, temple motif or the tearing of the veil of the temple at the hour of Jesus' death (15:38).

The actual Marcan interpretation of Jesus' suffering and death is to be found in the transformation of the royal title, "King of the Jews," which belongs to the original passion tradition, into an explicitly christological title. This occurs at several high points in Mark's story: at the crucifixion where it is placed in the mouths of the high priests and scribes who ridicule Jesus (in 15:32a: "The Messiah (or Christ), the king of Israel"), at the actual death of Jesus where the title is employed by the Roman centurion (in 15:39: "Truly, this man was the Son of God"), and, in anticipation, at the interrogation of Jesus by the Sanhedrin (in 14:61-62: "Are you the Christ, the Son of the Blessed? Jesus said, 'I am'!"). Moreover, the oldest evangelist has inserted into the passion tradition he has received another motif (a typically Johannine one) — "believing without seeing," — and he has done this in the same two verses descriptive of the crucifixion, namely 15:32b and 15:39. Both these themes — that of the christological titles and of "believing without seeing" reflect Mark's actual understanding of Jesus' suffering and death: Mark's passion narrative is the proclamation and confession of Jesus' messiahship, of the Messiah or Christ who died and rose again.

Conclusion: Suffering and Death - A Mystery

In the light of Jesus' suffering and death, we realize that suffering and death are a mystery involving us all. If we make of suffering and death a *problem*, we will never be able to come to terms with this bitter riddle which haunts our so-called good creation. A problem always calls for a solution. The fact is, however, that humanity has no solution for the problem of suffering and death, and for human history as the history of the finitude of death. The history of humanity's attempts to interpret suffering and death testify to the failure of both reason and praxis in this regard. Our human experience makes very clear to us that the elimination of all suffering and death is beyond our powers. God will not, therefore, keep us *from* suffering and death, but *in* suffering and death. Hence, we shall and indeed, we cannot do other, than participate in suffering and death as in a *mystery*, that is, as in a human question which is in search of an answer, in search of meaning or interpretation. Just as a problem calls for a solution, so does a question call for an answer. *God's* answer to humanity's question about the meaning of suffering and death is nothing less than the suffering and dying Jesus. The ultimate meaning or interpretation of the mystery of suffering is, therefore, given us in the story of the life and death of Jesus Christ: God did not shield him *from* suffering and death, but kept him *in* suffering and death. In the story of Jesus' life and death, it becomes clear to us that suffering and death are opened up, so to speak, into a "passage," a way to life. The example of Jesus' life has taught us that life without death is an impossibility, that glorification is not possible without the cross. In this respect, he has gone before us as no other. In word and deed he has shown us that no one can understand something of the cross and death apart from resurrection and glorification. Conversely, he has shown us that no one can understand something of resurrection and glorification apart from the cross and death. For that reason, the cross hangs in our homes as the sign of our redemption; for that reason, we make the sign of the cross over ourselves and one another; for that reason, we baptize our children with the sign of the cross.

The meaning or interpretation of the mystery of suffering is, therefore, given us, by God, in the story of the life and passion of our Lord Jesus Christ. The story of his life and death calls us to imitate him and to take our place alongside the suffering and dying, and to accept our share in this life's suffering and our inevitable death. So it is that suffering and death become a mystery in which we are all involved, without exception. On the one hand, we shall share, as far as possible, the suffering of *others*, and this, on the natural, interpersonal, and social levels, by struggling courageously against all forms of suffering, whether in nature, in life, or in society. On the other hand, we shall strive to see *our* suffering as the form our faith and love assume in the most difficult circumstances that go to make up our creaturely existence. Here, in these situations, the total surrender to God and the complete service of humanity find place in the willingness of each, acquired in the course of life, to suffer and die for the other. There is, then, no real love unless it proves itself in suffering and death.

In conclusion, I would like to summarize my view of suffering and death as follows. Not only is there no definitive solution to the problem of suffering and death, there is also no final *human* answer to the question of its meaning: suffering and death are, in themselves, meaningless — they are not meaning-full. In this case, meaning will have to be "found," "experienced" as gift, "received." Suffering and death, which have no meaning in themselves, can "acquire" meaning. A final solution or a conclusive justification of suffering and death are not possible. Christians will affirm that suffering and death may acquire meaning when they are set in the meaning-giving context, or the meaning-giving story, of Jesus' suffering, death, and resurrection. For that reason, this story ought not, must not, ever be forgotten.

In sum, my view is that suffering acquires its final meaning for humanity *from God*, that its ultimate meaning is given us *through God* in the story of the life and death of Jesus Christ. Jesus shows us that the way towards one another is through solidarity in suffering — *passio* which means love as well as suffering. This way frees us from ourselves, and brings us close to one another; this way brings us to the suffering Jesus and his defenseless and powerless God; finally, it brings us to our glorification, to the other side of that hill "where the grass is always greener" — the hill of Golgotha.*

* Translated from the Dutch by Terrence Merrigan.

PAUL AND SUFFERING

Jan Lambrecht

As is well known, Paul emphasizes in his letters the preaching of Christ crucified, the word of the cross (cf. especially 1 Cor 1:18-25). Very frequently he speaks of his own suffering, sometimes also of that of Christians. The so-called lists of tribulations, *Peristasenkataloge*, are famous. We find them in the two letters to the Corinthians, in Philippians and in Romans. There are seven or eight lists, some of them brief, others long.[1] They depict Paul's apostolic sufferings.

In 2 Corinthians 11 Paul boasts of himself: "Let no one think me foolish, but even if you do, accept me as a fool so that I too may boast a little" (v. 16). In verses 21-23, he writes: "Whatever any one dares to boast of — I am speaking as a fool — I also dare to boast of that. Are they Hebrews? So am I. Are they Israelites? So am I. Are they descendants of Abraham? So am I. Are they servants of Christ? I am a better one: I am talking like a madman — with far greater labors, far more imprisonments, with countless beatings, and often near death." So we see that what started as foolish boasting about Jewish privileges becomes very soon the paradoxical boasting of Christian, apostolic suffering

---

1. Rom 8:35; 1 Cor 4:10-13a; 2 Cor 4:8-9; 6:4b-10; 11:23b-29; 12:10; Phil. 4:12. R. Hodgson, "*Paul the Apostle and First Century Tribulation Lists*," in *ZNW* 74 (1983) 59-80, finds two lists in 2 Cor 6 (vv. 4b-5 and 8-10) and counts thus eight lists in all. Of course, there are still other verses which must be taken into consideration for this subject, although they can hardly be called lists or catalogues. See, e.g., 2 Cor 7:5 and Phil 4:11-12. Hodgson distinguishes between the "simple lists" (Rom 8:35; 2 Cor 6:4b-5; 11:23-29 and 12:10) and the "antithetical lists" (1 Cor. 4:10-13a; 2 Cor 4:8-9; 6:8-10 and Phil 4:12) (see pp. 63-64).

and weakness: "Five times I have received at the hands of the Jews the forty lashes less one. Three times I have been beaten with rods; once I was stoned. Three times I have been shipwrecked; a night and a day I have been adrift at sea; on frequent journeys, in danger from rivers, danger from robbers, danger from my own people, danger from Gentiles, danger in the city, danger in the wilderness, danger at sea, danger from false brethren; in toil and hardship, through many a sleepless night, in hunger and thirst, often without food, in cold and exposure. And, apart from other things, there is the daily pressure upon me of my anxiety for all the churches. Who is weak, and I am not weak? Who is made to fall and I am not indignant?" (vv. 24-29). In verses 30-33 Paul, moreover, refers to the Damascus incident, his humiliating escape, his flight from Aretas' governor: "I was let down in a basket through a window in the wall" (v. 33). [2]

The long section 2:14-7:4 is usually entitled "Paul's Apology." [3] Within it 6:3-10 may be called *l'apologie miniature*, the miniapology (J.-F. Collange). From the context it appears that by means of this list of trials Paul wants to illustrate how his ministry is without obstacle: "As servants of God we commend ourselves in every way: through great endurance, in afflictions, hardships, calamities, beatings, imprisonments, tumults, labors, watching, hunger... in honor and dishonor, in ill repute and good repute. We are treated as impostors, and yet we are true; as

2. Verses 32-33 "are a crowning illustration of the weakness and humiliation of which Paul speaks and boasts" (C.K. Barrett, *A Commentary on the Second Epistle to the Corinthians.* BNTC, London 1973, p. 303). In Acts 9:32-35, the same incident is dealt with, but quite differently. It must strike the reader that Luke depicts here a first example, not of Paul's weakness, but of the way in which God frees him out of the hands of his enemies (here the Jews).

3. As a matter of fact the long interruption 2:14-7:4 often possesses an apologetic tone. In 7:5 Paul takes up the narrative part which he interrupted at the end of 2:13. Compare 2:12-13: "When I came to Troas to preach the gospel of Christ, a door was opened for me in the Lord; but my mind could not rest because I did not find my brother Titus there. So I took leave of them and went on to Macedonia", with 7:5-6: "For even when we came into Macedonia, our bodies had no rest but we were afflicted at every turn — fighting without and fear within. But God, who comforts the downcast, comforted us by the coming of Titus."

unknown, and yet well known; as dying, and behold we live; as punished, and yet not killed; as sorrowful, yet always rejoicing; as poor, yet making many rich; as having nothing, and yet possessing everything" (vv. 4-5, 8-10). Whereas in chapter 11 Paul compares himself with his opponents, in chapter 6 he proves the quality of his ministry. Two very impressive catalogues of apostolic tribulations!

The most intriguing text, however, is probably that of verses 8-9 in 2 Cor 4:7-12: "We have this treasure (= the ministry) in earthen vessels, to show that the transcendent power belongs to God and not to us" (v. 7). Then verses 8-9 follow: "We are afflicted in every way, but not crushed; perplexed, but not driven to despair; persecuted, but not forsaken; struck down, but not destroyed." Paul continues: "always carrying in the body the dying of Jesus, so that the life of Jesus may also be manifested in our bodies. For while we live we are always being given up to death for Jesus' sake, so that the life of Jesus may be manifested in our mortal flesh. So death is at work in us, but life in you" (vv. 10-12). The expression "the dying of Jesus," *hê nekrôsis tou Jêsou*, occurs but once in Paul's letters, namely in 2 Cor 4:10: "always carrying in the body the dying of Jesus, so that the life of Jesus may be manifested in our bodies." How can Paul identify his suffering with the dying of Jesus? And how is this suffering, in a paradoxical way, the manifestation of Jesus' life?[4]

These very questions constitute the topic of our paper which will contain three parts. First we give an analysis of 2 Cor 4:7-15; then we examine how Paul himself saw his suffering; the third part will present critical remarks which may lead to reflection. In

4. See J. Lambrecht, *"The Nekrôsis of Jesus. Ministry and Suffering in 2 Cor 4,7-15,"* in A. Vanhoye, *L'apôtre Paul. Personnalité, style et conception du ministère.* BETL 73. Louvain, 1986, pp. 120-143, for a more technical treatment of this pericope and for bibliographical references. In his recent publication *Suffering and Hope. The Biblical Vision and the Human Predicament,* Philadelphia, 1987, J.C. Beker devotes two brief chapters to Paul ("Paul's Gospel of Redemptive Suffering", pp. 57-67, and "Paul's Response to Tragic Suffering", pp. 68-79). His approach, however, is very different from ours.

this paper we not only provide detailed exegesis of one specific passage but we also deal with a central issue of Paul's theology.

Analysis of 2 Cor 4:7-15

There are good reasons to take the passage 2 Cor 4:7-15 of Paul's second letter to the Corinthians as a small pericope which, together with 4:16-5:10, is part of the second main section of the apology 2:14-7:4. What is the reasoning that Paul develops within 4:7-15?

Line of Thought

It would seem that we can propose a threefold division for 2 Cor 4:7-15: the unequal units verses 7-12, verses 13-14, and verse 15. For each unit we first present the RSV-translation before discussing the text.

Verses 7-12

> 7 But we have this treasure in earthen vessels, to show that the transcendent power belongs to God and not to us. 8 We are afflicted in every way, but not crushed; perplexed, but not driven to despair; 9 persecuted, but not forsaken; struck down, but not destroyed; 10 always carrying in the body the death of Jesus, so that the life of Jesus may also be manifested in our bodies. 11 For while we live we are always being given up to death for Jesus' sake, so that the life of Jesus may be manifested in our mortal flesh. 12 So death is at work in us, but life in you.

The first person plural within the whole of this pericope (vv. 7-15) is "epistolary" and thus points to Paul (and his fellow workers). Verses 7 through 10 form one long sentence. The "treasure" in verse 7 means Paul's apostolic ministry which was dealt with in 4:1-6. The breakable vessel, that is, the fragility of the apostle, is required so that it may appear that the great power of this service does not come from humans but from God. In verses 8-9 this idea is worked out by means of four antithetical pairs: the eight present participles constitute a list of tribulations. Verses 10 and 11 are more or less parallels. With its participle "carrying", verse 10 still depends on the main clause in verse 7; verse 11, however, is an independent, explanatory sentence. In both verses there is a final clause: "in order that". Paul connects his suffering, as well as the continuation of his life, with the dying and life of Jesus. He suffers Jesus' dying; because of Jesus he is delivered to death so that Jesus' life may be manifested in him. The apostolic suffering is thus a christological manifestation; it is the epiphany of Jesus' life. Verse 12 is a conclusion: "so". But in the meantime a shift has occurred. In verses 7-11 Paul was only speaking of himself, in verse 12 he suddenly also mentions the addressees, the Corinthians: death is at work in us, life is at work in you![5]

It must strike the reader that Paul uses the name of Jesus four times in verses 7-12 and, moreover, twice in verse 14. This is unlike Paul. He certainly remembers the suffering and death of the earthly Jesus.[6] However, in the light of the broader context and the expression "the Lord (Jesus)" in verse 14 one should not assume that the "life of Jesus" in verses 10-11 refers only to the mortal life of the earthly Jesus. No, Paul equally means the life of the risen Christ. The long period of verses 7-10, but also verses 11 and 12 — the final clauses included — deal with Paul's present situation, his life before death. "Vessels" in verse 7, as well as "body" and "mortal flesh" in verses 10-11, does not signify the body without the soul, but the whole person of Paul, albeit with special attention to his mortal fragility which, of course, becomes particularly visible in the body.

Verses 13-14

> 13 Since we have the same spirit of faith as he had who wrote, "I believed, and so I spoke," we too believe, and so we speak, 14

5. In contrast with 1 Cor 4:8 and 2 Cor 11:19-21, neither irony nor sarcasm seems to be present here.

6. But 2 Cor 1:5 (cf. Phil 3:10) has "the sufferings of Christ" (*ta pathêmata tou Christou*) and warns us not to force this often used distinction between the earthly Jesus and the risen Christ.

knowing that he who raised the Lord Jesus will raise us with you into his presence.

In v. 13 we have a new start. The Greek writes a *de*: "But since we have ...". Verses 13 and 14 form together one long sentence. The main verbs are "we believe" and "we speak". In verse 13 Paul cites only three words of Ps 115:1 (the Septuagint): *episteusa, dio elalêsa* ("I believed, and so I spoke"). In all probability "speaking" points here to Paul's apostolic proclamation. Just as the psalmist, Paul, out of the same spirit, believes and, therefore, he speaks — notwithstanding his sufferings.[7] He cannot do otherwise (cf. 5:14a: "The love of Christ controls us"). Thus faith is the first motivation. Verse 14, however, adds a second reason, his hope. For Paul is certain of his future resurrection. God has raised Jesus. "With Jesus" God will also raise him.[8] God will "present" (*parastêsei*) Paul together with the Corinthians. It is not stated explicitly whose presence is meant. Most probably Paul and the Corinthians will be brought into the presence of Jesus (cf. RSV translation: "into his presence").[9]

Verse 15

15 For it is all for your sake, so that as grace extends to more and more people it may increase thanksgiving, to the glory of God.

"For" at the beginning of verse 15 indicates that Paul wants to further explain the phrase "with you" which stands at the end of verse 14. The expression "for your sake" underlines once more the apostolic dimension of Paul's whole existence (cf. "it is all"). The solemn, somewhat overloaded purpose clause of verse 15 is

7. It should be noted that both Paul's believing and speaking differ from those in the psalm where, moreover, the Septuagint text greatly diverges from the Hebrew original.

8. In v. 14 Paul twice uses the verb "to raise" (*egeirô*) and twice, it would seem, in an eschatological sense: the past resurrection of Jesus and the future resurrection of Christians. Thus the sense of the second use ("will raise") is not metaphorical, not pointing to new life before death.

9. Cf. 5:10: "... we must all appear before the judgment seat of Christ ..."; and 1 Thess 4:14: "... so, through Jesus, God will bring with him those who have fallen asleep."

undoubtedly concluding. Paul points to the ultimate aim of all
ministry: God's glory which increases through human thanksgiving.

Comparison of Verse 10 and Verse 11

Our first reading was, as far as verses 10-11 are concerned, a little
too fast. Although the expression "the dying of Jesus," *hê nekrôsis tou Iêsou*, is a hapax legomenon in the New Testament and
thus underlines the importance of verse 10, special attention must
also be devoted to verse 11. In verse 10 the participle "carrying"
has the same grammatical status as the numerous participles in
verses 8-9. Grammatically, verse 10 still belongs to the sentence
which started at verse 7. The adverb of time *pantote* ("all the
time") repeats as it were the phrase *en panti* ("in every way") at
the beginning of verse 8; "the life of Jesus" corresponds to "the
transcendent power" of verse 7; and the whole purpose clause of
verse 10b, moreover, is with regard to the content and somewhat
also to the form the parallel of the purpose clause in verse 7b.
The point of verse 10 consists firstly in the christological identification (the concrete sufferings of Paul are but the dying of
Jesus) and secondly in its paradoxical statement (suffering and
death are needed in order that Jesus' life be manifested precisely
in that concrete existence of Paul).

Verse 11 is grammatically independent. Through its "for" it is
intended as an explication of what precedes. The similarities
between verse 10 and verse 11 are striking. We may present a very
literal version:

> 10a all the time carrying in the body the dying of Jesus,
>   10b in order that also the life of Jesus in our body be manifested.
> 11a For always we, the living ones, are delivered to death for Jesus'
>   sake,
>   11b in order that also the life of Jesus be manifested in our
>   mortal flesh.

Both verses begin with an adverb of time: "all the time, always"
(*pantote, aei*). Just as in verse 10, there are in verse 11 two
clauses. Verse 11b, is like verse 10b, a final clause which, again

like verse 10b, contains the verb "manifest" in the passive and the expression "the life of Jesus." Just as verse 10, verse 11 twice has the name of Jesus, and in both verses there is an opposition between death and life.

Yet no pure reiteration is provided. As already stated, verse 11 is grammatically independent. The verb in verse 11a ("we are delivered") is in the passive, whereas the participle "carrying" in verse 10a is in the active. In verse 11a Paul writes "death" (*thanatos*) instead of "dying" (*nekrôsis*). In verse 11a there is no longer a strict identification: we are delivered "for Jesus' sake." In verse 11a "in the body" is missing; Paul speaks here of "we, the living ones." Verse 11b runs more parallel to verse 10b than verse 11a to verse 10a. Yet even here the parallelism is not complete. One must look at the position of the verb (last in v. 10b; middle in v. 11b) and at the phrase "our mortal flesh" (v. 11b) instead of "our body" (v. 10b).

All these changes modify the structure of verse 11 when compared with that of verse 10. Three particular features should be noticed. (1) We can detect in verse 11 a chiastic outlook: the verbs in verse 11a and verse 11b stand in the middle; at the beginning of verse 11a and the end of verse 11b we have "we, the living ones" and "in our mortal flesh"; at the end of verse 11a and at the beginning of verse 11b we find "for Jesus' sake" and "the life of Jesus". (2) Unlike what is found in 10a (death) and 10b (life), the opposition between death and life is made explicit in *both* clauses 11a and 11b: "we, the living ones ... to death" (v. 11a) and "life ... mortal" (v. 11b). [10] (3) Whereas in verse 10 the *nekrôsis* of Jesus stands over against his life, in verse 11 the opposition is rather between *we*, the living ones, who are always

10. See the dicussion of v. 11 in A. Plummer, *A Critical and Exegetical Commentary on the Second Epistle of Saint Paul to the Corinthians*. ICC, Edinburgh, 1915, p. 131: He calls "we the living ones" a "pointed insertion" and paraphrases: "we are ever a living prey." Further, 'in our mortal flesh' "comes at the end in a tone of triumph and repeats the paradox of *v.* 10 in a stronger form; so that, while the first half of *v.* 11 elucidates the first half of *v.* 10, the second half intensifies the second" (*ibid.*).

being given up to *death* (v. 11a) and the *life* of *Jesus* which is manifested in our mortal flesh.

Our analysis shows that the thesis put forward by Paul in verse 10, namely that he carries in his body the dying of Jesus, is commented on by means of v. 11 in a careful, skillful way. This analysis will prove of great help for our further investigation.

The Suffering of the Apostle

On page 51 we stated that Paul in verses 10-11 points to the whole of his human existence with the expressions "body" and "mortal flesh". All the lists of trials and many other passages from his letters confirm this. Paul suffers not only in his body but also in his soul.[11] We can now proceed to three questions which greatly concern the content. How does Paul evaluate and, intellectually as well as existentially, master his suffering? What is its function and aim? How does Paul want to endure his hardships?

Patterns of Thought

In our passage Paul employs the category of participation. His solidarity, his union with Christ, brings about the result that he himself suffers. Paul's suffering is the dying of Jesus. At the beginning of the same letter to the Corinthians he already had written: "we share abundantly in Christ's sufferings" (1:5) and at the end of that letter he will proclaim: "we are weak in Christ" (13:4). In Gal 2:20 he says: "I have been crucified with Christ",

---

11. Although in 4:16 Paul uses dualistic terminology ("our outer nature is wasting away, our inner nature is being renewed every day") the following verses 17 and 18, as well as the context, make clear that "the inner nature (*anthrôpos*, person, is to be added in Greek)" does not constitute the spiritual part but the whole person who is renewed eschatologically, who becomes "a new creation" (5:17).

and in 6:17: "I bear on my body the marks of Jesus".[12] In Phil
3:7-11 he deals with his union with Christ and his communion
with Christ's sufferings and resurrectional strength. According to
verse 10 Paul will know Christ "and the power of his resurrection;" he will share "his sufferings, becoming like him in his
death." In all probability one must understand this union and
unity in the framework of the Jewish notion of "corporate
personality." Just as the first Adam in a certain (but real) sense
contains in himself all descendants, so also does the second
Adam, Christ. However difficult it may be to specify that unity, a
kind of ontological union with Christ is presupposed by Paul and
referred to frequently in his writings: see, for example, Rom 5:11-
21; 1 Cor 15:20-22 and 2 Cor 5:14-15. That unity with Christ can
be considered in different ways. It was realized through the
historical salvation of Jesus on the cross; it is given to believers
sola fide; it is sacramentally appropriated in baptism;[13] it is
developed in Christian life, more specifically in that of the apostle;
and, finally, the Christian looks forward to it in eschatological
hope. Thus, at its deepest roots, apostolic suffering goes back to
that participation. Hence also the legitimate counterpart of the
statement: Christ manifests himself (epiphany). No opposition
between epiphany and participation (or union) can be detected.

Chapters 8-10 of 1 Corinthians deal with the tension present in
the Corinthian community between the "weak" and the "strong"
regarding the eating of sacrificial meat. In chapter 9 Paul

---

12. 2 Cor 4:10a and Gal 6:17 are very similar. Compare:

2 Cor 4:10a	with	*Gal 6:17*
carrying (*peripherontes*)		I bear (*bastazo*)
in the body		on my body
the dying		the marks
of Jesus		of Jesus.

Besides *hê nekrôsis tou Iêsou* ("the dying of Jesus", 2 Cor 4:10) and *ta stigmata
tou Iêsou* ("the marks of Jesus, Gal 6:17") Paul also uses the phrase *ta pathêmata
tou Christou* ("the sufferings of Christ") in 2 Cor 1:5.

13. The dying of 2 Cor 4:10-11, however, is not "the burial into death" by
baptism (as in Rom 6:3-10), but the process of dying during the entire Christian
life.

attempts to solve the dispute by pointing to himself and his mode of apostolic living as an example to be imitated by all. At the end of the whole discussion he repeats that idea: "... just as I try to please all in everything I do, not seeking my own advantage, but that of many, that they may be saved. Be imitators of me, as I am of Christ" (10:33-11:1). A similar tension is treated in Rom 14:1-15:13. In 15:3 it is Christ who is proposed as an example to the "strong." For Christ did not please himself. Then in 15:7, it is said: "Welcome one another, therefore, as Christ has welcomed you, for the glory of God."

2 Corinthians 8, the section dealing with the collection taken up in Paul's communities, also presents a motif of imitation. Again it is Christ who is to be imitated: "For you know the grace of our Lord Jesus Christ, that though he was rich, yet for your sake he became poor, so that by his poverty you might become rich" (v. 9). In 1 Thess 1:6 we read: "and you became imitators of us and of the Lord, for you received the word in much affliction, with joy inspired by the Holy Spirit." We note how the themes of imitation and suffering are connected here. To this list we could also add Phil 2:5-8, where the renunciation, the *kenôsis*, of Jesus is presented as an example to all Christians. Paul uses this hymn in a paraenetic sense: we must follow Christ's way of acting.

One more passage should be mentioned: 1 Cor 4:6-16, a passage which, like 2 Cor 4:5-15, also contains a list of trials. After Paul stated that the whole discussion of chapters 1-4 was carried out for the benefit of the Corinthians, that is, that they may learn by his example and that of Apollos (v. 6), he opposes in ironical terms community and apostles, puffed up Christians and despised ministers (vv. 7-13). Immediately afterwards, however, not without deep emotion, he pleads with his beloved children: "I urge you, be imitators of me" (vv. 14-16). Apostolic existence is the concrete example to be imitated by the Corinthians. The catalogue of sufferings (vv. 9-13) is thus presented as exemplary conduct, an object of imitation. Of course, God in his wisdom and power has ordained that apostolic suffering and weakness, just as Christ crucified himself could not use wisdom according to human standards. So persecution and labor intrinsically belong to the apostolic vocation. Yet it should be duly recognized that in 1 Corinthians 4 Paul uses that catalogue not, it would seem, to prove his unity with Christ, but to provide his Christians with an example.

All these texts point to an ethic of example and imitation, a *Vorbildethik*. But what precisely induced Paul in 2 Cor 4:10 to connect his missionary suffering with the dying of Jesus? We have already answered: the union of Christ and the apostle. Is it perhaps also the imitation of Christ? Maybe, but in 2 Cor 4:7-15 we do not find the category of imitation. No explicit call to human will and involvement is mentioned. Paul depicts an existing situation and interprets it. Suffering is a reality which is already there, which is not chosen but appears to be intrinsically related to his vocation. Paul considers that reality in some way identical with or at least intimately connected with Christ's passion and death. Thus, our first impression is that the notion of imitation has nothing to do with our attempt to explain 2 Cor 4,7-15. Yet can we be sure that it is completely absent? Verses 11 and 14 warn us.

For Paul, real union with Christ never means the disappearance of the Christian nor the loss of one's identity. In verse 11a Paul almost spontaneously admits a clear separation between Jesus and the apostle. The apostle is always being given up to death "for Jesus' sake". The reason for his tribulations is his faith in Jesus and the preaching of Jesus' gospel (cf. 4:5). Here Jesus' dying is no longer directly present in that of the apostle. By means of the technical term *paradidometha* ("we are being delivered") he most probably compares his own existence with that of Christ. For Paul, his sufferings are, it would seem, a likeness of those of Christ. Paul thus easily uses categories other than direct union in order to explain his connnection with Christ. This is in verse 11a all the more striking, since in verse 11b Paul preserves the union language of verse 10b: "the life of Jesus" is manifested in the body of the apostle. Although Paul believes that those who

are in Christ will be made alive (cf. 1 Cor 15:22), in 2 Cor 4:14 by
the different tense and the parallel placing of Jesus and "we" the
distinction between apostle and Jesus is evident.[14] Paul seems to
point to a being together with Jesus after his own resurrection.

Paul thus somewhat mixes two patterns of thought in 2 Cor
4:7-15. This should warn us against a too radical exclusion of
other concepts than union (such as imitation or conformation
which, admittedly, are not explicitly expressed here).[15]

Function and Aim

How does Paul evaluate his hardships? Do they have a function?
In 2 Cor 4:7-15 Paul is very explicit with regard to these questions. He provides us with a fourfold answer. First, according to
verse 7, there must be suffering in the apostle so that it may be
evident how the all-surpassing power does not come from himself
but belongs to God. God's trancendency will thus be ensured.
This theological reason is at the same time christological. The
identification in verses 10-11 of Paul's suffering with the dying of
Jesus makes this clear. Jesus' life is manifested in the apostolic
existence. Verse 11a, moreover, states plainly that Paul suffers
"for Jesus' sake." Thirdly, in verse 12 the missionary aspect
suddenly appears: death in us, life in you. Although it is not
explicitly stated, in the antithetic verse 12 the apostle's dying
brings about life in those addressed. This is made evident by verse
15a: "it is all for your sake." Between the two clauses in verse 12
there must be a causal link in the mind of Paul. The apostolic
dimension is also present in the "so we speak" at the end of verse

14. The expression "with Jesus" is an anomaly. There is no simultaneity;
Christ is already risen. Paul seems to point to a being together with Jesus (and the
Christians) after his own resurrection.

15. In Rom 6:5 no union language is used, although that language is present in
the context. Within Phil 3:10 Paul moves from union to a "conformity" category.
See also 2 Cor 5:14-15. Further, one should note that in 2 Cor 1:3-11 the category
of union with Christ is present (cf. v. 5); but no "manifestation, epiphany"
language appears nor is there any paradoxical identification of affliction and
comfort.

13. Fourthly, in verse 15b the final theological aim of all missionary endeavor as well as apostolic suffering is indicated: God's
glory. The ultimate horizon is abundance of grace and more and
more prayers of thanksgiving to the glory of God!

Our passage certainly contains a theology of suffering, a *Lei-
denstheologie*. Is it meant polemically, against those who prefer an
apostolic existence of splendor without affliction? Can Paul's
reflection here thus be compared with that of 1 Corinthians 1-2
where the "word of the cross" and "Christ crucified" are a
stumbling block to the Jews and a folly to the Gentiles (cf. 1:23)?
This is not at all unlikely but difficult to specify as long as the
identity of Paul's opponents in 2 Corinthians is not better known.

Attitude and Spirituality

We have tried to place Paul's suffering in a theological thought
system. We have also tried to explain Paul's view of God's aim in
connection with the apostolic hardships. All this provides us with
valuable insights. But how has Paul endured his suffering, in what
attitude and with what spirituality? To this last question the brief
pericope of 2 Cor 4:7-15 again supplies us with a surprisingly
comprehensive answer.

In 4:13 Paul considers *faith* as a compelling power: I believe,
and because of this I speak. He compares this faith with that of
the psalmist. Paul's faith, which started at his conversion, is an
enduring gift from the *past*. This faith clearly enables the apostle
to suffer while proclaiming the gospel.

Paul could and can suffer also because in the midst of his
tribulations he truly experiences God's power and Jesus' life. In
verses 7-12 Paul depicts this paradoxical reality. Notwithstanding
the death which besieges him and is at work in him, there is in an
inexplicable way still remarkable life, visible, not to be denied. In
the midst of weakness there is strength, already now, before
physical death. Despite affliction, perplexity, persecution and
assaults without end, there is, thanks to God, no total despair nor
destruction. One can rightly infer that the daily experience of life
and deliverance expressed in verses 7-12 means for Paul an

encouragement to continue and endure (cf. 1:10). "I can do all things in him who strengthens me" (Phil 4:13). In 2 Cor 12:1-6 Paul boasts of his revelations and visions. But in 12:7-10 he writes: "... a thorn was given me in the flesh, a messenger of Satan, to harass me, to keep me from being too elated. Three times I besought the Lord about this, that it should leave me; but he said to me, 'My grace is sufficient for you, for my power is made perfect in weakness'. I will all the more gladly boast of my weaknesses, that the power of Christ may rest upon me. For the sake of Christ, then, I am content with weaknesses, insults, hardships, persecutions, and calamities; for when I am weak, then I am strong." We cannot understand such language without supposing in him the presence of God's controlling love to which Paul responds with generous *love*, day by day, in the *present*. [16]

But besides that strange mixing "in one another" of power and weakness, of life and dying, there is also "one after the other." The *future* and *hope* are just as much ingredients of Paul's spirituality. The apostle will not go down in death. Resurrectional life is a property in expectation, the eschatological future. In verse 14, using traditional expressions (cf., e.g., Rom 8:11 and 1 Cor 6:14), Paul points to his inner conviction that God who raised the Lord Jesus will raise him also with Jesus and place him in Jesus' presence together with the Corinthians. Both Jesus' resurrection in the past and Paul's own resurrection in the future help the apostle to continue in spite of hardships. His present experience of Jesus' life is but the anticipation of his own future resurrection. That spirituality definitely is based on life already present as well as eschatologically promised. Paul speaks extensively of this hope in 5:1-10. But already before that passage, Paul, immediately after 4:15, betrays his amazingly daring spiritual attitude: "So we

16. In 2 Cor 13:4 Paul says that he will show God's power during his third visit to the Corinthians (cf. 12:14 and 13:1). The future tense "we shall live" does not point to Paul's future resurrection (as in 4:14; see note 8). Cf. J. Lambrecht, "*Philological and Exegetical Notes on 2 Cor 13,4*," *Bijdragen* 46 (1985) 261-269: "... at his third visit to Corinth he Paul will be strong! The reader pauses and suddenly realizes that Paul strikingly presents this strength as anticipative resurrection power" (p. 269).

do not lose heart. Though our outer nature is wasting away, our inner nature is being renewed every day. For this slight momentary affliction is preparing for us an eternal weight of glory beyond all comparison, because we look not to the things that are seen but to the things that are unseen; for the things that are seen are transient, but the things that are unseen are eternal" (4:16-18).[17]

Critical Considerations

Up till now this paper has treated Paul's suffering and, through Paul, that of the apostles. Does Paul also deal with the suffering of Christians? Does suffering in Paul encompass the everyday adversities of life, for example, human tensions, natural calamities and various illnesses? Must a function be given to all suffering so that all sorrow can become fruitful? Is suffering for the Christian inevitable, intended by God? What call for the Christian goes out from Paul's letters as far as suffering is concerned? The consideration of these five questions brings us to critical remarks and may contribute to an in-depth debate.

The Suffering of Christians

There can be no doubt that in 2 Cor 4:7-15 Paul deals with his own suffering. It is that of the apostle; it is specifically rooted in his missionary life. The fact that the "treasure" in verse refers to the ministry, together with the distinction between "we" and "you" throughout verses 12-15, makes this clear. But we should not postulate an opposition between two kinds of suffering, apostolic and Christian.[18] Already in 4:16-5:10, the distinction

17. Also in 1 Cor 15:30-32 Paul argues that he would not have endured his apostolic suffering without his hope of the resurrection: "Why am I in peril every hour? I protest, brethren, by my pride in you which I have in Christ Jesus our Lord, I die every day! What do I gain if, humanly speaking, I fought with beasts at Ephesus? If the dead are not raised, 'Let us eat and drink, for tomorrow we die'" (cf. v. 19: "If for this life only we have hoped in Christ, we are of all men most to be pitied").

18. This distinction is sustained by, e.g., Scott J. Hafemann, *Suffering and the Spirit*. WUNT, Tübingen 19, 1986, p. 75.

between Paul and his Christians disappears. In 5:10, the "we all" encompasses all of them alike (cf. 3:-18). It is most probable that the widening of this "we" already starts in 4:16-18, a section which speaks of the same affliction as that in 4:7-12.[19]

An even more persuasive argument for the relation between apostle and Christian is provided by the paragraph at the beginning of the same letter, 1:3-11. This "eulogy" (cf. 1:3) is similar to our passage in many respects. Not only do we find here much of the vocabulary of 4:7-15, but many of the ideas are also analogous. According to 1:3-11 Paul, the apostle of Christ, suffers; he shares abundantly in Christ's suffering; his suffering is for the sake of the Corinthians; his suffering goes to the limit of death but God always delivers him; his weakness makes him rely not on himself but on God alone who raises the dead; and the purpose clause of 1:11 strikingly resembles that of 4:15 both in form and content. In 1:6-7 it is twice explicitly stated that the Corinthians endure the same suffering which Paul suffers: "If we are afflicted, it is for your comfort and salvation; and if we are comforted, it is for your comfort, which you experience when you patiently endure the same sufferings that we suffer. Our hope for you is unshaken; for we know that as you share in our sufferings, you will also share in our comfort."

The two most evident passages in Paul's letters are those which speak of imitation. In 1 Thess 1:6 the vocabulary is still general: "And you became imitators of us and of the Lord, for you received the word in much affliction, with joy inspired by the Holy Spirit." But in 1 Cor 4:9-13, in the midst of an emotional and somewhat bitter, incriminating passage, we find a list of trials: "For I think that God has exhibited us apostles as last of all, like men sentenced to death; because we have become a spectacle to the world, to angels and to men. We are fools for Christ's sake, but you are wise in Christ. We are weak, but you are strong. You are held in honor, but we in disrepute. To the

19. Barrett, *2 Cor* (n. 2), p. 126, commenting on v. 18, points to the ease with which Paul moves from apostle to Christians: "the transition is one that is inherent in Paul's thought."

present hour we hunger and thirst, we are ill-clad and buffeted
and homeless, and we labor, working with our hands. When
reviled, we bless; when persecuted, we endure; when slandered,
we try to conciliate; we have become, and are now, as the refuse
of the world, the offscouring of all things." In verses 14-15 he
goes on: "I do not write this to make you ashamed, but to
admonish you as my beloved children. For though you have
countless guides in Christ, you do not have many fathers. For I
became your father in Christ Jesus through the gospel." And
then, in verse 16, there is the appeal which cannot be misunderstood: "I urge you, then, be imitators of me."

The suffering of the Christian is undoubtedly of the same kind
as that of the apostle. Yet the apostle does have his own suffering
connected with the specificity of his vocation. So, in 2 Cor 5:18-
19, Paul in all clarity presents his vision of the apostle's position
within God's salvific work. But then again one should realize that
every person, as soon as he or she becomes a Christian, must be
seen as a potential apostle and is already an apostle in some real
sense. It would therefore be unwise to radically divorce the
apostolic hardships of 2 Cor 4:7-15 from those of all Christians.

All Sufferings

Whoever reads the whole of Paul's letters, especially all his lists of
trials, cannot escape a twofold, at first sight rather contradictory,
impression. The sufferings which Paul has in mind and also
mentions most frequently are persecution, Jewish opposition and
punishments, care and anxiety, toil and trouble, hunger, thirst,
labor and sleepless nights: apparently all sufferings which are
related to his apostolic mission. But, on the other hand, Paul
quite easily regards the negative aspects inherent to human nature
or God's creation as part of that suffering: frictions and adversities, wind and weather, illness and decay, robbers and numerous
dangers.

In Rom 8:17 Paul states that we as children of God, together
with Christ, will be heirs of God, "provided we suffer with him in
order that we may also be glorified with him." In verse 18 the

horizon broadens: "I consider that the sufferings of this present time are not worth comparing with the glory that is to be revealed to us." Obviously, Paul does not exclude any type of suffering.

Meaningful, Fruitful?

Paul was certainly convinced that his suffering contributed to the fecundity of his ministry. Suffice it to refer again to 2 Cor 4:12 and 15. A great number of New Testament passages, as well as traditional Catholic doctrine, state that the Lord Jesus, in a much more eminent way than his disciples, has suffered as an apostle and that his passion and death produced unexpected rich fruits: remission of sin, destruction of the curse, redemption and salvation.

Many Christians today ask the question whether all kinds of suffering, also those hardships which are not directly connected with missionary life, also the absurd, meaningless pain which should be avoided as much as possible, whether thus all sufferings can be made meaningful and fruitful. The traditional assumption is a decisive yes. It would seem that Paul subscribes to such a view, and rightly so.

No human suffering must remain caught in senselessness. To be sure, absurd, dull suffering itself does not become meaningful; moreover, it is not always removed. But through the Christian way we endure our sufferings, we are able to transform them as it were and make them function in a life with sense and purpose. "For this slight momentary affliction is preparing (*katergazetai* = brings about) for us an eternal weight of glory beyond all comparison" (2 Cor 4:17).

Necessary Suffering?

Through his suffering and death Christ has redeemed us. Since we are united with him, we too will have to suffer. One finds this conviction in Paul and elsewhere in the New Testament. It has become classic in Christianity. Is suffering then necessary for a

Christian? Must suffering perhaps even be sought and cherished? Is the suffering of a Christian an essential part of what is called the theology of the cross, *theologia crucis*?

Modern sensitivity avoids answering these questions too quickly or in an easy, too positive way. Perhaps today, more than in the past, we better realize that suffering as such should never be glorified. Suffering belongs to this passing world. Since grief and pain can "separate us from the love of Christ" (Rom 8:35), suffering possesses its own great danger. Suffering is negative and in itself evil. Poverty, hunger, tyranny, violation of human rights and war must be avoided and removed in all possible ways. We must, moreover, not forget that the majority of people find their vocation and daily work precisely in the fight against all kinds of suffering, in the striving for a better world, material and social as well as spiritual.

Yet both philosophical reflection and common sense teach us that there will always be suffering, not only natural catastrophes, illnesses, loneliness and depression, decay and death, but also hate and personal failure, and moral misery caused by human persons themselves. Alas, suffering can only be partly avoided. Many people, it should be kept in mind, take upon themselves the suffering of others in a spirit of sacrifice and outgoing, active compassion. In Colossians Paul says that he rejoices in his sufferings for his fellow Christians and wants to complete in his flesh "what is lacking in Christ's afflictions for the sake of his body, that is, the church" (1:24).

The disciple is not above the master (cf. Matt 10:24). Christians, therefore, call their concrete suffering — the misery which cannot be healed as well as the consciously chosen hardships — necessary because of their union with Christ. With "necessary" they mean that this suffering is not just fatal. An amount of suffering must be taken up in the project of their life, in their spirituality. It belongs to the pattern of the redemption. "The foolishness of God is wiser than men, and the weakness of God is stronger than men" (1 Cor 1:25). Christians duly recognize that such a vision, part and parcel of Paul's preaching of the cross, a scandal or a folly for this world, is easier to proclaim than to practice.

The Appeal

The foregoing considerations of the value and non-value of suffering should enable us to better realize how difficult and delicate the balance will be between the continual fight against suffering and its conscious acceptance. Fatalism or stoic impassivity cannot be a recommended attitude for a Christian. Faith in Christ crucified tells us that no suffering must remain mired in despair. All suffering can become fruitful in an apostolic way. To believe in such a message is a great comfort; it is also a challenge, an appeal. Followers of Christ, past and present, show us the way.

At the end of this essay our attention goes back to Paul's exposition in 2 Cor 4:7-15. In this pericope Paul emphasizes the apostolic, christological and theological functions of his suffering. As it were by accident, he also exposes to the reader what his inner inspiration is. He points to God as the source of the power that drives him.[20] This power comes from his union with the Lord Jesus, his experience of love now in the present. It also comes from the faith that although received long ago in the past remains very much alive. It is equally present in the hope of the future, of things that are eternal: his own resurrection, that of his fellow Christians, and the presence of the Lord Jesus Christ for ever. Our redeemer Christ "will change our lowly body to be like his glorious body, by the power which enables him even to subject all things to himself" (Phil 3:21).

According to Paul and the whole New Testament, suffering is not a dead end. The suffering of the apostle and that of all Christians is not the last word. Paul does not admit dualism. What lies in the eschatological future is risen life, life without suffering, and, through all this, God's greater glory.

---

20. Cf. Hodgson, "*Tribulation Lists*" (n. 1), p. 66: "In describing the paradox and way of Paul's diakonia ('ministry') it aims primarily at establishing God as the source of the power which transforms affliction, perplexity, despair, and persecution into conditions for the possibility of authentic ministry".

THE THEME OF THE "SUFFERING" GOD: AN EXPLORATION

Marc Steen

To speak about the terrible suffering of a human being and its relationship to God is a difficult undertaking. A thematic approach of God's relationship to human suffering is at least equally difficult. Despite the difficulties, many such attempts have now been made. Quite striking is the ease with which discourse on a "suffering" God seems to find acceptance at the present time.

A Surprising Change

The growing interest in the theme of the suffering God, with both Judaeo-Christian theologians or philosophers as well as spiritual thinkers, causes some surprise. *The Crucified God* of the German theologian Jürgen Moltmann has become widely known. The phrase of process-philosopher Alfred North Whitehead about God as the "fellow-sufferer who understands" has become sort of common knowledge. Many people know about the publication of *La Souffrance de Dieu* by the French Jesuit François Varillon. These three represent a clear indication of a completely new movement of thought, which has been gradually developing since the nineteenth century.[1]

All in all, this is a remarkable change of direction. For centuries

1. W. McWilliams, *The Passion of God: Divine Suffering in Contemporary Protestant Theology*, Macon, 1985, pp. 5 and 14; R. Bauckham, "Only the Suffering God Can Help: Divine Passibility in Modern Theology," *Themelios* 9 (1984) 6-12; P. Schoonenberg, "Lijden van God?," *Ons Geestelijk Leven* 56 (1979) 33-44, p. 33.

Christian tradition very firmly asserted the impassibility of God.[2] The fact that contrasting voices arose on the fringes, did not detract from the indisputable axiom regarding the *apatheia* of God.[3] In the third century patripassianism was branded as heretical.[4] That God the Father would have suffered in Christ's death on the cross was resolutely dismissed. A couple of centuries later it was proclaimed by some that "God has suffered."[5] This "theopaschitism" (observe the derivation from the Greek words *theos* (God) and *paschein* (to suffer)) resounded especially in circles, in which the divinity of Christ and the unity of his person were emphasized. Burning theopaschite disputes were settled at the Council of Constantinople (553). The Church accepted the idea that Christ, who is truly God, has been crucified "in the flesh." By no means did this affirmation make the claim that the divine nature as such was passible. The tendency to deny suffering to God himself has clearly remained dominant in the history of Christian thought. However much Luther's theology of the cross resulted in the notion of a crucified God, the Reformed line of thought remained faithful to the tenet of an impassible God.

Whence, then, the reversal since the nineteenth century? That

2. J.K. Mozley, *The Impassibility of God: A Survey of Christian Thought*, London, 1926; G. Wondra, "The Pathos of God", *The Reformed Review* 18 (Dec. 1964) 23-35.

3. H. Küng, Excursus II: "Can God suffer?," in *The Incarnation of God as Prolegomena to a Future Christology*, transl. by J.R. Stephenson, Edinburgh, 1987, pp. 518-525.

4. The patripassianists — we especially think of Noetus and Praxeas (Tertullian strongly opponed to the latter) — held a monarchian modalistic view, in which the unity of God is over-accentuated. In this conception Father and Son are merely seen as manifestations or modalities of the deity, which is essentially and undifferentiatedly one.

5. The sentence "Who was crucified for our sake" (*ho staurootheis di' hèmas*) that Peter Fullo added to the *Trishagion* ("Holy God, Holy Strong One, Holy Immortal One, Who was crucified for our sake") aroused the theopaschite controversy in a heated way. Scythian monks aimed at an ecclesiastical approval of this theopaschitism. In the end of the fifth ecumenical Council (Constantinople, 553) a theopaschitely souding formula was accepted, though with this very important amendment: *en sarki* (in Greek) or *carne* (in Latin). Cf. W. Elert, "Die Theopaschitische Formel," *TLZ* 75 (1950) 195-206. and the dissertation of M. Feitsma, *Het Theopaschitisme*, Kampen, 1956.

the classical theologoumenon of the *impassibilitas Dei* (impassibility of God) is being critically questioned and that by many contemporary thinkers — albeit not always that explicitly and systematically — a "growing consensus about divine suffering" is to be perceived, points to what Daniel Day Williams calls a "structural shift." [6] That — however — not everyone falls in with this trend, is apparent from the controversial propositions that the question "Can God suffer?" elicits on many fronts. [7]

In this essay, however, we are not so much going to enter that (otherwise fascinating) arena. Rather we will make a short "propaedeutic" exploration. We will first probe some of the impulses that have made possible the new orientation. Then, in a second moment, we will consider some of its semantic aspects.

Three Approaches

In our opinion the present-day theopaschite discourse has come about under the impulse of three factors, which actually work in convergence. [8]

Biblical and Christological Theological Discourse

A first line of approach in the suffering-of-God-position is of a specifically theological nature.

In the biblical-theological movement a static concept of God has been exchanged for a dynamic perspective in which God is conceived as personal, loving, and history-making; as such, He is

6. "Growing consensus about divine suffering," in W. McWilliams, *Passion*, p. 16; "structural shift," in D.D. Williams, *What Present-day Theologians Are Thinking*, Westport, 1978 (1st. ed. 1952) p. 138. For the opposition against the impassibilitas-tradition, see, among others, T.E. Pollard, "The Impassibility of God," *Scottish Journal of Theology* 8 (1955) 353-364.

7. J.K. Mozley, *Impassibility*, p. ix speaks of "a controversial question."

8. Cf. P.S. Fiddes, *The Creative Suffering of God*, Oxford, 1988, ch. II: "Why belief in a Suffering God?"

72   MARC STEEN

involved with his creation and his people. It is striking that God
is represented in an "anthropomorphic" manner in the bible.
Even such human feelings as love, anger and sorrowful regret
are attributed to Him. Hence theologians increasingly wish to
valorize the so-called "anthropomorphic" and "anthropopathic"
God.[9] So the living God of the Bible comes into focus. In this
atmosphere a theology regarding the suffering of God has been
able to take root. Without scrutinizing the scriptural data in every
detail, we can mention some of its leitmotifs.[10]

In the Old Testament, attention is readily drawn to the alliance
of Yahweh with his suffering people, as is narrated in Exodus,
and also to the divine pathos, which is especially revealed in the
prophetic experience. This latter aspect has been especially highlighted by the Jewish thinker Abraham Heschel.[11] According to
Heschel the prophets of the Old Testament experienced God not
as an unmoved *Absolutum*, exempt from all suffering, but as
Someone who participates of his own free will and interest in the
history of his "partner." Greek philosphy's apathy-principle
with regard to the concept of God was erroneously adopted by
Jewish philosophers like Jehuda Halevi, Maimonides, and Spi-
noza. If, however, one wants to do justice to the Semitic experience of God's passion, then that priciple must be broken down.
From the Old Testament perspective the pathic God, who shares
the fortunes of humans, is assented to by sym-pathetic people.
Here we are apparently facing the antipodes of the Stoic ideal of

9. We allude to the work of H.M. Kuitert, *De mensvormigheid Gods*, Kampen,
1969. Opponents of the idea of divine passibility argue that anthropomorphic
statements about God have to be interpreted figuratively, symbolically or meta-
phorically. For an illustration, see L.J. Kuyper, "The Suffering and Repentance of
God," *Scottish Journal of Theology* 22 (1969) 257-277.
10. Some biblical clues are, for instance, indicated by D.D. Williams, *The
Spirit and the Forms of Love*, New York & Evanston, 1968, ch. II and III and in
his article, "The Vulnerable and the Invulnerable God," *USQR* 17 (1962) 223-229.
See also the interesting publication of T.E. Fretheim, *The Suffering of God: An Old
Testament Perspective*, Philadelphia, 1984. We can find further references in W.
McWilliams, *Passion*, pp. 7-9.
11. A.J. Heschel, *The Prophets*, New York, 1962; J.C. Merkle, *The Genesis of
Faith: The Depth Theology of Abraham Joshua Heschel*, New York, 1985.

apatheia. A dipolar theology comes into light. God is the almighty, supreme celestial Lord as well as the humble Partner of the Alliance, who has attached himself in passionate, unique solidarity to Israel and all indigent people, says Heschel.

From the New Testament's point of view, reflection is consistently carried forward in the awareness of faith that "God is love" (1 John 4:8). That love has been revealed in a preeminent way in Christ. He is the privileged and normative point of departure for every truly Christian doctrine of God. Emboldened by this principle, theologians draw from the concrete history of Jesus far-reaching conclusions with regard to their understanding of the trinitarian being of God himself. The center of gravity of divine love is often recognized in the preaching of the Cross. The christological concentration upon the expiatory passion of God's Son is therefore considered by several authors as the deepest ground for attributing suffering to God. The current theopaschite tendency has to an important degree been prompted by the christocentric theological discourse about the history of the cross of Christ. It is notable that the impulse for this has principally come from Anglo-Saxon circles. [12] More precisely, Anglican reflections about the notion of sacrifice have ushered in and catalysed this tendency. The theme of the cross on Golgotha was spontaneously associated with the heart of triune God. Even though some Roman-Catholic theologians were involved, discourse about a passible God more readily found a home in recent expositions of the Protestant *theologica crucis* (theology of the Cross). [13]

12. Cf J. Moltmann, *The Trinity and the Kingdom of God*, transl. M. Kohl, London, 1981, ch. II, 3. For an excellent account of the emergence of new theopaschite tendencies in British theology of the nineteenth century, see A. Van Egmond, *De lijdende God in de Britse Theologie van de negentiende eeuw. De bijdrage van Newman, Maurice, McLeod Campbell en Gore aan de christelijke theopaschitische traditie*, Amsterdam, 1986.

13. Most important Catholic representatives are H. Küng (see footnote 3); F. Varillon, *La souffrance de Dieu*, Paris, 1975; H.U. von Balthasar, "Mysterium Paschale," in *Mysterium Salutis*. Grundriss heilsgeschichtlicher Dogmatik III, 2, 1969, pp. 159-166; K. Rahner, *Theological Investigations* IV, London, 1966, pp. 112-120; H. Mühlen, *Die Veränderlichkeit Gottes als Horizont einer zukünf-*

74 MARC STEEN

The New Metaphysical Ideas of Process Thought

A set of metaphysical concepts, as they find expression in process thought, offers the basis for a second approach to the idea of divine passibility.[14]

The key to the interpretation of all reality is the human experience, characterized by communication and historicity. Thus Whiteheadian process thought, which is a philosophy of "organism." Everything takes its place in a creative development. The massive impact of the theory of evolution also bears witness to this. According to process thinkers, God forms no exception at all to this general rule of relationality and temporality. He is eminently a communicative event. He evolves in close connection with the world, in a history of gift and receptivity. So he takes up the weal and woe of the world-process in his own becoming.

That this sort of image of God involves passibility is probably obvious. Therefore process thinkers act vigorously against classical metaphysical theism, in which the single pole of God's immutability and impassibility is sustained.[15] They hold the view that their metaphysically founded concept of God corresponds more adequately not only with the standards of a global vision that is rational, coherent, and based on experience, but also with the authentic biblical message. A protest against blending the

---

tigen Christologie. Auf dem Wege zu einer Kreuzestheologie in Auseinandersetzung mit der altkirchlichen Christologie, Münster, 1969; J. Galot, Dieu souffre-t-il?, Paris, 1976; J. Kamp, Souffrance de Dieu, vie du monde, Tournai, 1971. For the contribution of Protestant theology, see, for example, W. McWilliams, Passion.

14. Good introductions to process thought are E.H. Peters, The Creative Advance, St. Louis, 1966; J.B. Cobb & D. Griffin, Process Theology: An Introductory Exposition, Philadelphia, 1976. For a credable commentary on the theme of a suffering God in (Whiteheadian) process thought see J. Vanhoutte, "God as companion and fellow-sufferer. An Image emerging from Process Thought," Theodicea Oggi?, Archivio de Filosofia 56 (1988) n°1-3, Roma, 191-225. See also J. Van der Veken, ed., God and Change. Process Thought and the Christian Doctrine of God, (Center of Metaphysics and Philosophy of God), Louvain, 1987.

15. According to their dipolar metaphysics, process thinkers reject classical theism, which has the bad habit of attributing "metaphysical compliments" to God, so that the pole of mutability and passibility is disregarded.

typically Judaeo-Christian dynamic message with the static mental categories of the Hellenic tradition, is frequently heard.[16]

We are also obliged to reflect on the contribution of Hegel to this matter. Has he not indissolubly correlated the historical and the tragical with the self-becoming of the Spirit? Among those who opt for a suffering God, a Hegelian ferment is often — if only latently — at work.[17]

Among the process thinkers who explicitly speak about the suffering of God, we can mention Alfred North Whitehead, Charles Hartsthorne, Edgar Brightman, F.R. Tennant, Henry Nelson Wieman, Bernard Meland, W. Norman Pittenger and Daniel Day Williams.

The God Question which Proceeds from Human Suffering

The existential experience of human suffering constitutes a third possible point of departure for speaking about a suffering God.[18]

The God question which emerges from human suffering is very critical. How are "God" and "suffering" to be harmonized? The theodicy question remains ultimately unresolved. It is notable, however, that several contemporary thinkers fix their attention less upon the divine origin of suffering than on a divine response to suffering.[19] If God is truly love, then He must be affected by so many violent forms of misery and pain. "How can we believe

16. Criticism of classical theism and the demand for a "dehellenisation" of the Christian idea of God are characteristic of proponents of the idea of divine passibility, also in circles outside the so-called "process philosophy." See, e.g. T.J. Van Bavel, "De lijdende God," *Tijdschrift voor Theologie* 14 (1974) 131-149, p. 141.

17. Some critics recognize an implicit Hegelianism in Moltmann's theology: cf. R. Bauckham, "Moltmanns Eschatologie des Kreuzes," in M. Welker, ed., *Diskussion über Jürgen Moltmanns Buch "Der gekreuzigte Gott"*, Munich, 1979, 43-53, esp.pp. 44-45.

18. Paul Tillich thinks the problem of the (im)passibility of God may not be avoided and this "in view of the question's significance for the most existential problem of theodicy." See P. Tillich, *Systematic Theology*, Vol. III, Chicago, 2nd. ed. 1964, p. 404.

19. W. McWilliams, *Passion*, pp. 3-4.

that God is love if it is to be thought that our suffering does not
affect him in his eternal being?" François Varillon wonders.[20] An
apathic God who, staying in his own bliss, is the unmoved
observer of misfortune "is by contemporary man justly experienced as cynical and readily dismissed," says Brantschen.[21] So
the idea catches on: God's response to suffering is to be found in
his sympathizing and compassionate love.[22] He heals our suffering by sharing in it.

Undoubtedly "personal experience and culture" plays a
role in the possible sensitivity to something like a suffering
God.[23] So the speculations of the Spanish poet and philosopher
Miguel de Unamuno (1864-1936) about the tragic attitude to life
(*congoja*) and God's corresponding sorrow are anchored in personal experiences of anxiety.[24] That the American James Cone
embraces the theme of the God of the oppressed, affected by
suffering and fellow-combatant, is partly due to his experience of
the oppression and the emancipatory strength of the black in
America.[25] Moreover, the two World Wars offer a strong
impulse for a fresh revival of the theme of the suffering God. As
regards the First World War we find, for example, the very
influential book, *The Hardest Part*, by Studdert Kennedy, the
English preacher and poet.[26] In 1946 Kazoh Kitamori, a Japa-

20. F. Varillon, *Souffrance*, p. 14: "Comment croire que Dieu est Amour, s'il
faut penser que notre souffrance ne l'atteint pas dans son être éternel?"
21. J.B. Brantschen, "Die Macht und Ohnmacht der Liebe. Randglossen zum
dogmatischen Satz: Gott ist unveränderlich", *Freiburger Zeitschrift für Philosophie
und Theologie* 27 (1980) 224-246, p. 226.
22. Cf. K. Surin, "Theodicy?" *HTR* 76 (1983) 225-247. H.W. Robinson argues
the relevance of a suffering God to suffering people in *Suffering, Human and
Divine*, New York, 1939.
23. W. McWilliams, *Passion*, p. 187: "personal experience and culture."
24. Cf. J. Moltmann, *Trinity*, ch. II, 4.
25. Esp. J.H. Cone, *God of the Oppressed*, New York, 1975. Cf. W. McWilliams, *Passion*, pp. 51-95, p. 187.
26. Cf. J.K. Mozley, *Impassibility*, pp. 157-160, esp. p. 160: "The thoughts of
The Hardest Part came to its author on the battlefields of the West, and their
intensity, both in idea and expression, reveals clearly enough the pressure and
tension of such tremendous experiences."

nese, finished his epoch-making work about the sorrow of God, which "signaled a new interest in divine suffering."[27] Dietrich Bonhoeffer's theopaschite statements also are marked by the terror of war. His conviction that "only the suffering God can help" natured in prison.[28] We are moved by the story of the Jew Elie Wiesel — who himself has gone through the horrors of Nazism — who places God on the side of the victim: "He is hanging there on the gallows".[29] After Auschwitz the image of God as a potentate is best smashed to pieces. Equally influenced by his personal afflictions, Jürgen Moltmann arrived at his theology of the suffering God. He testifies: "Shattered and broken, the survivers of my generation were then returning from camps and hospitals to the lecture room. A theology which did not speak of God in the sight of the one who was abandoned and crucified would have had nothing to say to us then."[30]

One of the frequently recurring "topics" in the complicated network of issues related to our theme, is the question, whether God's compassionate, loving response to the extreme distress of humans necessarily implies sorrow for himself. A positive answer seems to be suggested by the current success of the idea of a "suffering" God. Nonetheless, we must limit this essay to a few introductory issues. However, the point of view of Francis Fio-

27. W. McWilliams, *Passion*, p. 22. The English translation of Kitamori's book is *Theology of the Pain of God*, London, 1966 and the German translation is *Die Theologie des Schmerzes Gottes*, Göttingen, 1972. Thanks to these translations, the attention to the theology of the suffering God has been increased in the West.

28. D. Bonhoeffer, *Letters and Papers from Prison*, New York, enlarged ed., 1976, p. 361.

29. We can find the frequently quoted story of Elie Wiesel in his book *Night*, London, 1972, pp. 76-77: "The SS hanged two Jewish men and a youth in front of the whole camp. The men died quickly, but the death throes of the youth lasted for half an hour. 'Where is God? Where is he?' someone asked behind me. As the youth still hung in torment in the noose after a long time, I heard the man call again, 'Where is God now?' And I heard a voice in myself answer: 'Where is he? He is here. He is hanging there on the gallows....'"

30. J. Moltmann, *The Crucified God: The Cross of Christ as the Foundation and Criticism of Christian Theology*, transl. by R.A. Wilson & J. Bowden, London, 1974, p. 1.

renza is indeed relevant: "In discussing the pain of God, we must be aware that we are first of all dealing not with God directly but with a question of our language about God."[31] Hence, the second part of our introductory overview will consist of a discussion of some of the linguistic aspects of the issue.

Semantic Exploration

The obvious way to grasp the full import of the term "(im)-passibility" is to start from the semantic components that lie contained in the original Greek lexical field around *pathos*, the equivalent of the Latin *passio*.[32] A broad and variegated vista quickly opens up: "The semantics of *pathos* breaks up into a multitude of significations."[33] We can distinguish three significant circles.

The Three Fields of Meaning of Pathos

A first fundamental sphere of meaning can be associated with the

31. F.P. Fiorenza, "Joy and Pain as Paradigmatic for language about God," *Concilium* 10 (1974) 67-80, p. 75.

32. We think of the Greek words which are cognate to *pathos*: *pascho, pathêma, pathêtos, apatheia*... and the Latin terms, circulating around *passio*: *pati, affectus, impassibilitas*... The following lexicographical investigation is based on R. Eisler, "Passio," in *Wörterbuch der Philosophischen Begriffe*, Zweiter Band (2nd. ed. 1904) p. 80; A. Heschel, *Prophets*, pp. 247-265; H. Küng, *art. cit.*; A. Lalande, "Passion," in *Vocabulaire technique et critique de la Philosophie* (1972) pp. 745-747; G.W.H. Lampe, *"apatheia-apathês, pathêtos-pathos,"* in *A Patristic Greek Lexicon* (1961), pp. 170-172 and 991-996; H.G. Liddell & R. Scott, *"Pathos,"* in *Greek-English Lexicon* 2 (1948) p. 1285; W. Michaelis, *"pascho...,"* TWNT 5 (1954) pp. 903-939; W.L. Reese, "Passion," in *Dictionary of Philosophy and Religion: Eastern and Western Thought* (1980) p. 415; H. Reiner, "Apathie," in J. Ritter, ed., *Historisches Wörterbuch der Philosophie* 1 (1971) pp. 429-434.

33. "Le sémantisme du pathos éclate en une multitude de significations," in H. Parret, *Les Passions. Essai sur la Mise en Discours de la Subjectivité*, Brussels, 1986, p. 11.

notion of "suffering" in its strict sense. "Suffering" speaks of a painful event, of sorrow and distress. This tendency is found in the original Greek discourse, where very specific meanings are linked to the *pathos*-lexical group. There are allusions to "disease," "dying," "punishment," and "defeat."

A second meaning of *pathos* pertains to the emotional field. The concept is profiled in terms of feeling and sensibility. Again a whole spectrum of possible specified meanings unfolds. *Pathos* can stand for affect, passion, sexual impulse or — in a outspokenly negative direction — an irrational, if not guilty, emotion or desire.

In the third place *pathos* also functions in the general sense of "experience." In that way it is an ontological concept, which points to an event with receptive character, to "undergoing" and "being acted upon." With Aristotle we find the notion as a category, opposed to that of action. *Pathos*, interpreted as receptivity, is a modality of change. More precisely we think about being affected by external factors. In this respect traditional metaphysics could conceive impassibility as a form of immutability (or: *passibilitas* as a *species* of the *mutabilitas*).[34] Thus "suffering" — broadly understood — can obtain the signification of "being influenced."

Towards a Positive Connotation of Pathos

The classical Greek *pathos*-concept is characterized by a predominantly pejorative overtone. Connotations of disaster, irrationality, and passivity which deprive humans of their freedom, adhere to it. In tradition this element is hardly to be overestimated. Among the present advocates of the idea of a "suffering" God, however, little of the concept's negativity can be perceived. With respect to the three levels of meaning discussed above, *pathos*

---

34. Cf. R.E. Creel, *Divine Impassibility: An Essay in Philosophical Theology*, Cambridge, 1986.

80   MARC STEEN

even acquires a positive potentiality of meaning. The shift towards this new content of *pathos* in the modern range of thought about the suffering God gives food for thought.

1) From pathos as evil fate to suffering as accepted solidarity

Insofar as one's perspective is Greek, the traditional notion of *pathos*, conceived as "suffering" in the strict sense, displays dominant negative characteristic. In it looms the doom of chaotic and harmful fatalism. However, those who favor the notion of divine passibility refer to a distinction between suffering as a purely fatal, passive and paralysing event and suffering as a free, constructive act of solidarity and openness.[35] We find the plea for a "pathic," vulnerable attitude to life in, for example, the writings of Dorothee Sölle. By way of illustration, we can mention a few of her main ideas.[36]

In basic agreement with Simone Weil, Sölle cites three dimensions of evil: physical, psychic and social suffering.[37] Only the interweaving of these three elements, of which social suffering forms the decisive and intensifying factor, leads to the total experience of isolation and despair. Two attitudes towards suffering are possible: patiently born silence, which culminates in apathy, and the "productive" strength to suffer which makes possible the retrieval of communication.[38]

A morbid position in the presence of suffering is that of

35. J.Y. Lee, *God suffers for Us. A Systematic Inquiry into a Concept of Divine Passibility*, The Hague, 1974, pp. 41-42: "Suffering which is due to evil" opposite to "suffering which is due to vicarious sacrifice" — "redemptive suffering"; J. Moltmann, *Crucified God*, p. 230: "But there are other forms of suffering between unwilling suffering as a result of an alien cause and being essentially unable to suffer, namely active suffering, the suffering of love, in which one voluntarily opens himself to the possibility of being affected by another."
36. Our comments are based on some passages of D. Sölle, *Suffering*, transl. by Everett R. Kalin, London, 1975 and Sölle, *Sympathie. Theologisch-politische Traktate*, Stuttgart-Berlin, 1978.
37. Sölle, *Suffering*, pp. 13-16.
38. Ibid., p. 168.

"purely passive endurance."[39] When misfortune is experienced as an inevitable destiny, the human is stuck in a resigned dullness, mesmerized and thrown back upon the self. This attitude to suffering is sealed in the bourgeois ideal of apathy, because of which a creative, humanizing approach to suffering is excluded.[40] In the contemporary industrialized consumer culture a "panic fright for suffering" is unchained, as Leszek Kolakowski puts it.[41] The cry to be free from suffering is overwhelming.[42] Immediately, however, the concern to involve oneself with others on a deeply human level floats away. Through apathy we inwardly deny our own suffering and we are rendered incapable of compassion for the outside world.[43] This double face of apathy — the deadening repression of one's own pain and a cool, resigned indifference towards the other — reveals an absurd stagnation, through which all sense of community is nipped in the bud. The apathic structure eventually demonstrates a "necrophilic orientation."[44]

Rare and extremely precious is the "suffering that can humanize" people "in a productive way."[45] Passibility is then no longer shunned, and paralyzed by a defensive retreat or a sterile,

39. Ibid., p. 75.

40. Sölle, *Sympathie*, p. 9: "A-pathie als die wahre Bürgertugend;" Sölle, *Suffering* p. 38: "in keeping with middle-class ideals"; p. 101: "Socially and politically expressed, tranquility is an ideal for the upper classes, just as the apathetic God is not the God of the little people and their pain."

41. Sölle, *Sympathie*, p. 32: "panischen Flucht vor dem Leiden". Cf. "Le projet du monde moderne, je le sais, est antitragique", in F. Varillon, *Souffrance*, p. 23.

42. Sölle, *Sympathie*, p. 36.

43. Ibid. p. 34: "Apathie als Leidverleugnung nach innen, Apathie als Mitleidunfähigkeit nach aussen."

44. Sölle, *Suffering*, p. 37. The author joins here Erich Fromm. See also: Sölle, *Sympathie*, p. 9.

45. Sölle, *Suffering*, p. 75; cf. p. 167: "a humanizing suffering"; pp. 167-168: "The number of those who dare to understand suffering at society's hand, as well as their own suffering, as a productive force is too small; the attempt to avoid suffering too great." However much Sölle prizes suffering in solidarity, she considers the removal of suffering as the ultimate aim: "It is axiomatic for me that the only humanely conceivable goal is the abolition of circumstances under which people are forced to suffer, whether through poverty or tyranny" (p. 2).

fatal indifference; rather it is embraced as the capacity that makes a person stronger than anything that comes along.[46] Thus, as the inherent counterpart of a fundamental "yes" to life, a "meaningful" way of suffering is outlined.[47] Driven by love for life, the active acceptance of grief and the sensibility for one's own and other people's pain stimulates communicative human existence.[48] In that way, humans accept one another as fellow-sufferers. Only through sym-pathy does a transformation and structural change of meaningless suffering become possible.[49] Authentic passibility generates solidarity. With this we are far removed from "the ancient concept of fate" and the exclusively negative atmosphere with which the traditional Greek notion of suffering is surrounded.[50] The consequence for Sölle's doctrine of God is clear: "We have to dimiss this God who in independent apathy stands above everything; (...) he does not want to be powerful in any way other than through solidarity with the weak."[51]

2) From the apatheia-ideal to pathos as affectively-motivating force

In ancient Greek philosophy the emotional sphere was discredited.[52] Supremacy was clearly given to reason, the preeminent capacity which elevates human beings and connects them to the

46. Ibid., p. 102.

47. Ibid., p. 107; p. 170: "(...) loving life so much that our affirmation includes the injury and the pain!"

48. Sölle mentions "the capacity for acceptance" (ibid., p. 167), which is diametrically opposed to submission or resignation.

49. Sölle, *Sympathie*, pp. 9-10.

50. Sölle, *Suffering*, p. 100.

51. Sölle, *Sympathie*, pp. 37-38: "Dann ist diesem Gott, der unabhängig-apathisch über allem steht, der Abschied zu geben; (...) der nicht anders stark sein will als durch die Solidarität der Schwachen."

52. P. De Labriolle, "Apatheia," in *Mélanges de Philosophie, de Littérature et d' Histoire Anciennes offerts à Alfred Ernout*, Paris, 1940, pp. 215-223; A. Heschel, *loc. cit.*; A. Lalande, *art. cit.*; W. Michaelis, *art. cit.*; H. Parret, *Passions*, pp. 9-15; H. Reiner, *art.cit.*; A. Vögtle, "Affekt," in T. Klauser, ed., *Reallexikon für Antike und Christentum* 1 (1950) 160-173; H. Vorgrimler, "Gelassenheit, Apatheia, Indifferenz," *LTK* 4 (1960) 631-632.

divine. In contrast, passion pertains to the lower regions of mortal existence. This subordination of "affect," which has broken through in Plato's teaching on the soul, takes concrete shape in the ideal of a-pathy.[53] This ideal was propagated by such trends of thought as Cynicism, Skepticism, and, above all, Stoicism. The Stoic view of life holds *pathê* (passions) to be irrational, unnatural movements of the heart, which are principally to be blamed on misjudgments. Everything called *pathos* is, in that view, excessive and "pathological;" it leads one along a path which threatens selfdetermination. The search for a serene state of happiness (*eudaimonia*) of the soul — a typical feature of all Hellenistic philosophy — requires liberation from morbid affects. In its most forceful expression the *apatheia*-ideal aims for a total annihilation of passion under the direction of reason. As a positive counterpart, *ataraxia* is pursued; this is an undisturbed spiritual peace of mind.

This ideal of apathy has made its mark, even though various approaches and corrections have arisen both inside and outside Stoic circles. Philo of Alexandria presents his own Judaeo-Christian interpretation of *apatheia*. Supported by God's help, the faithful Jew aims at a life that is averse to sinful *pathê*. Clement of Alexandria integrated the ideal in his vision of Christian Gnosis. In Eastern patristic and monastic circles the *apatheia*-theme is played upon readily and with a good many variations.[54] Latin Christian authors, nevertheless, entertain serious reserves against the postulated *impassibilitas*, though most of them cannot completely avoid it.[55] The impact of the ideal of apathy is clearly felt in Western moral theorization. We even recognize Stoic reminiscences in Cartesian, Spinozist and Kantian texts.

The prevalant classical degradation of the pathic-emotional level was gradually shaken by the modern philosophical climate.

53. According to Aristotle — who in contrast with Plato emphasizes the unity of the soul — the *pathê* are *in se* neither good nor bad. However, he acknowledges the indisputable sovereignity of reason.

54. We think of Origen, Athanasius, Basil, Gregory of Nyssa and particularly of Evagrius Ponticus, theorist of Eastern monastic life.

Descartes, who preceded this development, still represented the traditional idea of passions as *perturbationes animi* (perturbations of the soul). The tide turned with Post-Cartesian thinkers who no longer describe passions as destructive disturbances of the soul, created by invasions from the body, but as actual, energetic motives of personal and inter-personal action, as Amélie Rorty demonstrated.[56] This revalorization of passion takes a clear shape, for instance, in the "naturalistic" view of the English empiricist David Hume.[57] As the deepest source of human activity, passions are also treated by the Romantic thinker Charles Fournier.[58] The motto of Hegel reads: "We may affirm absolutely that nothing great has been accomplished without passion."[59] The idea that pathic sensibility constitutes an essential and motivating structure of personality is well received by today's supporters of the thesis of divine suffering. In their view, emotional apathy evokes an insensitivity that weakens vitality and degenerates community; hence it is stigmatized by a negative judgment. In this way *pathos* appears in a favorable light.[60]

55. Among others, Lactantius, Jerome, Augustine, and Thomas Aquinas criticize the ideal of apathy, understood as *insensibilitas* (insensibility).

56. A.O. Rorty, "From Passions to Emotions and Sentiments," *Philosophy* 57 (1982) 159-172.

57. According to David Hume, passions are essential to "human nature."

58. W.L. Reese, *art. cit.*, p. 415; A. Lalande, *art. cit.*, p. 746 (footnote): "Les philosophes ont toujours vu dans cet état une faiblesse et non une force, une impuissance de l'âme... Cela est vrai sans restriction jusqu'à l'époque de la philosophie romantique, mais à partir de ce moment on commence à laisser dans l'ombre le caractère passif des impulsions affectives, et l'import péjoratif qui s'attachait au mot passion tend à disparaître."

59. A. Heschel, *Prophets*, p. 256; W.L. Reese, *loc. cit.* .

60. This viewpoint is corroborated by an authentically biblical vision, thus A. Heschel, "The source of evil is not in passion, in the throbbing heart, but rather in hardness of heart, in callousness and insensitivity... There is no disparagement of emotion, no celebration of apathy. ...Pathos, emotional involvement, passionate participation, is a part of religious existence... The characterization of passion as a state of passivity would hardly be consonant with biblical experience. Passion was regarded as a notive power." (*Prophets*, p. 258) See also F. Varillon, *Souffrance*, p. 14: "Impassible, cela veut dire insensible, donc indifférent...;" p. 90: "La sensibilité délicate est une qualité de l'être spirituel. Qui se veut invulnérable ne porte pas l'autre en soi;" p. 91: "Etre sensible, c'est donc être proche."

3) From autarkeia-ideal to relational-historical receptivity

The Greek tradition of thinking hangs an aura around the principle of self-determination, the so-called *autarkeia*.[61] Typical is Aristotle's statement: "For it is felt that the final good must be a thing sufficient in itself."[62] Perfection exists in a substance that is considered to be independant and finds the ground for its being entirely in itself. Diametrically opposed to this, *pathos* appears to be something which is "undergone." The influence of exterior forces manifests imperfection, for there would then occur a disturbing infringement on the natural, sovereign source of action.[63] Given the options of Hellenic-classical metaphysics, *pathos* as a specific form of change by definition implies imperfection.[64]

The ontological idea of the active, unaffected "being-in-itself" apparently stands out in stark contrast to the present appreciation of the dynamic-receptive "being-in-relationship."[65] The identification of *pathos* with a passivity that curtails one's freedom is no longer maintained. Processes of interdependence are regarded as enrichments. This appreciation of receptive reality is fully shared by authors who are in favor of the idea of a suffering God. The older objective-metaphysical jargon fairly often and significantly gives way to categories with an anthropological and personalistic color. "Passibility" in the broad sense becomes

61. Y.J. Lee, *God Suffers for Us*, pp. 30-32; A. Heschel, *Prophets*, p. 254; p. 248: "... the dignity of man was seen in the activity of the mind, in acts of self-determination."

62. *Nicomachean Ethics*, 1097 b: "*to gar teleion agathon autarkês einai dokei*," in *Aristotle* in twenty-three volumes, XIX, *The Nicomachean Ethics*. With English translation by R. Rackham, London, Cambridge, MA, 1968, pp. 28-29.

63. Cf. H. Parret, *Passion*, p. 12.

64. Cf. A. Heschel, *Prophets*, p. 262: "The principle that change is incompatible with true being..."; J.B. Brantschen, "Macht und Ohnmacht," p. 231: "... metaphysisch gesehen schliesst jede Veränderung (weil Veränderung immer als Übergang von Potenz in Akt gesehen wird) Unvollkommenheit mit ein."

65. "In-sich-selbst-Seins," "In-Beziehung-Seins," in D. Sölle, *Sympathie*, pp. 118-119.

nearly synonymus to a sensitive, responsive capacity of adaptation to the other.[66]

(Im)passibility as a Divine Attribute

1) From divine "impassibility" to divine "passibility"

The modification of the *pathos*-concept and its presuppositions is notably reflected in theological thought. A traditional line of thinking considers the desirable a-pathy to be supremely realized in the divine reality: the supreme being is free from grief, obscure emotions and passivity. God is thought of as completely blissful, absolutely contemplative and autarkic, pure act. The attribution of *apatheia* or *impassibilitas* to the transcendent reality is a fundamental and constant element in the classical doctrine of God. Contemporary thinkers, who apparently want to change this outlook have a modified interpretation of the so-called "passibility." The positive capacity of an experience of identification and solidarity with sufferers, an emotional involvement and a personal concern is attributed to God. This turnabout has raised many questions. One consideration may suffice here.

On the one hand, a clear distinction forces itself upon us, namely, between the traditional understanding of the terms "impassibility" and "passibility" with respect to the idea of God, and the interpretation of these terms in recent thought on divine suffering. "Apathy" as it used to be understood, is not necessarily identical to what is understood by it now.

In the first systematic text treating our topic, namely, in the Gregory Thaumaturgus' third-century treatise addressed to Theopompus, we are informed that a loving God must be "impassible."[67] Nowadays the reverse reasoning is in vogue: if God

66. Cf. D.D. Williams, *Spirit*, p. 182: "... suffering means being acted upon or being conformed to another in relationship."

67. The Latin title of this treatise, which is originally written in Syriac, is: *Ad Theopompum: De Passibili et Impassibili in Deo*. We can find further bibliographical references in R.E.Creel, *Divine*, p. 223. For a comment on this text of the

is love, then He must be "passible." A misunderstanding of this conceptual difference leads to a veritable tower of Babel. Fighting traditional theism at the present time as if it introduced the notion of an "apathic," that is a cool and indifferent God, often seems to be a battle like Don Quixote's. It is, in any case, necessary to recognize that the term "(im)passibility" does not always and everywhere have one and the same connotation.

On the other hand, the dialogue between the classical point of view and this newer outlook, must not be omitted. A clean break with tradition opens the door to massive one-sidedness. [68] Setting apart some outdated presuppositions, the tradition of the *impassibilitas Dei* — which has, after all, acquired a certain permanence and coherence — points to some relevant aspects of the problem. Moreover, it is doubtful that the contemporary idea of God's suffering has completely changed the idea of "passibility" into a positive concept. A priori swearing by the traditional view alone is not a fruitful attitude either. Critical judgment requires that the new sensitivity be examined in all openness so that valuable discoveries can be made. It is not unthinkable that the classical theologoumenon of impassibility and the current divine attribute of passibility are to a certain extent compatible.

2) The function of discourse about an impassible, or possible God

Traditionally a remarkable simultaneity occurs. Alongside classical metaphysical considerations about God's impassibility, the theme of God's suffering is occasionally found in devotional and liturgical contexts. [69] This is not necessarily a contradiction. The

Alexandrian theologian Gregory Thaumaturgus: see J.K. Mozley, *Impassibility*, pp. 63-72.

68. Ibid., p. 1: "Whether the idea of a 'suffering God' be true or false, exponents of this conception would have been well advised to discuss it in the light of Christian tradition."

69. W. McWilliams, *Passion*, p. 188: "... a study of Christian piety, especially through its devotional writings and hymnody, would probably reveal a greater willingness among lay people to accept divine suffering;" D.D.Williams, *Spirit*, p. 125: "... we remember that in spite of much of the formal ontological language

observation can make us appreciate the right to co-existence of different language games, each with its specific and irreplaceable role.[70] It is unwise to draw from pious religious discourse direct conclusions for ontological-theological discussions.[71] Every linguistic register possesses its own rules, each has its proper task to fulfil. Did not the traditional ontological theory of God's *impassibilitas*, for instance, demonstrate a vigorous attempt to protect divine transcendence? On the other hand, we should not overly exaggerate the discrepancy between different linguistic registers.[72] Modern trends of thought tend to level things out, so that overlooking the differences may be a dangerous shortcoming.

Like all language, speech about God contains a social dimension of significance and a performative force.[73] As an illustration, we can present two different views.

The German sociologist Niklas Luhmann highlights the social function of religion, more particularly of theology.[74] He demonstrates how a theological system exists in Christian culture which functions as an established complex of meaning for the faithful community. The theological construction finds an evident climax

about God in traditional theology, the language of devotion has been modelled very largely on the acceptance of God's hearing, responding, sharing, and suffering with its creatures... ."

70. J.K. Mozley, *Impassibility*, p. 6: "... one is bound to remember the wide difference between a context of religious exhortation and a context of philosophical discussion."

71. Ibid.: "Language of a liturgical or devotional character must not be pressed into the service of theological theory."

72. Ibid.: "Moreover, if either context is sharply isolated, there is grave danger of one-sidedness, and, therefore, of inadequacy;" J.B. Brantschen, "Macht und ohnmacht," p. 225: "... galt es, diese Diastase zwischen Theologie und Frömmigkeit zu verhindern, denn sie wäre tödlich für beide Seiten."

73. F.P. Fiorenza, "Joy and Pain." The fact that words get their use in social context is related to the ideas of Wittgenstein, such as they are stated in his work *Philosophical Investigations* (written during the years 1936-1945 and 1947-1949). The performativity of language was especially elucidated by the English language philosopher John Austin (1911-1960).

74. N. Luhmann, *Die Funktion der Religion*, Frankfurt, 1977.

in the conviction: "God himself has suffered for us."[75] This dogmatically explicated awareness serves as a frame of reference, in which an effective religious sense of healing and consolation is disclosed for the human being who is afflicted by suffering.

Less positive towards the thesis that God suffers is the approach of Francis Fiorenza.[76] Fiorenza contends that religious language functions in a meaningful way within the community, because it provides a global interpretation of life. The judgment about suffering figures as a decisive factor. "Religious discourse must come to terms with the human experience of the ambiguity of suffering," claims Fiorenza.[77] Only religious language that does justice to the actual negativity of suffering is adequate. It is precisely that aspect which is lacking in direct speculation about the suffering God, according to Fiorenza. With that notion, suffering tends to be eternalized and receive a pretended conceptual solution. Fiorenza opts for a kind of religious discourse which maintains the absurdity of pain, so that a corresponding personal recognition and commitment can be had.

3) Affirmative and forbidden speech about the Other

Whoever speaks about an impassible or passible God cannot pass over the fact that the transcendent Reality can never be directly profiled. It is possible to speak about God but always with reservation. With anthropomorphic terms, we build a bridge from "similarity" to the "Other," well aware that He ultimately goes beyond all of our affirmations. In a short but interesting article Almeida devotes attention to what he calls "the auto-correction of religious speech."[78] It is inherent to religious language to see

75. See ibid., p. 199: "Besonders folgenreich war die Möglichkeit, die sich der christlichen Religion darbot: den alten Gedanken der Leidenssubstitution zu erneuern, jetzt aber als Substitution durch ein Höherwertiges Objekt: Gott selbst hat für uns gelitten."
76. F.P. Fiorenza, "Joy and Pain."
77. Ibid., p. 79.
78. I. Almeida, "Discours inter-dit, discours transitionnel: réflections méta-sémiotiques sur la nature du discours religieux," in J.P. Van Noppen, ed.,

to it that all descriptive propositions about God are ultinately limited by accompanying prohibition signs. Because of this important negative moment, the Other is respected in his otherness and his exteriority. Linguistic "dis-course" about God is at the same time permitted and forbidden. Only in this paradoxical interplay can something be said about Him, but this goes together with unknowing, with silence in the presence of the ever transcending and ineffable Mystery. The restriction in our use of language for God cannot be sufficiently emphasized when the attribute of divine impassibility or passibility is being discussed.

Open Questions

The change that has occured is intriguing. What is at stake in the abrupt change from the nearly undisputed traditional affirmation of God's impassibility to current theopaschite discourse? We have only ventured a beginning of an answer. May it serve as an incentive for further reflection! Yet now the question is above whether the notion of a "suffering" God does not constitute a *contradictio in terminis*. With regard to suffering humans, the question can be worded otherwise: does the language of a suffering God still refer to "God," the One from Whom we ultimately expect to receive salvation?

Authors, like Richard Creel, who react against the tendency of a passible God, think that one cannot experience real awe for a suffering God.[79] Is there not, for that matter, in people who expect God to suffer a hidden jealousy and an urge for manip-

---

Theolinguistics, Brussels, 1981, pp. 47-62, p. 47: "l"auto-correction' du discours religieux."
79. R.E. Creel, *Divine*, pp. 123-126.
80. Ibid., pp. 147-148.
81. Ibid., p. 155, and *passim*.

ulation?[80] Moreover it is difficult to understand what advantage accrues to a suffering person from the idea of a suffering God! Religious people who are afflicted by suffering do not need a weak fellow-sufferer; they are looking to a God who is effectively able to help and save, a God who experiences and communicates an unmitigated bliss.[81] To transfer suffering onto God makes everything seem even more hopeless.[82]

Thinkers who sympathize with the idea of a possible God suggest, on the other hand, that God justly deserves no reverence if He cannot be truly affected by people's suffering. The suffering of God must not thought to be the result of a megalomaniac human lust for power; it is the self-determined choice of God himself.[83] This divine suffering is, moreover, recognized as the factor which transforms human suffering. Often the conviction is expressed that only a God who is really com-*passionate* (a fellow-*sufferer*) is able to offer a response to a suffering human.[84] To provide some clarification, Human analogies can be cited.[85] "One who does not suffer, only helps one who suffers half-way," says François Varillon.[86] Daniel Day Williams phrases it as follows: "The discovery of the other who bears the consequences of my suffering and shares my condition is a powerful mode of personal communication and healing".[87] In his judgment, three

82. This objection is stated by F. Varillon, yet he himself has tried to refute it: *Souffrance*, p. 23: "Dramatiser Dieu même, est-ce opportun? L'idée d'un Dieu qui souffre n'aggrave-t-elle pas le scandale en l'amplifiant jusqu'à l' Infini?" Cf. R. Mackintosch: "An unhappy God would mean a bankrupt universe, a demonstrated pessimism" (quoted in J.K. Mozley, *Impassibility*, p. 171).

83. See W. Robinson in W. McWilliams, *Passion*, p. 19.

84. According to Paul Schilling, the suffering of God is "the most profound of all responses to human anguish", quoted, ibid., p. 191.

85. R.E. Creel, who is, however, a convinced defender of the doctrine of the impassibility of God, writes in *Divine*, p. 219: "My wife, Diane, has pointed out that sometimes what most helps people in grief is for their friends to cry with them."

86. F. Varillon, *Souffrance*, p. 112: "Celui qui ne souffre pas n'aide qu'à demi celui qui souffre."

87. D.D. Williams, "Suffering and Being in Empirical Theology," in B. Meland, *The Future of Empirical Theology*, Chicago, 1969, pp. 175-194, p. 188: "The discovery of the other who bears the consequences of my suffering and

elements help to clarify suffering as a process of healing.[88] A first element of transformation is the fact that my suffering is being objectivated and taken up by and in the other who experiences my suffering without rejecting it and without being harmed by it himself.[89] Further, there is the healing event of the companion who offers communion in spite of my suffering. His suffering can become an expression of solidarity. Finally, the suffering that someone bears for me also is presented as an expression of love, and as such it becomes a profound source of energy for the healing of my suffering. In this way, the suffering of the other can bring about a transformation of my own suffering. It is along these lines that help from a suffering God ought to be interpreted, says Williams.

The newer trend, in which God is readily spoken of as our fellow-sufferer, can open up promising sources of consolation, especially to the degree that God's solidarity with suffering humans is taken seriously. Must, however, a participating God necessarily be called a "*wounded* Healer?"[90] Surely, the suffering religious person longs for a "sympathetic" God. That only a "suffering" God could meet this demand is, however, not so sure.[91] According to Max Scheler, even on the level of anthropology only the component of solidarity, expressed in the prefix "*com*," confers a positive moral value on *com*passion.[92] Pain or suffering as such and in themselves can never have any value. Only a response of love and solidarity brings consolation to the un-

shares my condition is a powerful mode of personal communication and healing;" see also D.D.Williams, *Spirit*, p. 136: "If the life in communion is the essential nature of man, this includes transformation by participation with the other, and the acceptance of suffering with and for the other."

88. Williams, "Suffering and Being," pp. 187-189.

89. D.D. Williams refers to the healing interaction in a psychotherapeutic relation; see also: *Spirit*, p. 184.

90. We allude to Henri Nouwen's phrase "The wounded Healer."

91. J.K. Mozley, *Impassibility*, p. 182: "Is the alternative to a suffering God an unsympathetic God?" Cf. K. Surin, *Theology and the Problem of Evil*, Oxford, 1986, pp. 142-143.

92. M. Scheler, *The Nature of Sympathy*, transl. from the German by P. Heath, London, 1970 (repr. of the 1954 ed.).

happy. Moreover, further consideration needs to be devoted to the idea of whether the idea of God as fellow-sufferer can still be meaningfully related to the idea of God's omnipotence.

These and other questions are a challenge for discussion, but let us never forget that no theological answer will be able to dispel or conclude the existential "why?" of the person who is suffering. The question "why?" remains an open one.

FROM THEODICY TO ANTHROPODICY
The Contemporary Acceptance of Nietzsche and the Problem of Suffering

Georges De Schrijver

In recent times a number of authors have called themselves post-modern. They reject the monopoly of the great stories and choose the fragment. Their very existence is justified by the interpretation which they themselves give to it. This choice reveals their Nietzschean background which, however, is only fully understood in the light of the great philosophical systems against which Nietzsche reacts: Hegel, and Leibniz before him. Leibniz and Hegel are the respected classic proponents of theodicy, yet post-modern authors denounce their justification of God as illegitimate. For them, life is light and bearable — and this we could call an *anthropodicy* — only if it is successful in throwing off the chains of the great systems with the help of irony. Thus a few words need to be said about the comprehensive way of thinking found in the rational theodicies of Leibniz and Hegel.

Rational Theodicy

Leibniz' Rational Construction of the Best of All Possible Worlds

We all know the passage in which Dostoevski has Ivan Karamazov say that he is returning his ticket to life to the creator because there is so much innocent suffering in the world. Ivan is repelled by the idea that all suffering is justified from the perspective of a higher harmony from which it derives its ultimate meaning. Perhaps we do not realize that the strictly logical presentation of this argument comes from Leibniz, the philosopher who coined the term "theodicy" in 1710. For Leibniz, the mathematician, the lesser evil is always taken up in the divine calculation of that greater good which is the whole.

In contrast to Augustine[1] and Thomas Aquinas,[2] who also use this argument, Leibniz is not concerned with the personal solace which the sufferer seeks by placing his or her suffering within a larger perspective so that a particular misfortune becomes somewhat relativized. No, Leibniz is a systematician who from the very beginning lays down the law of the universal, and has particular events submerged in it by regarding them as building blocks for the whole. Characteristic is his comparison with the battle field by means of which he illustrates his goal-oriented thought on harmony: "It is logical," he says, "that a general by far prefers a great victory with few casualties to a stalemate which involves neither victory nor defeat. In the same vein, a world with evil is better than a world without evil."[3] Within the best of all worlds which is ours, evil and suffering will thus always be a concomitant phenomenon *necessary* to lift the whole to a higher perfection.

Leibniz is a deist who puts himself in the place of the architect of the universe and reconstructs the logic of his thought on the basis of calculations of probability. According to this logic, God's will is bound by the rational laws of non-contradiction and of compossibility. God cannot, for example, create a square circle. Neither can he attach too much importance to the rights of the particular, because the latter derives its goodness from its belonging

1. *De ordine*, 2,11-13
2. 2 *Sent*, dist. 32, qu. 1, art. 1
3. G. Leibniz, *Essais de Théodicée 1710*, edited by M. Jacques, Paris, 1882, p. 310.

to the overarching whole. Pain in a part is necessary in order to make the whole more powerful. From this point of view, physical suffering is the price we must pay for the benefit of being embodied, and moral suffering is the price of human freedom. This double toll is inherent in our finite condition, which may be regarded as either metaphysically "good" or "bad." We simply do not possess God's a-historical perfection and insufferability, because we are imbedded in history and matter. To be dissatisfied with one's finite condition, which also includes physical and moral suffering (and from which, after all, the best of all worlds results), would be clear evidence of folly.

That is to say that suffering is always relative, that is, it is related to a larger good with which it is intertwined (I would not be able to burn my finger, had I not a finger). For Leibniz it is further evident that, while the energy in this world may diminish locally with the result that there is regression in one of its parts, the upward spiral of the global evolution is not affected. The world possesses enough energy to maintain its own impetus as an evolving totality. Partial deterioration, in other words, does not abolish the best of all possible worlds. From the perspective of the whole, the shadows of pain and struggle add color and variety to the otherwise monotonous picture of harmony. Beauty is constituted by harmony and variety (disharmony). Hence God is always justified. Suffering in the best possible world is always justified by the ultimate goodness of the whole. Whoever realizes this will respect the mathematically calculable general laws which govern the development of nature and history. These laws function as a kind of providence.

Hegel's Theodicy of History

The optimistic theodicy of Leibniz received a severe blow from the 1755 earthquake in Lisbon. It was sharply criticized by Immanuel Kant, who saw through Leibniz' supposed identification of logic with providence and demonstrated its dangers for moral action. According to Kant, if one believes too much in a "God-world reason" who would stand as the guarantor of ultimate harmony, one just might begin to act immorally by not treating the other as a subject, as an end in him- or herself.[4] Shortly thereafter, however, Hegel again picked up Leibniz' line of thought; he posited that the "philosophy of history" is the "true theodicy." The logic of history reveals the good order of things by reconciling understanding and reality.

The link with Leibniz is clear. The particular facts of history, according to Hegel, derive their intelligibility and their justification from their belonging to the overarching whole: "The Truth is the whole." This exchange between the whole and the constituent parts has for Hegel, however, an explicitly dialectical effect. Hegel does not only analyze how human actors come to acquire a historical consciousness, that is, by externalizing themselves into the "other than themselves" (in work, culture, language); he also demonstrates, with various historical material, just which dialectical movements in history are necessary to bring consciousness and civilization to what they are. Historical periods come together in a single unity to which the various parts contribute. The transition from one period to the next (from the Ancien Régime to the French Revolution, from Napoleon's empire to the Prussian state) is governed by a logical insight which works itself out through periods of crisis until it establishes the truth of the new historical consciousness. Without certain irreversible leaps, civilization would never progress. Modernity would never have become what it is without the breakthrough of civil law which protects the free market as well as private property, without the establishment of a capitalist mode of production which does away with family craft enterprises, or without the rise of a centralized state which has the power and the means to enforce a national policy of the common good against internal and external enemies. Each of these is an expression of the "objective spirit" of

4. I. Kant, "Über das Misslingen aller pilosophischen Versuche in der Theodizee," *Berlinische Monatschrift* (Sept. 1794) 194-225. See I. Kant, *Werke*, VI, edited by W. Weischedel, Darmstadt, 1975, pp. 103-124.

history as well as of the "subjective consciousness" of the people who tune in to it.

Some call Hegel one of the first great sociological thinkers. Yet Hegel has also a strong theological interest, albeit in the form of a rational reconstruction of the logic of divine wisdom. According to Hegel, reason is capable of reconstituting the dialectical steps which the divine wisdom has made use of in order to bring about new historical eras. What God intends with his creation can be deduced from the logical unfolding of history, set in motion precisely by a generation's free yet necessary commitment to a better future.

Whereas theology had previously been more concerned with the reconciliation of an individual with himself, neighbor and God, a basic pattern of reconciliation now becomes perceptible in a historical and logical form. Indeed, the logic of history not only determines just which are the general agencies capable of bringing about unity and reconciliation among people, but also which are the physical and psychic pains which individuals and groups must suffer in order to find their place in a society which is reconciled with itself. As for the latter, Hegel emphasized — partly on the basis of Christian beliefs — the need of self-emptying as a way to reach a higher harmony. This implies that people have to give up their previous cultural habits, however painful this may be, because this sacrifice hastens the breakthrough of a new historical phase in society. To submit oneself to the evolution of the historical whole is an expression of reverence for the divine wisdom which reveals itself in history. If Leibniz could still say "accept your pain because otherwise you revolt against your corporeality," or "do not be surprised to be now and then betrayed, because otherwise you would not realize the price of human freedom," Hegel filled in those words of solace with more social terms. His message was: consider the pain of your effort, work, disillusion and illness as a process of self-emptying which is necessary to insert yourself into the rhythm of the new time. The place you occupy in this new harmony is good. Accept your pain and the emptying which are necessary to help civilization as a whole progress in a way which is indispensible for the growth of a new historical consciousness.

All of this has to do with God. "There was a time," says Hegel, "when it was fashionable to admire God's wisdom in animals, plants and the separate events of life. When, however, one assumes that God's providence is revealed in these things, why not extend this to the history of the world? To some, this approach seems too all-encompassing. Since, however, divine wisdom (= reason), is one and the same in the great and in the small, we should not consider God so weak that He could not apply his wisdom to the great. The dynamics of our human knowledge requires that we realize how strongly the goals of the divine wisdom are revealed not only in nature but also in the area of the historically active and working spirit. As such our reflection is a theodicy, a justification of God, in the style of Leibniz, although he has worked this out in categories which are still too metaphysical and abstract. This reflection allows us to grasp how evil in this world is to be understood and how the thinking spirit is to be reconciled with it. To come to this reconciling insight, there is no greater challenge than that of the history of the world." [5]

Suffering under Theodicy as Suffering under the Repressive Logic of History

Feuerbach and Marx became ardent atheists because they did not accept Hegel's thesis that the logic of history (as Hegel perceived it) was necessarily coincident with the God's will. Marx, especially, raged against the way in which Hegel's theodicy always allowed, in a priori fashion, that the conservative powers in society are in the right. For Hegel, it was part of God's plan that the Prussian workers of his day did not have the right to vote and

---

5. G. Hegel, *Vorlesung über die Philosophie der Geschichte* 1805, Einleitung, 1, edited by F. Brunstäd, Stuttgart, 1961, p. 56.

that a strongly centralized, military state could machiavellistically determine what was good and evil. Exactly what is a good ethos in society, and which sacrifices have to be made because of this (social inequality and oppression of the basic rights of life), are elements dictated by institutions in power which appropriate God's name. Submission to a worldly power which assumes divine prerogatives becomes a source of immeasurable misery for many. The persistence of Leibniz' thought in Hegel raises the suspicion that theology blesses the existing power and ignores the cry of the oppressed. From now on, theodicy becomes suspect as a theory of legitimation.

This leads to an important social issue. Many contemporaries assume atheistic stances because of their discontent with a political system which legitimizes itself religiously. They doubt the good order of the world and reject God and religion. Only very recently — and this is an exception to the rule — has theology also criticized, in the guise of liberation theologies, those social systems which justify the repression of the poor on the basis of a rational theodicy. In the 19th and even in the beginning of the 20th century, bishops and Catholic intellectuals inculcated believers with the idea that they had to obey regime in power and submit to the will of God.

In 1806, one of the Belgian bishops, a Fleming, declared in a sermon that social injustice is ordained by God and inscribed in the laws of nature, so that from this, the greater good of charity could follow: "God uses the poverty of the lower classes to recommend them to the generosity of the rich."[6] Joseph de Maistre (1753-1821) also preached this same submission in the face of an irreversible fate: "The social condition sprouts from a state of affairs which is willed by God. . . Indignation does not help. We can only lighten our destiny by accepting it with love and not by grimly fighting against it."[7] Submission, rather than

6. Cited in H. Gielen, "El sufrimiento humano y el compromiso cristiano," *Christus. Revista de teologia y ciencias humanas* (March-April, 1984) p. 17.

7. J. De Maistre, *Du pape et autres écrits*, edited by J. Pauvert, Paris, 1957, p. 23.

resistance, is preached. This last approach is despised by those who understand that it is merely a matter of justifying a political system in the name of God.

Nietzsche

The Death of God and the Recovery of Life

Moving from here to Nietzsche, we realize from the very beginning that Nietzsche does not so much denounce social injustice as he defends the vital life-force which had been repressed under the influence of modern rationality. Nietzsche's polemic expression "God is dead" announced that the God of rational legitimations must sooner or later collapse (his death struggle has already started) because this God denies the vital (dionysian) power of life within us. The western rational God who seeks to keep all spontaneity under control is the enemy of life. He feeds on a corrupted "Will to Power." If this will should rise in its pure form, it would impart a creative impulse to life's dynamism.

Nietzsche pleads for a new mythology which would end the monopoly of the God manipulated by the state. His point of departure is a desire for life which frees itself from the yoke of imposed systems of meaning and which radically opts for an interpretation which is to be personally constructed. Personal choice grows because the subject becomes aware of a more profound understanding of things and of an artistic power which prompts a reviewing of reality with ever new eyes. The more eyes the person has, the richer the interpretation of life will be. The multitude of perspectives attained by one person serves to do away with the "monotheistic" constraint of one God, one state, one reality, principles which since Hegel have determined the sense of normativity of good and evil. This explains Nietzsche's leap to an ecstatic experience beyond Good and Evil, which frees a person from an impersonal monotonous existence and over-powers him with a joy which makes him dance. This is a theme which Heidegger also will later emphasize: the ecstasy of Being delivers us from the grip of an all-consuming Being unto Death.

Nietzsche was one of the first authors to react against what some authors of the Frankfurt School later described as the terror of instrumental reason. He reacted against any form of rationality which tried to justify the unjustifiable: the subjugation of conscience to the reason of a government which dictates to individuals their duties and their rights. As the son of a minister Nietzsche expressed his unease by transposing his feelings of hatred onto Christianity, which, in his eyes, encouraged believers to submit to the inevitability of the will of God.

Nietzsche saw in Christianity the psychological soil for the herd-mentality of collective submission. Not generosity and power, but furtiveness and jealousy inspire the Christian to "virtue."[8] In God's Kingdom on earth, there seems to be only room for meek personalities who bow down before the once and for all determined laws of good and evil. This "genealogy of morality" is, however, quite suspect. A morality of resignation does not only cripple creative fantasy, it also concentrates power in the hands of "logocentric" institutions which feed on the subordination of their subjects. The power apparatus wielded by a state or a Church desires nothing more than to control the thought of a culture and is not disturbed by the violation of conscience. It insist upon obedience and a sense of sacrifice for the greater good of the whole. Yet, what meaning could such sacrifice have for a person who has no say in determining his or her own happiness?[9]

---

8. G. Deleuze, *Nietzsche et la pilosophie*, Paris, 1962, p. 139.
9. F. Savater, *Panfleto contra et Todo*, Madrid, 1982, pp. 82-83.

Nietzsche's Theory of Interpretation

Nietzsche wanted to shake the domination of the universal logos. His suspicion was inspired by a breath of resistance which gathered its forces from the creative impulses of the will to life. In opposition to the tyranny of imposed laws of thinking, he presented a doctrine of interpretation which would allow as many perspectives in the interpretation of history as possible. From the standpoint of the artist, the depth of existence is inexhaustible. Hence Nietzsche, in accord with (but also going beyond) Schopenhauer, argued that the "world" and our existential view of it are the fruit of an exuberant will to life, exteriorized in a multitude of representations. The will to life has such a powerfully expansive force that it presents itself in ever new and unexpected perspectives of beauty, and as such allows a person to see his or her situation in life under the sign of beauty. The eruption of these creative representations rescues those who risk drowning in the tragedy of existence. Pain and suffering are only exorcised if one is able to fit them within a frame of interpretation to which one may adhere. The will then assimilates the polar tensions of life and transmutes them into a momentary fragment of meaning. This vital though fragmentary interpretation provides more satisfaction than the ready-made answer dictated by the universal logic of institutions in power. In the conclusion to his *Genealogy of Morals*, Nietzsche demonstrated the power of the interpretation of life for one who tries to come to terms with destruction and death. For him, there is no doubt that life can be saved from total absurdity only through creative interpretation, however minimal the meaning which results from it may be. According to Nietzsche, uninterpreted suffering is more unbearable than any other. As human beings, we are mostly burdened by the pain which we cannot make bearable by means of a frame of interpretation. The first step toward a lessening of suffering consists in the determination to place it within a life-line which we ourselves have designed. At least, there thus emerges a perspective of freedom as "representation" and "appearance," which allows us to look at suffering with a view different from that of fatalism. If we do not have this minimal perspective of a will eager to create meaning through interpretation, then only nihilism and suicide remain as the ultimate abdication of life.[10]

Nietzsche takes this basic statement so seriously that he ironically remarks that Christianity, which (in his eyes) only preaches resignation, had after all an advantage in that it did at best offer an interpretation of life—and it is always better to have one than to have none. Through many generations Christianity has provided a counterbalance against the brutal weight of suffering, which, without the dogmas of the cross and resurrection, would not have been interpreted or made bearable at all. Yet Nietzsche returns once more, in a characteristic *volte face* to the attack on Christianity. For acquiescence, the Christian answer, is an inadequate interpretation which denies the true depths of the will to life and keeps people enchained in slavery.[11]

Nietzsche admires Christianity's story-technique, but not its story. He is convinced that only self-interpretation, self-expression and narrativity are capable of creating the horizon of meaning within which the sufferer escapes the destructive power of meaningless suffering. He believes, moreover, that Christianity has woven too many guilt-motives into its story. As a result, the fire of the vital creation of meaning, despite all efforts to resist the void, only remains smoldering. Self-interpretation in the Christian perspective implies that the will is saved, but with the consequence that the yes to life is internally poisoned and degenerates into a yes to self-torture which does not much differ from the impulse toward death. No amount of irony can do justice to this contradiction. Self-affliction as a price for life cannot constitute an ideal. This is why Nietzsche has recourse to the pre-Christian, non-Jewish affirmation of life which he encounters in Greek mythology. His model is Dionysus, the god who out of the

10. P. Moroney, *Nietzsche's Dionysian Aristocratic Culture*, Maynooth, 1986, p. 54.

11. F. Nietzsche, *Zur Genealogie der Moral*, III, par. 28 in Werke, VI, 2, edited by E. Colli and M. Montinari, Berlin, 1968, pp. 429-430.

abundance of life destroys that which he has built, and who as such creates a space for the emergence of even richer forms of expression. The power of the will to life manifests itself in the ability to reject old and extinguished values so that life can arise in new forms.

From this perspective Nietzsche opts for an acting subject who no longer allows its creativity to be paralyzed by the representation of an "I" which would be substantially unchangeable. The "I" is not determined by any fixed teleology. Substantial thinking suggests immobilization, and this leads nowhere. This basic insight will later inspire Whitehead and the process thinkers. Liberation from the self-torture of moralizing existence is possible only by letting go of straightforward goal-orientedness. It is not the "fixed being," which awakens guilt, that brings salvation, but the "eternal flow" of the innocence of becoming. Only the perspective of an ever new "becoming" does justice to our corporeality and to our creative imagination which form visions of a fulfilled life within history. The pulsation of the will to life cannot be dissociated from the sensations which rejuvenate our spirit. A spirit in the process of "becoming" must take its sensitive basis very seriously, because it is this element which moves the spirit toward change and renewal. Whoever forgets the mind's rootedness in the body necessarily experiences how the will to life is being blocked. Such a person becomes rusty, because the imagination is extinguished. Nietzsche's life is one great protest against the immobilization of life not only in culture, but also in himself. He cannot but be the Great Negator, because in his heart he is the Great Affirmer. His loyalty to the power of the will to life causes him to fight against the curse of the unchangeable. To break the fatality of the "sameness," he opts for that imagination which desires the different. The weapons of that imagination are cynicism and irony.

Neo-Nietzscheans such as Foucault, Derrida, and especially Savater have emphasized the importance of irony in Nietzsche's approach. Nietzsche employs irony because he understands that an ideology twists and turns to hide its own contradictions. He does not tolerate, for example, Christianity's presentation of itself as a religion of salvation while it regards corporeality, pleasure and beauty as taboo. How can a religion without pleasure save? Yet, Nietzsche uses irony against himself as well in order to prevent his overlooking the complexity of things. The Nietzschean soul has no visceral need to negate the tension between polarities. It clearly realizes that the ever-new perspective of interpretation leading to the innocence of "becoming" must remain in a tensional relation with the never-ending darkness of existence. However much the creative will to life may exorcize meaningless suffering through interpretation, it can, realistically speaking, never bridge the gap of the dramatic. Even if the will to life has worked itself up to the light, a background of darkness will always accompany human existence, a fact which shows how everything is connected with everything else. Despite this polar complexity, and this is Nietzsche's conviction, the will to life is still able to conjure up for itself a sensible horizon of beauty, which, however, must necessarily be fragmentary. That happiness is only fragmentary is existence's supreme irony.

The Meaning of the Expression: "Only as an Aesthetic Phenomenon is the Existence of this World Justified"

Nietzsche admits — and this demonstrates his insightfulness — the complexity of existence. Complete clarification is neither possible nor desirable. The justification of existence is possible only as anthropodicy, in the form of the partial meaning which the human subject achieves for him- or herself. Each person must create his or her horizon of meaning against the background of an ambiguity which is never completely resolved. If this limitation is forgotten, a possibility is created whereby all-encompassing justifications are put in the service of the existing powers. This is why Nietzsche rejects every rectilinear pattern of thought which lays claim to a total understanding of reality in the name of an absolute optimism or pessimism. Such a totalizing approach necessarily proposes black and white plans which cannot do justice to the polar tensions of reality. A fragmentary interpretive approach on the other hand attempts to stand within those very fields of tension which comprise life itself, and to appreciate how seemingly very opposite facts and emotions are fundamentally complementary. Whoever chooses the fragmentary view will more easily realize that he or she is both good and bad, or rather that one only becomes virtuous, because, from a different point of view, one is also a villain. Similarly someone is impetuously creative only when he or she is able to maintain some self-discipline. In short, only the confrontation of a multitude of feelings invigorates the power of life. The joy of the spirit is strong only when it is mixed with sensitive pleasure. Profound joy presupposes also deep suffering. Or, as Nietzsche puts it in his *Joyful Science*: "Happiness and pain are inseparable twin brothers: they grow together or remain small together; it is impossible to have one without the other."[12]

The affirmation of life manifests itself, according to Nietzsche, precisely in the deep emotions (*aisthesis*) which well up within us, when we realistically stand up amid the tensions of life and do not fear the pain in the midst of our happiness. This is not to say that pain is a priori overcome by happiness. Nietzsche believes that the powerful emotions, which result from the often desperate struggle to overcome pain, are such that they allow us to affirm life. It is not pain in itself, but the pain which we attempt to avoid, that awakens in us deep emotions which miraculously state that life as we see it now is justified. A miracle of assent thus emerges from the will to life which prompts a person to (again) interpret life as a phenomenon of rich sensations, despite the threat of paralysis. In a dense statement, Nietzsche formulates this as follows: "Only as an aesthetic phenomenon is the existence of the world justified." The words "only" and "phenomenon" are important here, because, logically speaking, the world as it exists

12. F. Nietzsche, *Die fröhliche Wissenschaft* IV, par. 338, in *Werke*, V, 2, Berlin, 1973, p. 247.

and is sustained by institutions with totalitarian pretences, remains the "worst of all possible worlds" (against Leibniz).[13] If one wants to existentially justify one's existence from within one's own life story, however, and not on the basis of an imposed text or context, this will be possible only through the impetus of powerful emotions which are also nurtured by pain, and which reinvigorate the will to life and thus the creative imagination.

It is impossible, however, to deduce from the foregoing an aesthetics which is coherent apart from one's vital experience. Leibniz' argument that pain and misery bring variety into an otherwise monotonous harmony is, in Nietzschean terms, non-sense. Such a systematic assimilation would legitimate the world and society in their objective forms, but this can and should not be. No, it is precisely that assent emerging from the will to life and the creative imagination which, for Nietzsche, provide the incentive for critique. The greatest affirmer is at the same time the greatest despiser who continues to express his contempt for the human and political powers which cripple the tensions of life. Nietzsche fulminates against every form of cultural monotheism, which he calls "*monotono*-theism."[14] He ridicules a dominant instrumental reason, which, in the effort to "humanize" people (!), imposes on them a straightjacket of uniformity. He criticizes the moralizing instances which affect the spontaneous powers of life by pre-programming everyone's ethos. He reacts against the dictates of that philosophy of history which exposes civilians to their masters' warring instincts under the banner "right and reason."

13. See F. Nietzsche, *Die Geburt der Tragödie aus dem Geiste der Musik*, par. 5, in *Werke*, III, 1, Berlin, 1972, p. 43; ibid., par. 25, p. 150.
14. F. Nietzsche, *Götzendämmerung*, in *Werke*, VI, 3, 1969, p. 69.

The Polytheism of Postmodernity

Nietzsche is the Coryphaeus of contemporary cultural critique. He is the pioneer of the post-modernists, who critically distance themselves from the great, dominating stories of legitimation. "The nostalgia for the lost story is itself lost for the majority of persons," says Lyotard.[15] Indeed, the younger generation will not easily be stirred by the story of the all-powerful God, creator of heaven and earth, who governs everything according to the Leibnizean and Hegelian precedence of the whole over the particular. How could they love a God who has sold his soul to the great institutions of power in this world and who has become apathetic toward the particular destiny of people in the daily circumstances of life? However much this God calls himself Father, he is in no way different from a Moloch who feeds on the blood of his children. No, no one who wants life can feel a nostalgia for such a God. Since God, for cultural reasons, has been connected to the dominating grip of the whole, so that individuals experience him as the repressor of their will to life, his name can no longer lead to an ecstasy which makes people dance and sing. This *mono*-theistic God, who grounds the monotonous atmosphere of murderous totalities, must die. He may not rise again; otherwise there will be no place for a new search which would allow individuals to affirm their uniqueness in the face of a totally regulated world. From now on, anthropodicy will be fashioned under the sign of the self-affirmation of the subject who defends his "differential uniqueness" against the centripetal pull of the all-determining whole.

Even though postmodernists sometimes give the impression of retreating into the intimacy of the I, some of the leading figures adopt outspoken social-critical stances. They owe this to themselves if they really want to proclaim themselves to be Nietzschean. Their claim to "differentiation" provides a perspective

---

15. J.-F. Lyotard, *La Condition Postmoderne*, Paris, 1979, p. 86.

from which they practice cultural criticism. This is evident in both
Jacques Derrida and Louis Borges. Their works are an appeal to
plunge again and again into the labyrinth of signs and to interpret them over and over again in an independent fashion, free
from the fetters of a streamlined tradition.[17] The option for
originality and for the forgotten detail is experienced as a liberation from the constraints of normative texts and contexts; it
implies a refusal to allow oneself to be absorbed by the monopoly
of an established logic which reduces all that is multiplicity to
unity. In a culture which despises the subject, this refusal is an
attempt to learn to see the falsehood of the slogan that "the
subject is dead," and to contest the thesis that all mental creation
is pre-programmed by the structures of language. The structura-
lists may be right if they argue that no one can express his or her
deepest feelings except through the medium of a given language;
the post-modernists nevertheless force themselves to use language
in such a way that their own different interpretation strikes home.
As such, they wish to prevent their life-stories from sinking away
into an anonymous story which belongs to no one in particular.

This option for a heretical, heterogenous standpoint is already
to be found in the Nietzschean doctrine of interpretation. In his
footsteps, the postmodern person wants to liberate him- or herself
from the boring emptiness bequethed her by cultural monotheism. Hence, the postmodernist is not satisfied with schemes of
solutions which are pre-programmed; on the contrary, he or she
remains faithful to the vital need to create one's own beautiful
image of the world which makes existence more or less bearable.
A person needs this "own" interpretation in order to be able to
hold on in a world which sometimes drives one to despair.
Without her own differential interpretation, the postmodernist
feels herself subjected to the blind games of anonymous powers.
But once the powers of the will to life and creative imagination
are released in her, she comes to view the world, or at least

16. M. Taylor-Erving, *A Post-Modern A/Theology*, Chicago, 1984, pp. 170-181
with reference to J. Derrida, *Writing and Difference*, Chicago, 1978, pp. 280-292,
and L. Borges, *Labyrinth*, New York, 1964, p. 51.

certain parts of it, through new eyes. The world of will and representation is then inhabited by a multitude of gods and goddesses who look with benevolence upon the person.

In *The Gods and the World* Fernando Savater welcomes a large number of gods and goddesses who console him: "I call upon the god of the great silences who only frightens me in the end; the god of the right word who uplifts and inspires; the god of the painful recollection who sharpens the memory; the god of your pale face; the god who does not make me shrink from who I am; the god who fools the almost infinite darkness; the god of the beggars who loves them because they wander, not because they are poor; the god of the stinging insects, who knows no privileges; the god who paid my ticket on the train from Beaune to Paris and continued to read his course in criminology; the ironical god of blasphemy; the god who sends us dreams and who enters into conversation with us during sleepless nights; the god of your mouth when you say 'nice;' the goddess of the mountains with her liturgy of eagles and snow; the god who wants to be neither father nor son, but brother; the goddess of deceitful childhood phantasies; the goddess who smiles to my boy when I am not there; the goddess who gives emotions and inspiration to the story-tellers." [17]

There is irony, critique and charm in this enumeration of gods. Phantasy is seen as a weapon against the dullness of existence, against suffering under the processes of an anonymous establishment of power which stifles the voices of human subjects. Irony becomes a principle of social criticism for Savater. For him ethics is based on the sting of the insect. The biting mosquito is, ironically, chiefly attracted by large bodies who are quite used to drawing everything to themselves.

17. F. Savater, *De los dioses y el mundo*, Valencia, 1982, pp. 24-26.

Strength and Weakness of Neonietzscheanism:
The Open Questions of Postmodernity

Irony and Ludicrous Action as Moderation of Utopic Dreams

It is striking that neo-Nietzscheans strive in their own way for a liberation from subjugation. Even though they are rather pessimistic about the possibility of liberating the whole whose killing power expands as a desert, they do succeed in once again creating oases of solace. They derive enough phantasy from the basic drive of their will to life to remain mentally strong ("Man is the preserver of Being," says Heidegger) and to stand up against growing absurdity. Moreover, they study this absurdity carefully. They make it a point of honor to unmask simulated appearance as hypocrisy. Savater, for example, condemns the dignified lifestyle of wealthy citizens insofar as it hides their complicity with regimes of terror in the Third World.[18]   This remark is ironically presented and openly mocks the elaborate way in which modernity narrates the great story of growing prosperity. Were this prosperity broad-based, it would eventually benefit all. The (deceitful) utopia of the great stories is debunked by the neo-Nietzscheans, regardless of whether it is presented in the political garb of the left or the right. For them, the great promises evoke no more than angry or restrained mockery. They satirize the monstrous contradictions between the words and intentions of certain politicians and economists who admitedly speak humanitarian words but whose deeds are conditioned by success in the international struggle for power. For them, rhetoric concerning great utopias and counter-utopias is not really thought-provoking.

The postmodernists thus feel forced to limit their own utopian dreams, lest they fall into the same struggle for power of which they accuse others. They are convinced that overly ambitious utopic world projects invariably end up in the desire to dominate others,

18. F. Salvater, *Invitación a la etica*, Barcelona, 1982, p. 142.

since the realization of such utopias depends upon the often brutal establishment of a counter-power. Neo-Nietzscheans think very realistically about the way political power is wielded. Since Machiavelli it has used the logic of total subjugation. Their alternative to the desire to dominate is playfulness, as well as lucid mockery. They seek, in other words, to draw their energy in large portion from creative phantasy, because precisely this allows them to create oases of meaning in a world which otherwise remains submerged in darkness. Phantasy and irony should overcome the impulsive imperialism of violence.

Thereafter neo-Nietzscheans proceed to organized actions. These take on a non-violent character, except perhaps for the verbal violence lurking in the irony which they employ, and its public expression through symbolical action. The calculated, yet ludicrous protest actions of the Greenpeace movement, such as the funeral of the dead Rhine, or their masquerading the undesirable visits of foreign presidents, correspond to the strategy of mockery which the lucid pessimists have developed in the social field. This playful note points to the fragmentary breakthrough of a creative imagination, but it also reveals the concomitant seriousness of a will to better the world. If this will is not released in a ludicrous way, it might turn into a morbid fury which strikes out blindly. Here a question can be raised as to the social relevance of the post-modernists: are their actions, as is sometimes scornfully said, the last convulsion before the final departure, or do they, on the contrary, point to new ways of resistance? Irony in this latter sense would then be the resurgence of reactive power rather than resignation.

Irony as Substitute for Religion?

More than ten years ago, when there was as yet no talk of postmodernism, Niklas Luhmann, from a sociological standpoint, asked whether in a highly developed society the ironization of existence could become a "functional equivalent" of religion.

As a functionalist, Luhmann took account of the fact that religion is always seeking new forms to fulfill its function. Religion's function today is to provide a support in an environment which, because of the disparate evolution of mutually conditioning systems, can offer nothing stable to hold on to. In principle, anything may lend itself to become such a support, even the symbolic actions which parody the sacred, such as satire, play and irony. Humor and mockery, as Kierkegaard already seems to have realized, often turn out to be disguised forms of religion. The figure of the holy fool emerges regularly throughout history.

The real issue is, however, whether the current wave of ironization can be self-sustaining so that its social impact can endure because of a sufficiently powerful group of sympathizers. Luhmann has his doubts about this. He considers humor and irony as phenomena of a sub-culture. Specifically he does not believe that a dispersed ironic strategy which focusses on separate facts can ever succeed in producing a sense of global wholeness. The creative impulse of irony can only be fractional. Hence, it can not pretend to offer an interpretation which would encompass the whole of existence, as a religion is expected to do. One may thus presume that the "ironizers of existence" remain a group of laughing anarchists, heretics who never succeed in founding a church.[19]

Even though Luhmann tends to underestimate the combative character of the heretics who resort to irony on the basis of lucidity, he nonetheless puts his finger on the issue. The question is whether the ironization of existence, which is essentially fractional, can offer a new and encompassing support for today's world. We see concretely how the magic formula of the ironic is powerless against the chaotic experiences of life. Irony cannot exorcize any and every irruption of evil, misery, misfortune and pain out of the world. The more lucid ironists realize this. The post-modern recipes of mirth and jeer are not the solution for

19. N. Luhmann, *Funktion der Religion*, Frankfurt, 1977, pp. 47-48.

every mishap. Neo-Nietzscheans will be just as helpless as others when they discover that a newborn child has a heart-disease which will cause it to die young; they will be just as devastated when they see the misery of refugees' camps or when they hear the moaning of people emaciated by starvation, cancer, or AIDS. This will throw them into a kind of desperation against which, on the other hand, they struggle, empowered by their will to life.

For postmodernists, irony is the expression of a will to life which struggles against the absurd. This is why they will never make fun of someone's misfortune, whether this be the dying child, or the tortured person who writhes in pain. Such behavior would only abase them to the level of sadists, which is an attitude they resent. Whereupon, then, is their irony particularly focussed? Upon the contradictions of existence, more specifically, upon the institutions and persons who could have helped rid the world of many contradictions, but who instead only aggravate them. The postmodernists' irony goes hand in hand with the realization that life is full of paradoxes, and that no one can guarantee a smooth outcome. Despite this relativizing, however, the will to life incites them to use the weapon of mockery against a dosage of pain which could have been diminished in society had there only been more concern and ethical commitment.

In spite of Luhmann's sinister prognosis, postmodernists give expression to an ethical sensitivity which aspires to the realization of the common good. Yet they can only allow their concern for the whole to manifest itself fragmentarily in the contemporary, disrupted world. The vitality of the will to life prompts the postmodernists to criticize those political bodies and persons who present themselves as the benefactors of humanity, but who at the same time are guilty of corruption and the abuse of power. Irony becomes a savior of humanity, because it highligts those societal knots which should be untied. Hunger in the Sahel is a huge problem for which there is no immediate solution. Nonetheless the caption which postmodernists have attached to the photos of starvation speaks volumes: "No government has ever fallen over such trivialities."

Irony as Concretization of Love?

If the postmodernists' irony appears to refer beyond itself to a universal concern which can only be expressed in an indirect and fragmentary way, the question may finally be raised as to what extent the disarming strategy of mockery can contribute to making Christian love concrete. Indeed, inasfar as the strategy of mockery focusses upon absurd situations, it might just be a welcome supplement of (or a variation on) the "resisting love" to which recent theological reflections upon suffering call us. According to Gisbert Greshake and Jan Van Bavel, God, as the power of love, encourages us to continue to struggle against completely absurd evil.[21] In using the terms "supplement" and "variation" I would suggest both an affinity with and a difference from this view. Authors who emphasize the combative power of love connect this insight with the representation of a (com)passionate God whose powerful love combats the chaotic powers of misery and death, and who makes us partners in this struggle. There is an archetypal story about God, the creative power of life, who drives away darkness and continues to struggle against it. In this story, both God's (and our) energetic force, and God's (and our) defenselessness are merged.

Some neo-Nietzscheans will be able to identify with this story, especially because God is here seen and understood in the light of a will to life which also breaks through to us humans, and which prompts us to struggle against suffering. Yet we can also expect that these same neo-Nietzscheans will ask for greater clarification in sorting out whether we are here dealing with a long, general or with a short, concrete story. If it seems that the story is written with too many capitals (Love and God), which time and again are the grammatical subject of the sentence (God is Love who struggles with and through us), they suspect the narrators of being ideologists. Such a story serves a metaphysical system

20. J. Van Bavel, "De lijdende God," *Tijdschrift voor Theologie* 14 (1974) 145-148; G. Greshake, *De prijs van de liefde*, Antwerp-Amsterdam, 1980, p. 58.

which seeks to legitimate something, rather than being a guiding principle which can aid people in coming to terms with their situation through their own interpretation.

Postmodernists dislike metaphysical language because it strikes them as being too overarching and too abstract. If the story of a Love (with a capital L) which struggles with us becomes lifted to metaphysical heights, it takes on the function of a compelling universal scheme which concentrates all power in itself without consideration of individuals. This gives rise to the indoctrinating efforts of false prophets who abuse the generosity of people with the expression "God is with us" and, when they think it necessary, can send a whole nation to its death in a military exercise. A story received as universal law soon becomes fanaticism. This leads to disappointments which help no one. Moreover, for the postmodernists, metaphysical language is too vague, because it makes abstraction from the institutions of social and political power. These take such hold of the lives of citizens that in instances of corruption or failure, they only add an additional burden to the physical and moral suffering which is already present. When the postmodernists brandish the weapon of life-courage and mockery, it is in the struggle against this supplementary suffering, that suffering which could have been lessened, had there been no absurd yet remediable flaw in the structures of political and economic management.

In sum, a purely metaphysical view of the struggle between love and death risks overlooking the social and political aspects of the struggle. Postmodernists take this into account. This means that, at least in a limited way, they will probably be more efficient in lessening suffering than metaphysical thinkers have been. As a general category, love is an unspecified and vague weapon; irony and mirth may concretize this with regard to cultural and political life. In terms of anthropodicy, the concrete is characteristic of a justification of life in terms of the anthropodicy. On the other hand it would be wrong to so limit the concrete struggle to the fragmentary that the larger perspective, in view of which that struggle is fought, is lost sight of. It may be the responsibility of

Christians familiar with postmodern thought, to make continual reference, in the midst of all the attention which is given to the fragment, to the larger whole which is present in every fragment. Resistance and liberation on a small scale are, when considered closely, the embodiment of a combative love which (operative in us) comes from God, even though its full potential only reveals itself indirectly (*in obliquo*) and fragmentarily in the horizon of our lives.[21]*

---

21. D. Cupitt, *Life Lines*, London, 1986, p. 214.
* Translated from the Dutch by Catherine Cornille.

THE MEANINGLESSNESS OF SUFFERING AND ATTEMPTS AT INTERPRETATION

T. Johannes Van Bavel

It is not a little ironic that my attempts to prepare these reflections on suffering were hampered by my stay in hospital for an operation. There is, it seems, an opposition between suffering as a concrete experience, and suffering as a subject of discussion. That opposition immediately calls to mind a question: does it make sense to talk about suffering? Is suffering not something that has to be experienced personally? Asking questions about it does not seem to be particularly helpful. Would it not be better to remain silent, especially since humanity has never been able to find a satisfactory answer to the problem of suffering?

To Speak or to Remain Silent

The question of whether "to speak or to remain silent" has been posed in recent years especially with respect to unspeakable suffering, suffering that leaves us mute, that exceeds all our conceptual, imaginative, emotional and verbal capacities. There is suffering before which one can only bow one's head, and about which even the simplest word seems to be a betrayal. This is the suffering which is incommunicable. The Jewish author, Elie Wiesel, in particular, has wrestled with this problem. He has declared that, "a theological reflection on Auschwitz is blasphemy, for the non-believer and the believer alike." Nevertheless, after ten years, Wiesel broke his silence. Why? Because speaking about this suffering is less of a betrayal of the dead than remaining silent about it. The one who is silent promotes indifference, and the one who forgets becomes an accomplice. We may not rob the victims of their history. "The day shall come that the dead themselves will speak and on that day the whole earth will tremble ... The murderers triumphed the first time when they killed millions of Jews. They would triumph a second time and would kill them again should mankind cease to believe that the unimaginable was true." (Wiesel during the trial of Klaus Barbie.)

Wiesel is not the only one to wrestle with this question. Many contemporary theologians say of suffering that it is not a theoretical problem; suffering can never be understood, only combatted. Dorothee Sölle characterizes all traditional attempts to find an answer to the problem of suffering as "theological sadism." Nevertheless, I believe, with Wiesel, that we are obliged to speak about the unspeakable and to confront questions for which we have no clear answer. There must be a forum where one can raise questions about suffering, and give voice to one's anguish and fear in the face of evil, one's bitterness, and one's anger and remorse. My own experience has been that I reflected most deeply on suffering when it touched me, not when it was distant, and when I met others who asked "Why me?" And is it not the case that people in every age have posed questions and have continued to speak about suffering, even though they have not found a satisfactory answer?

Whence Suffering?

The two major questions which humanity has posed, relative to suffering, are the following: *whence* suffering, and *why* suffering. First, a few words about the question of whence. When I gazed from my hospital bed to the buildings on the other side of the street, I saw portions that were brightly illuminated and others that remained shrouded in a sinister darkness. The illuminated portions were still in use, the darkened, no longer in service, and hence, quite dilapidated. I saw in this an illustration of the question about the origins of suffering: which comes first — a lustrous and sound whole which degenerates into chaos, or a chaos from which, in time, good and useful elements grow? When what is at issue is a building, the answer to that question is not very important. When, however, what is at issue is the question of the origins of suffering, the answer is fraught with serious consequences, since it can put us on the wrong track when suffering is our lot. Many worldviews, be they religiously inspired, or philosophical in character, such as Platonism, have accustomed us to an image of the world as originally good, divinely good, even as paradisiacal. That world offered us the spectacle of a perfect harmony, a harmony to be found both within the individual and among human beings, nature and the animal kingdom.

Such a view or vision aroused in many the conviction that all was good in the beginning, and that it was only later — usually through the fault of humanity itself — that suffering and death were able to affect humankind. Take, as an example, the biblical story of creation. We are usually fascinated by the paradisiacal portrait of the person as a near perfect being, familiar with neither suffering nor death, and possessed of extraordinary insight, exceptional freedom, and the highest moral qualities. Then, however, we overlooked the second verse: "The earth was without form and void, and darkness was upon the face of the deep; and the Spirit of God was moving over the face of the waters." It is only afterwards that God creates order out of chaos, and that paradise emerges. From the outset, however, I must warn against reading the biblical narrative as a scientifically historical account of how things were and how they became. I am of the opinion that the biblical presentation of the first man is the portrait of an endpoint, of an ideal of how it really should be, rather than a picture of an historical beginning. The biblical narrative is a particular sort of theological answer to the question of the origins of evil. And this answer contains two important elements: 1. evil does not come from God, since creation is, in itself, good; 2. evil is in some way related to human freedom and responsibility.

Viewed from the perspective of modern science, humankind, *homo sapiens*, is the product of a long process of development, and there can be no question of a sort of intermediate state such as a paradise. Humankind is a growing, developing being. If, however, humanity is a latecomer on the evolutionary stage, then it is obvious that there was life of every sort before there were humans, and that that life was already involved in a struggle for existence marked by suffering and death. We must, therefore, make a distinction between the biblical and the scientific vision, and this distinction is significant for the question of guilt as far as suffering is concerned, a question with which many people still wrestle. Suffering and death cannot be attributed exclusively to humanity.

One thing is obvious: from time immemorial humanity has asked the question, "whence evil and suffering?" and has formulated a variety of answers. I cannot summarize all of these here. All, however, ranging from ancient Greek fatalism and Roman suicide to Islamic resignation and the more positive resistance to, and struggle against, suffering, bear witness to a certain protest against this persistent reality. People experience suffering as something negative, and strive to develop some attitude in response to it. Suffering in the broadest sense of the term is that which we regard as a threat to existence. A shortage of food, accidents, natural disasters, conflicts, wars, sickness and death, indeed, suffering of any sort ultimately signifies the destruction of humanity. Suffering is, in its essence, destructive of life. My point of departure in this reflection is that suffering, viewed in and of itself, is negativity. We, especially here in the West, are so accustomed to thinking in terms of cause and effect that the question of "whence?" is a constant feature of our inquiries about suffering. This is natural since, once we know the origins of a problem, we are often able to do something about it. A person who has just undergone an operation, and feels a peculiar pain, finds some peace in the explanation provided by the attending physician. There is, indeed, suffering that humanity can combat and even overcome, such as sickness and certain disasters.

Even if we accept the idea that all suffering is negativity, we must still make a distinction between different sorts of suffering. For the purposes of our discussion, the following distinctions are significant. There is suffering which derives from the reality within which we live, and which affects us because of our corporeality or the structure of our universe, and there is suffering which human beings inflict on one another. This leads us immediately to the distinction between inevitable suffering and suffering which can be overcome. There is suffering which can acquire meaning, but there is also meaningless suffering, suffering which is impervious to all attempts to make sense of it. There is structural suffering which is born of the existence of certain structures (e. g., economic), and which affects whole groups of people, and there is personal suffering which affects us as individuals. (Group suffering clearly includes personal suffering.) There is the suffering which afflicts the innocent, but there is also the suffering for which we ourselves must accept the blame. Finally, there is the suffering which we unwillingly undergo and the suffering which we willingly accept, because we wish to strive for greater justice in the world through our defense of others. Returning to the question, "whence suffering?," I would like to reflect on two answers.

Humanity Itself is Responsible for Evil

"Humanity" here obviously means myself as well as the other. That suffering is caused by one possessed of a power for evil, is an ancient answer to the question of its origins. That answer persists to this day, as it does, for example, in Africa. According to this view, sickness, death and disaster are not simply the product of chance. The one responsible for my suffering is one who desires to injure me and does so. It is not that those who hold this view simply believe that another is the source of their troubles. Rather, the victims believe that there are those who are, in some way, in league with the power of evil. Accordingly, they approach the witch doctor or cast lots to determine who is responsible for the evil they are forced to endure. Often, of course, this gives rise to a vicious circle of revenge and reprisal. We are perhaps more at home with the question of our own guilt. That question is still frequently asked, albeit in a somewhat veiled fashion. Since we are accustomed to think in terms of cause and effect, we are quickly inclined to look to ourselves as a possible cause for certain forms of suffering. The danger here is that we forge links which have no basis in reality, and thereby generate unwarranted guilt feelings.

Suffering and guilt are not necessarily related, though a stubborn prejudice to that effect continues to prevail. By this I do not mean only those familiar instances, cited in Harold Kushner's work, such as, "had I not sent my mother or father to an old-age home, this would not have happened," or "had I insisted that my husband have the operation," or "had I done this or that, such and such would never have happened." I mean more particularly the oft-repeated and vague question of the sort: "why did this have to happen to me?," or "what did I do to deserve this?," as, for example, in the case of the parent left alone at the death of a child. Such laments are, of course, a cry for help, but they also often reflect a supposition on the part of the victims that they are being punished for some fault. They look for a *moral* cause for what is a natural process. I cannot insist too strongly that the question cannot be posed in such a fashion, since it rests on the supposition that all suffering is the product of some moral failure. Were this the case, humanity would have suffering in its power. Innocence would mean the end of suffering. That this is not the case is evident from the protest of innocent sufferers, such as Job. A great deal of suffering can be ascribed to the reality within which we live, a reality in part determined by natural processes. We cannot live without gravity, but gravity can cause us to fall or cause something to fall on us. Sickness finds its roots in the inevitable deterioration of our body. There is no moral cause that can be identified to explain natural disasters and the random victims they make. Of course, we can console no one by pointing out that their suffering is the result of a natural process, but we can spare them the additional suffering of unwarranted feelings of guilt.

To attempt to free humanity from unreasonable guilt is not, of course, to maintain that humanity is always guiltless where suffering is concerned. It is evident that we can inflict suffering on ourselves, both moral-psychic and physical. So, for example, we can neglect our physical or mental well-being, or make ourselves unfree by one or another addiction. We can also be responsible for the suffering of others. Perhaps this is much more serious. I need mention only the concentration camps, political oppression, the torture of prisoners, organized crime, famine, napalm and atomic bombs. These have made more victims in our age than all the epidemics of the Middle Ages.

Evil is an Eternal Principle: The Gnostic Answer

As we have already indicated, humanity often experiences suffering as a power beyond its control. Suffering befalls us, it assaults us and forces its way into our lives in the fashion of an intruder. The good of this life is mixed with suffering. Good and evil cannot be reconciled, since the good cannot bring forth evil. Otherwise, the good would contradict and deny itself. For that reason, there must be two contradictory and independent primal principles grounding the universe and humanity: a principle of good and a principle of evil, or a good god and an evil god. This is the foundational proposition of Gnosticism, a movement which was quite strong in the first four centuries after Christ. Not that it has completely disappeared: it persists in some modern streams of thought such as theosophy, anthroposophy, the Rosicrucians and Christian Science. According to the Gnostic vision, the two principles are in conflict, and the good is, in fact, the weaker, since it has never learned to fight. The whole of reality is, therefore, rent by a division, that between good and evil.

I will not assert that this is a theory which can easily be dismissed. Its point of departure, the opposition between good and evil, is far too serious to allow facile rejection of it. Where Gnosticism does become more suspect is when it accepts a division, a dualism, within humankind itself, specifically, between spirit and body, between the immaterial and the material. Spirit and immateriality are the sparks of the good, of humankind's primeval bliss; materiality and corporeality belong to the realm of evil and are the source of suffering. The truly human consists, therefore, in the spiritual and especially in knowledge ("gnosis"). Liberation or redemption is achieved through partaking of a special enlightenment or knowledge, and leaving the material and the corporeal behind. Whereas many systems of thought, including Christianity, are at a loss for an answer to the question of the origins of evil and suffering, Gnosticism offers a most seductive reply precisely because it sounds so rational and radical.

At first sight, the Gnostic answer satisfies human reason, and this explains the centuries-old success of the system. Has it not paid too high a price, however? A closer look exposes two major weaknesses. In the first place, if one regards evil as an independent primal principle, one identifies the cause of suffering, but one also renders the situation of humankind more hopeless than ever. It leaves humankind even more powerless, and lessens its responsibility. Saint Augustine, who was for ten years a member of the Manichean sect, the most radical wing of Gnosticism, experienced it as follows: it is not I who act, but evil which acts in me. The second weakness of the Gnostic position is its identification of materiality and corporeality with evil. Does this not mean the dismissal of a large share of the human reality? And has not the positive valuation of materiality and corporeality been one of mankind's major triumphs? The truly human does not consist in the separation of spirit and body, but in their union. Must we not say with Eduard Schillebeeckx that the dismissal of the good that is creation represents a "doubling of the problem of evil?"

Why Suffering?

The question of "why" there is suffering might also be seen as a quest for the meaning of suffering. Is it possible to discover a purpose and a sense in suffering or to give it meaning? To repress this question would not be human since, as we have already indicated, this could lead to the emergence of an apathetic or a fatalistic attitude towards suffering. When, however, people ask the question "why," they are not always interested in a theoretical answer. Often they are expressing their pain, their desperation or desolation, or they are simply crying out for help. Are theoretical answers really meaningful in such a situation? I believe they are, because they can provide direction for our attempts to come to terms with suffering, and they prevent us from aggravating our suffering by interpreting it in an improper fashion — though it remains the case that no theoretical answer can spare us the task of coping personally with the suffering that touches our lives. I do not believe in the proposition that suffering is meritorious in itself. Nor do I believe that all suffering is meaningless. There are forms of suffering which we can render meaningful. That meaning must come from without though, that is, from something good that stands apart from suffering, and from a good, moreover, that transcends suffering. This latter is necessary if we are to be able to speak of justified meaningfulness. I would like to reflect on four responses to the "why" question.

The Meaning of Suffering Consists in its Punitive Character

Nietzsche wrote that: "The [Christian] explanation [of suffering], by viewing all suffering from the perspective of guilt, brought new suffering: a more profound, interior, poisonous and life-sapping suffering ... Despite everything, however, this proved to be man's salvation. He had found a meaning, he was no longer a leaf in the wind, the plaything of meaninglessness." Nietzsche need not have limited himself to Christianity, since this answer is as old as humanity itself. We can detect it in countless ancient myths, and in Greek philosophy: in Orphism (ca. 700 B.C.), Empedocles, Plato (though one does discern a certain development here), and in Plotinus. In all of these there is a recurring scheme of things: originally, humanity enjoyed a state of purity, devoid of suffering, and this was subsequently lost through humanity's own fault. Suffering was the punishment for this loss. This view of things is illustrative of the ease with which humanity links suffering and punishment (expiation). We have already pointed out that not all suffering can be explained in terms of human guilt. Similarly, all suffering cannot be regarded as punishment.

The big question is whether there was initially no suffering, whether suffering only came later as punisment for some infrac-tion. This view is scientifically untenable. It does not seem likely and I personallly do not think that the ancient myths were intended to provide an historical overview of things. Let us look once again at the biblical narrative of creation as an example. The author is concerned with giving a theological description of humanity alienated from God. That alienation is coincidental with creation. The biblical writer does not intend to provide an historically delineated or chronological account of events, to state that there was a time when there were no labor pains, no suffering and no death. When he presents these as punishments, he is revealing his own theological vision. One ought not conclude from this, however, that these things do not pertain to the essence of being human. Moreover, we must not forget that in both the Old and New Testaments (Job, and Jesus in John 9:1-3 and Luke 13:1-5, respectively), there is an outright denial of the notion that suffering is simply a punishment for sin. I am of the opinion that to regard suffering as a punishment is to miss completely the immediate causes of certain forms of suffering. Of those who maintain that AIDS is a punishment for sin, I ask why it is that this punishment was not imposed much earlier, when people did the same things that they are doing today?

The Meaning of Suffering is its Contribution to the Formation or Development of the Human Person

Suffering is often described as life's great teacher. To a certain degree this is true. Suffering can help us grow in wisdom and maturity. It can teach us a greater appreciation of the simple things of life. In particular, it can make us more sensitive to others, and thereby prompt in us the desire to suffer for a cause that is good and just. Bernard Kemp has expressed it as follows: "Suffering is perhaps the only wellspring of genuine love in the human person. Does not the mystery of evil and suffering consist in this, that without suffering people would no longer know what love is and would no longer be capable of it? For me, to love is essentially to suffer with another. I fear that where there is no suffering, love, too, has been banished." Dorothee Sölle, too, has objected to the fact that, in our day, suffering has been pushed as far aside as possible, under the pretext that it teaches us nothing. Sölle castigates, as due to the blindness of modern society, the view that suffering should cost us nothing. Pain, separation, disappointment can be ways to maturation, growth, and deeper knowledge. Despite its inhuman character, suffering can enable us to long for greater humanity. For that reason, Gisbert Greshake has entitled a recent book on suffering, *The Price of Love*.

Even within the biblical account of humanity's paradisiacal state, we can find some basis for the view that suffering can be useful for human development. There, we find a suggestion of the loneliness of the human creature, and we read that it is not good that the human person should be alone. There, too, in the story of the tree of the knowledge of good and evil, we read of the human experience of finitude as far as knowledge and freedom are concerned. Moreover, paradise was not devoid of temptation. The whole narrative of the Fall treats of the temptation to transgress the limits of creatureliness. Finally, paradise was not devoid of fear, either fear of ignorance or fear of death. So it is that the tempter says: "[If you eat of this tree], you will not die ." Loneliness, finitude, temptation and fear are, according to Genesis, forms of suffering which pertain to the essence of humanity, and which may not simply be dismissed as pointless or meaningless. Instead, they are, as it were, openings or lacunae which ask to be filled out or fulfilled, which ask to be given meaning. Loneliness leads to the discovery of the other, and teaches us the value of human love-relationships: humanity is a joint venture. Were it not for the experience of our own finitude, we would have all we desired, and nothing would be forbidden to us. Then, too, however, there would be no longing whatever, no place for wonder, surprise, or thanksgiving. The door to boundless egotism would be wide open. Temptation makes us aware of our frreedom to choose. It is precisely in this freedom that a portion of our greatness lies, since while it enables us to opt for evil, it also allows us to choose the good, the true, the just — to choose love. The fear of destruction and death not only instructs us in the dangers in life. It summons us to an untold creativity and commitment on behalf of life. As J. B. Metz expresses it, "Humanity must learn to accept itself ... in and through the spiritual adventure of its own becoming via the many stations that lie between birth and death."

Of course, there are limits to the view of suffering as a factor promoting human becoming. What we have said in this regard is appropriate in the case of the death which follows a richly-filled life. It is not so in the case of the death of a child or of the victim of violence. It is appropriate where the loneliness experienced is the "normal" loneliness of existence, it is not so when we consider the loneliness of the abandoned elderly or of women and children left to fend for themselves. It is appropriate as far as the limitations under which one labors are normal, it is not so where there is a question of undernourishment, oppression because of one's minority status, or some handicap. It is appropriate in the case of normal fear, it is not so in the case of the fear of atomic weapons, or the fear that results in despair or suicide. It is appropriate in the case of the pain that harbingers some ailment, it is not so in the case of an excess of pain. The deficiency of this model is that not all suffering is formative. There is suffering which engenders bitterness in the human person.

The Meaning of Suffering Consists in its Contribution to Progess

In addition to the view that suffering is formative for the personality, there is also the view that suffering is necessary for human progress in the broad sense. Suffering, in this scheme of things, is subsumed under faith in the inevitability of progress. The suffering of the past, it is asserted, was due largely to ignorance, the deficiencies of science, superstition, passivity, and a lack of ingenuity. The generations before us were convinced of the inevitability of hunger, infant mortality, contagious diseases, poverty and natural disasters. Contemporary humanity is different: we believe in human progress and we effect such progress ourselves through the elimination of the negative. This is not to suggest that evolution does not require sacrifice. Development includes the negative, elements which cannot be integrated, failure, waste. Cancer, new virusses, miscarriages, accidents and floods are the necessary corollaries of evolution. In this respect, life in the plant and animal kingdom, where life is dearly bought, serves as a model for human evolution. The struggle for life is the motor of a self-regulating existence, but its ultimate aim is, the achievement and development of that very existence. If we desire progress, we must be prepared to make some sacrifices.

Translated into the language of the natural sciences, this means that evil is the price of a better functioning reality. Our ability to interfere in natural processes enables us to control suffering itself. This is true to a degree, and it is certainly not my intention to deny the results of science and technology. What does strike me as problematic is the presupposition upon which this faith in progess rests, namely, that the universe is a rationally comprehensible and organized system, such that any and all development is necessarily positive. There is, today, the growth of a more critical spirit, a spirit which no longer views the universe as a harmonious whole governed by unchangeable laws, but as a place also marked by indeterminateness and even chaos. This view has shocked that faith which saw progess as a perfectly predictable and controllable process. That there are limits to the exploitation of nature and experimentation with human persons, is more and more apparent in the destruction unleashed when either humanity or nature are treated purely as instruments of progess. To sacrifice the person to a system which views progess as a higher norm than humanity itself is nothing short of a justification of suffering.

The same is true where faith in progress is linked to a particular vision of the state. The state shall provide for the happiness of the individual person, and hence, the state lays claim to absolute power so as to eliminate all obstacles to the realization of its goal. In such a scheme of things, the fear of those in power is justified, and the question of the person's well being is suppressed. It is all well and good to posit as an ideal a classless society which may be achieved at some point in history's evolution, but this must not be purchased at any price. When countless individuals are sacrificed as cogs to some greater wheel, society in this case, the matter becomes quite problematic indeed. Victims cannot be expected to accept or approve their suffering because it is said to be the way to a better future. Mass graves do not disappear because progress has been achieved. The theory of progress is, therefore, only partially true. One cannot console the victims by means of it. As far as many of the "why" questions are concerned, for instance, why cancer, why miscarriages or floods, we would do better to answer that we simply do not know.

Suffering Acquires Meaning in the Context of an Higher Harmony

According to this view of things, all that is evil, suffering included, has its place and acquires meaning within some greater whole whether this be the world order, the logos as universal principle, or God. This stoic answer to the problem of suffering has been widely disseminated. It has been advocated by various philosophers and Church Fathers, as well as by certain modern authors such as Leibniz and Hegel. Ultimately, even evil and suffering find their place in some higher coherence. Within the context of this comprehensive whole, these can not only be neutralized but even accorded a positive role. This conviction rests on both the insight that all that exists is somehow related, and on the demand for justice — somewhere, somehow, good and evil must be balanced out. The beauty of the world is revealed most gloriously precisely in oppositions. Suffering exists, finally, in service to the good. That we are not able to recognize this is to be attributed to our lack of insight, since we always see only portions of the whole. Various analogies are invoked to illustrate this view of things. These include the example of a painting in which the interplay of light and darkness contribute to the effect of the whole, and the beautiful patterns on the surface of a woven carpet which are achieved by the confusing crisscross of threads on the underside. I imagine that Elizabeth Kübler-Ross departs from this vision when she maintains that the child who dies has achieved fullness, that it is ready to return to God.

The ability of this vision to console many undoubtedly consists in its demand for justice. Moreover, by relativizing suffering, it serves as a summons to people to integrate suffering into a broader context. It is not without dangers, however. This is especially true as far as border-line cases are concerned. The vision of a greater harmony fails when great systems collapse, when innocents are prey to destruction and death, when there is senseless suffering. If this vision were a true one, even the most horrible facts would be accorded a place. Even a higher order, however, can never justify horrendous suffering. It is difficult to maintain that the meaning of the atomic bomb is sufficiently explained by the fact that it brought an end to the war, or that the meaning of Auschwitz was its role in the foundation of the state of Israel. Hiroshima and Auschwitz are, instead, absolute defeats for humanity.

I am not able to see how these sorts of things can be integrated into some higher principle without making that principle somehow sadistic. For this very reason, there has long been vociferous opposition to this theory. The most famous declaration of opposition is, perhaps, that voiced by Dostoevski's character, Ivan: "Eternal harmony is not worth one tear of that tortured child in that stinking toilet, the child who beat her breast with her tiny fists and who, with unrequited tears, begged the dear Lord for help. The fact that those tears went unrequited makes that whole harmony worthless ... I do not want any harmony and I refuse it out of love for humanity ... That harmony is too costly, we cannot afford the admission fee. And for that reason, I hasten to return my ticket." Kushner makes the same point even more radically, when he reflects that a person who causes undeserved suffering in the name of something higher ends up in prison.

I would like to conclude with the following question. Where do we draw the line between suffering to which we can give some meaning and meaningless suffering? There are those who maintain that suffering to which we can give a meaning is not suffering at all. I do not agree with this view. Perhaps we can formulate it as follows: the line is drawn where suffering ceases to be serviceable to life. I realize, however, that this principle remains an abstract one. One person is able to come to some meaningful terms with more suffering than another. It is not only the suffering which is determinative, but the person. I do not think that all suffering can be regarded as serviceable to the growth and development of humanity. Humanity is capable of much — it can distinguish what contributes to life and what brings death, what builds up and what destroys, and it can even, up to a point, promote life. I do not, however, think that humanity is always able to make the negative serviceable to the positive, death serviceable to life. It is a fact — there is suffering which leaves us mute.*

* Translated from the Dutch by Terrence Merrigan.

WHERE IS GOD WHEN HUMAN BEINGS SUFFER?

T. Johannes Van Bavel

When fifty children perished in a car accident in France in 1982, one newspaper headlined the news as follows: "Where was God last night?" Many people, together with Stendhal, have already drawn the following conclusion: "God has only one excuse, namely, that He does not exist." Reading modern literature, such as, for example, the essay written by a Dutch author entitled, *The Incredible Cruelty of the Supreme Being*,[1] one more than once encounters the sentiment expressed by Georg Büchner in 1837: "Suffering is the rock of atheism." If there is a God, then it is a very bad God, according to the late actress, Romy Schneider, whose child fell out of a window and died.

Adolphe Gesché recently wrote that the exclamation, "There is no God, otherwise such suffering would not exist," is not so much a protest against God, as against evil. I believe, however, that this is not always the case, and that one cannot make it into a general rule. In my opinion, the question is more serious. I am alarmed by the considerable apostasy of some people because of the problem of suffering. A theologian cannot be silent in the face of this problem. I am aware that many of my colleagues say that one does not have to justify God vis à vis human suffering, and that this is, in any case, simply impossible. Theodicy, that is, the justification of God, has always failed in the past and never offered a solution. This is true if one conceives of theodicy as a justification of suffering by some such appeal to God as the

---

1. Karel van het Reve, *De ongelooflijke slechtheid van het opperwezen*, Amsterdam, 1987, p. 27.

following: God allows suffering because He, in His providence, knows what is good for a human being. However, is it not possible to see theodicy in another way, namely, as an attempt to purify, as far as possible, our own ideas about God? This is the perspective I wish to adopt in this article.

My starting point is Elie Wiesel's statement that, "One does not understand Auschwitz *with* God; one does not understand Auschwitz *without* God." These words mean that a denial of the existence of God is no solution to the problem of suffering, just as belief in God provides no definitive answer. The attitude of atheists deserves our respect insofar as they base themselves on humanitarian motives and on love of human life, as is expressed in the following text: "There is only one cult left [for us]: the cult of kindness and of courage — the courage to accept the undeniable madness of life without resorting to suicide, a cult of human kindness which finds its nobility in being certain that we will not be rewarded." However, it still has to be admitted that such an attitude does not diminish the amount of suffering in the world. With or without God, questions about suffering remain. The atheist, Ernst Bloch remarks acutely: "There are questions which also remain in atheism, in as far as atheism is no unhistorical, unreal or foolish optimism." Indeed, one can reverse the problem: if God disappears as the one responsible for suffering, who then becomes responsible? Must we direct the accusation to humanity itself? If we are forced to substitute the justification of humanity for the justification of God, has anthropodicy not replaced theodicy? If God is not allowed to exist because of suffering, are human beings then allowed to exist? This does not get us very far.

The Almighty God

A First Distinction

In speaking of God and suffering we will begin by making a distinction between suffering caused by human beings and suffering which human beings encounter, but have not caused. It is self-evident that we ourselves are responsible for the suffering we have caused. This responsibility is situated on both a personal level — for example, hatred of others, discrimination, physical violence, egotism — and on a broader social level — for example, support for unjust structures such as those involving exploitation, commodity dumping, and oppression of every sort. The question, "What are we doing with our freedom and knowledge?" is still both topical and urgent, though it was addressed to Cain as long ago as the beginning of human history. Georges De Schrijver, in another essay in this book, has pointed out that it is precisely this question which Latin-American liberation theologians put to the Western world. These same theologians criticize traditional Western answers by stating that: Westerners should attach more importance to concrete and personal suffering and that they should pay more attention to moral evil because they themselves make victims. In this context, the words of 1 Peter 4:15 still hold force: "Let none of you suffer as a murderer, or a thief, or a wrongdoer, or a mischief-maker."

It is obvious that the God of the Bible is a God who does not will moral evil. We can never cover up human sins by making an appeal to Him. It is simply impossible to regard the whole course of human history as the reflection of God's own deeds. In such a case, everything, the most horrendous no less than the finest, would reveal Him. Dorothee Sölle has written that, as far as the Holocaust is concerned, it is unthinkable that God should choose the side of the executioners rather than that of the victims. To seek to discover a divine message in such a catastrophe is to accord victory to the perpetrators. Undoubtedly, there is suffering that could be eliminated from the world if all people were to do the good. For that reason, we cannot simply hold God responsible for all the world's suffering. I cannot agree with C. S. Lewis' assertion that all suffering is God's "amplifier," a bitter medicine which offers the wicked a unique opportunity for conversion. Such a view leads us immediately to a cruel God. On the other hand, I am well aware that, alongside the suffering born of human freedom, there is also suffering which transcends human power, such as sickness and death, natural disasters and accidents. Is this kind of suffering within the power of almighty God?

The Dilemma of Omnipotence and Love

According to Lactantius, Epicurus formulated the dilemma of God's omnipotence and His love as follows: "Either God wishes to abolish suffering and cannot; or He can abolish it and does not wish to do so; or He does not wish to abolish it and cannot do so; or He wishes to abolish it and can do so. If He wishes to do so, and cannot, He is powerless, which is not proper to God. If He can do so, and does not wish it, He is merciless, which is equally alien to God. If He does not wish to do so, and cannot, He is both merciless and powerless, and therefore not God. If He wishes to do so and can — and this is the only thing fitting as far as God is concerned — whence comes evil and why does God not abolish it?"[2] This text makes it abundantly clear that we are not able to combine God's omnipotence and love in our thinking, or to reconcile them with one another.

There are reasons for this. In the first place, our God-talk remains imprisoned within the horizon of the possibilities proper to human language. This is self-evident, but it is no less significant for that reason. In fact, it has far-reaching consequences. Our speech about God always departs from our own experiences. So, for example, we say that God is a person and not a thing,

2. *De ira Dei*, 13; PL 7, 121.

that He is love and not hatred, that He is freedom and not slavery, that He is meaning and not nonsense, that He means happiness and not misery, that He is powerful and not powerless. In fact, on such occasions, we are speaking about person, freedom, happiness, love and power as we experience and know them. Moreover, we often use these expressions unquestioningly, as if their meaning was self-evident. However, even in our daily experience, this is not the case. Who is able to say what actually constitutes real personhood, authentic love, genuine freedom, or real power? The problem emerges even more acutely when we seek to apply these notions to God. Our speech about God can, necessarily, only point towards, or tend towards, Him. Is it merely coincidence that "utopian" God-talk is to be found in all theologies, theistic, process, and post-theistic alike? This indicates that we cannot say anything and everything about God. What is not worthy of humanity is also not worthy of God. No one wants an inhuman God, that is, a God who is less than a human being. I ask myself if this is not a good criterion for guarding our representations of God from arbitrariness. Seen in this light, our speech about God's omnipotence creates special difficulties.

When we hear the word "power" — and even more so, when we hear the word "omnipotence" — a warning light begins to flicker for many of our contemporaries. We have, not unjustly, become apprehensive of power. A powerful person is often a dangerous person. The word "power" is derived from the Latin *possum*, which means the capacity to do something. Omnipotence means the capacity to do every thing, to suppress everything that stands in opposition. This, however, immediately calls to mind thoughts of arbitrariness, dictatorship, or abuse of power. The notion of power always includes the possibility of oppression, cruelty, capriciousness, violence and injustice. Nevertheless, we often (perhaps unconsciously) conceive the power of God in terms akin to human power. The question is whether this does not lead to an impoverished representation of God. The God who emerges from such categories is one who is responsible for everything: death no less than life, sickness no less than health, accidental death no less than survival, evil no less than good. God becomes the puppeteer who pulls all the strings. A sudden jerk here and someone dies, a jolt there and an accident occurs, a twitch here and an handicapped child is born, or an earthquake takes place. The upshot of such a view of things is obvious: God is responsible for all suffering. He is much more akin to an unjust despot (how otherwise do we explain His choice of victim) than a loving Father.

From such a perspective, God is easily indicted. Take, for example, the words of Karel van het Reve: "If one accepts an omnipotent God — and I don't really know if there are Christian churches which do not hold that God is almighty, and if there are such churches they must lead a hidden life since one never sees or hears them on radio or television — if, as I said, one accepts that God is almighty, and that without Him not even a sparrow falls from the roof, then He does a great number of things every day which, in the case of a person, would make him or her a villain." It would seem that van het Reve has not read any contemporary theologians. Otherwise he would realize that many of them have serious doubts and questions about God's omnipotence. To quote only one of them, H. J. Heering: "Is contemporary theology not obliged to speak of God's omnipotence in a more subdued fashion? Must we not show a little more respect for an Etty Hillesum who, in the concentration camp at Westerbork, found that the good God needed a little help? Would it not be better, after Stalin, Hitler and the atomic bomb ... to keep silent about God's omnipotence?"

It seems to me that it is time to redefine the notion of divine omnipotence. Should we not deal with the question of God's omnipotence in the same way as we deal with the question of His freedom? Even the most classic theology holds that God is not free in the fashion that a human being is free, since He can neither sin nor will evil. Should we not think of divine omnipotence along the same lines? In any case, omnipotence, in and of itself, is an empty notion. Unless and until we determine its object or its content, power is neither good nor evil. Mere power is nothing other than unbridled violence. Viewed in these terms alone, one cannot say if the Almighty One is a god or a devil, a lover of life or a monster of destruction. If human power is only good when something good constitutes its goal and determines its limits, must not the same be said of God's power (Jürgen Moltmann)? André de Halleux is of the opinion that the biblical term *pantocrator*, usually translated as "almighty," originally meant something else, namely, the all-embracing one or the one who surrounds everything with His solicitude.

At the very least, these reflections make it clear that caution is needed where the word omnipotence is concerned. Indeed, must we not say, with Piet Schoonenberg, that, "I resist the thought that God *in abstracto* can do everything." Schoonenberg's observation is not simply a product of modernity. Sixteen centuries ago, Augustine declared that, "God is not mightier than Himself."[3] This text is not only food for thought, it brings us to the theme of creation. To say that God is not mightier than Himself means that when God gives creation its own freedom, He cannot simply abrogate the laws of that creation.

Creation as Risk

We confess that God is creator of heaven and earth. Creation, however, is not a simple notion. Etymologically, the word "create" means to make something, to give it form, to give it existence. Here, too, our human experience comes into play. To make something is to call into being something that differs from oneself. It is to give to someone or something the space within which they themselves can exist. Consider the case of couples who do not wish to remain alone, but desire children. They not only give their children life, they also give them the possibility of an independent existence. Consider, too, the case of the artist who

3. *De Genesi ad litteram* 9, 17, 32; PL 34, 406.

creates a masterpiece. The parents and the artist are well aware of the fact that the child and the work of art are not them, even though they are the source from which both issue. They realize that by the act of generation they give to the "other" an independence and character proper to it. These two traits, independence and proper character, immediately suggest freedom and risk. Parents cannot foresee if their children will always love them; neither can they prevent those children from making the wrong choices in life. By the same token, they cannot protect their children from sickness and death. (The same is true, *mutatis mutandis*, of a work of art).

Must we not think of God's creative act along the same lines? God does not wish to remain alone in inviolable and unapproachable exaltation. He wishes to give existence to something outside Himself, something possessed of a certain freedom and autonomy. His wish is for people who can choose Him in freedom, since real love always involves a free choice. Love is only experienced as a wonder, as a delight, when another freely chooses me. That same freedom means, however, that the other may not choose me. It is this which constitutes the risk. Applying this line of thought to God, one can speak of God's self-limitation, a limitation born of His loving wish that the world exist alongside and over and against Him. God creates by relinquishing his will to be everything. We ought to be grateful that humanity and the world are not crushed under the weight of God's omnipotence, for then there would be no freedom for either humanity or the world. Indeed, there would be no future for either.

Omnipotence is, therefore, not a matter of caprice, of arranging everything from on high, but of sharing, of allowing the other to be. God's plan is not immovably fixed, such that everything is preordained and our freedom is robbed of all meaning. Such a vision can only lead to an unchristian fatalism: "it had to be so," "one gets what one deserves," "when one's time has come it has come." Must we not see creation much more as an appeal to our freedom and "creativity?" In the perspective of such a vision, we become co-responsible for creation in its finitude and incompleteness. Moreover, we are more easily able to interpret creation as a continuing process. The old framework within which the idea of creation was situated, that is, that of "making and causality," is discarded to be replaced by another, that of a God "who is ground of our existence and who calls us to being." Creation is then neither exclusively past- nor exclusively future-oriented; it finds place now, in this instant, though only where the good is realized. It is my opinion that the foregoing reflections can enable us to pose the problem of suffering more acutely, and to view it in another light. They are not, however, able to provide us with the final satisfactory answer.

There is one objection which is raised from many sides: could God not have made a better world, a quite different world, a world without blood and tears, without sickness and death? Plotinus in antiquity, and Leibniz in the seventeenth century, both believed that this world was the best of all possible worlds, that a better world was simply an impossibility. It is, however, possible to raise two objections to this theory of the best of all possible worlds: 1. concretely, it is obvious that there is a surplus of suffering which ought not and need not exist; 2. this theory was devised to exonerate God of all responsibility for suffering and evil, to place God beyond the pale of the question of suffering.

It is also necessary to see clearly the consequences of the postulate of a better world. Usually we dream of a world where neither freedom for evil (either cosmic or human freedom) nor finitude exist. Would such a world be this world however? Would it not be something quite different, something we could not imagine in even our wildest fantasies. Everything would have to change instantly. To take but one example: were no one to die, the propagation of the human race would become an impossibility, simply because the earth would be too small. To put it plainly: a person might long to be unlimited and immortal, but it must not be forgotten that he or she would not, then, be a person at all. (Imagine that all mice wished to be elephants since

elephants are larger and stronger, and live longer. The fulfilment
of their wish would mean that mice simply ceased to exist.) Two
conclusions can be drawn from what we have said up to now: 1.
God cannot simply shift the parameters of creation, since this
would mean the end of creation as it now exists, with its own
particular characteristics of freedom and independence; 2. viewed
from the standpoint of humanity, the longing for a world without
limitation and finitude is, in fact, the longing that our world cease
to exist, since it is nothing other than a refusal of our reality. And
this calls forth another consideration: to be or not to be, that is
the question.

Is Non-existence Better than Existence?

It would have been better had God created nothing, since this life
is nothing but misery. There are those who not only think as
much, but cry it out in the fashion of Job: "Let the day perish
wherein I was born, and the night which said, 'A man-child is
conceived.' Let that day be darkness! May God above not seek it,
nor light shine upon it .... Yea, let that night be barren; let no
joyful cry be heard in it" (Job 3:3-4, 7). Job's lament contains
two thoughts which are significant for our consideration: non-
existence as darkness, and the cry of joy from parents when their
child is born. To be born into the human family means to be
invited into existence. We did not decide to live, we received life.
There is such a thing as wonderment at existence. I remember
how, during my childhood, I would lay in bed in the evening
alongside my younger brother, amazed that *I* was alive, and that
my life was not the same as his. What I thought was not what he
thought. Was it pure chance that I was alive? I might not have
been. I tried to imagine how it would be if I was not. The only
thing I could then call to mind was an absolute, unfathomable
darkness, one devoid of all consciousness. Indeed, had we never
lived, we would never have been aware of anything, we would
never have enjoyed anything, neither nature nor persons; we

would never have seen, or heard or felt anything, nothing evil but nothing good either; we would have known no difficulties but neither would we have known love.

When one is required to speak of suffering, the disadvantage is that all attention is focussed on the negative dimension of our existence. Almost everyone is aware, however, that this is not completely justified. There are positive sides to existence. There is war but there is also reconciliation, hunger but also seed and harvest, natural disasters but also sunrises and sunsets, sickness and death but also healing and comfort at the end, loneliness and desperation but also feasting and joy, crime but also justice, hatred but also friendship, ugliness but also beauty, disloyalty but also fidelity, falsehood but also truth. Our reality imposes limits on us. When, however, we accept those limits, we can also enjoy the good that life brings; without such acceptance, life is nothing other than a perpetual torment (Antoon Vergote). Viewed from the point of view of our reality, one must even say that, without life death would be neither important nor possible, without health there would be no sickness, without justice there would be no injustice. Augustine was not wrong when he wrote: "Despite all our unhappiness [at the death of our loved ones], still we love life." This draws me to ask the question: Does not one moment of love or affection balance out death? However, while this thought can serve to comfort us, it is not enough in some cases. There are those who never arrive at a truly conscious experience of love and affection. In such an instance, this thought does not constitute a satisfactory answer.

The God Full of Love Who Is Present to Us

One might ask whether, by subjecting the notion of omnipotence to a criticism, by describing creation as a risk, and by accenting the value of life, we have not placed God completely beyond the pale of the question of suffering. We think not. What we have achieved is a state where it is no longer possible to attribut all suffering to God. However, as long as we believe in God as creator of heaven and earth, we are not able to explain the fact that finitude and death are essential features of our existence. As creator, God must be involved in some way or another with these realities. Could He not have done it differently? The question might seem absurd, but I am prepared to venture an answer: No, it could not have been different. If God wishes another than Himself, then that other will necessarily differ from Him. Otherwise, it would not be an "other," and God would only be reproducing Himself. If the Infinite calls into existence something outside itself, that something will necessarily be finite and perishable. Moreover, if it is really to exist as another, it must be possessed of its own freedom and autonomy. So it is that God gives up some of His power, and limits Himself. In terms of humanity, this means, positively, that the creature is responsible (or at least co-responsible) for creation. On the other hand, it also means that God cannot simply abrogate the human freedom and finitude which characterize this existence without contradicting Himself. Still, if even a finite existence is superior to complete non-existence, it becomes possible to place creation in the perspective of a loving, and not a cruel, God.

God, the Fellow-Sufferer

In view of the sort of considerations we have already discussed, many contemporary theologians have shifted the accent from an almighty God who can simply abrogate the limits of creation, to a God who is almighty in love. In this way, the notion of omnipotence acquires a different content (Kierkegaard). Of course, love, no less than omnipotence, is a human characterization of God. There is, however, one important distinction. Our notion of power is decidedly ambiguous, since, in and of itself, it says nothing about good and evil, while our notion of love (noncommercial love at least) is unambiguously positive; it is to will the good for another. When we speak of the "power of love," we use the word power in a very particular sense. All of us know that love is not without effect. So, for example, our personality is always the fruit of the love of others: our parents, educators, teachers, our friends and loved ones. As Martin Buber expresses it, "The I blooms by the grace of the Thou." To love is to recognize and respect the value and dignity of the other, to receive the other with thanksgiving as a gift, not only when all is well, but also in the nakedness of suffering. Love is no less present in suffering, and shares the burden of that suffering. For that reason, all love is creative.

In Greek philosophy, the divine first principle is often represented as uninvolved with the created order, as impervious to suffering. The divine principle does indeed set everything in motion, but it remains itself unmoved, since, as the fullness of being, it cannot be subject to change. The question which immediately arises here is whether one can regard self-absorption and all absence of relation as perfections. Although the Greek idea of God strongly influenced early Christian thought, it is not in harmony with the biblical view of God. The bible always sees God in active relationship with humanity and the world. That relationship is not viewed as incompatible with the notion of omnipotence. The contradiction is not to be found here, but on the part of those who insist on God's omnipotence and, at the same time, steadfastly reject the notion that He can enter into relationship (He can do everything except this — that is, enter into a relationship of love). Love, at least as we have experienced it, is to be always involved with others, either by sharing our lives with them or by sharing in their lives. Can we think of God as in some sense less than a human being? If God is love, then He must be involvement at its highest. If He is such, it is not odd that He is affected by human suffering, and that He shares in the legitimate joys and the suffering of innocent people.

Considerations along these lines have brought a great number of Jewish and Christian authors to the idea of a suffering, or

more accurately, a "fellow-suffering" God. Among Jewish
authors, we find, for example, Abraham Joshua Heschel, Harold
Kushner and Elie Wiesel. To take the last-named, most people
are by now familiar with his gripping story "Night," which
describes the execution, in the concentration camp at Buna, of
two adults and a child. Wiesel recounts how he was forced to
march past the gallows where the child hung for an hour sus-
pended between life and death, and how he heard one of his
fellow prisoners behind him ask three times, "Where is God
now?" In that instant, he heard a voice within him answer,
"Where is he? He is here. He is hanging there on the gallows ... "
Those who wish to interpret Wiesel's story in terms of the death
of God or of God's complete absence were confronted by Wiesel
himself in 1985.[4] In an article written at that time, Wiesel defends
the view that God is omnipresent, even in suffering, and that He
suffers with us, since our suffering affects Him. He does, however,
ask a critical question: "What does it mean that God suffers?
Does this not increase our suffering?" Wiesel answers: "No, God
is free to choose. And, without understanding it, all we can do is
to strive to be worthy of that choice. It is certainly not a
justification of the evil of Auschwitz." This last observation seems
to me to be of great importance, since even with a changed
representation of God, that is, that of God the fellow sufferer, we
could easily revert to a model of harmony by effecting a cheap
reconciliation between God and suffering. There are two reasons
why we may not do this. First, God is opposed to all suffering
which people cause one another, all horrible and senseless suffering.
Secondly in God there is not the suffering powerlessness which is
characteristic of humanity. We must not elevate the chaos of our
history into a perpetual process in God Himself. If God voluntarily makes Himself powerless in certain circumstances, this is to
make room for a freedom outside Himself, but He remains
almighty love which redeems.

For Christians, the idea of a suffering God finds form in Jesus'

---

4. E. Wiesel, *Die hundert Namen Gottes*, Freiburg, 1985.

death on the cross. In Jesus one encounters the suffering God-Father in the most intense fashion. Here, too, however, we must be wary of incorrect interpretations. Jesus' violent death must not be regarded as a glorification of suffering. The violence done to Jesus was, in the first place, a crime. It was not God who killed Jesus; it was people who saw in him an obstacle to be eliminated. His suffering was not redemptive because he was tortured; it was redemptive because it was the final consequence of his loving commitment to others. Only love, not pain, is redemptive. Moreover, when we say, and quite correctly, that God suffered with Jesus, we do this by analogy with human suffering. That is to say, the one who suffers *with* another does not endure suffering and death as brute facts, in all their physicality, but as psychic torment, and this because of the love-identification with the other which the fellow-sufferer feels. The pain is not less intense because it is psychic, as the case of parents who suffer with their sick children illustrates so well.

Discriminatory Death and Christian Resurrection-Hope

It is often said that death is the great equalizer, that all must die and that there is justice in this. Death, it is said, does not discriminate. This is not true, however. It makes a great deal of difference whether an elderly person dies after a richly-filled life or a child dies in an accident, whether one dies peacefully like a waning candle or expires in pain, whether one dies surrounded by those who are dear one or one perishes alone in a concentration camp. Death is quite clearly unjust. It is therefore not surprising that resurrection faith arose out of the following consideration: if death is the last word, then there is no justice, since the fate of the executioner and that of his victim are one and the same, and this life is nothing but madness and meaninglessness, as some atheists maintain. Christianity, together with other religions, protests against such negativity. Christianity proclaims a God who wishes to redeem all of humanity out of and through love. It tells a big

story, because there are obviously no little stories (since even
when a system of thought professes to do otherwise, it still
endeavors to provide a comprehensive meaning for our history).

Is death indeed the end, and is destruction the last word? When
our rational system fails — and that happens most absolutely in
the case of death and meaningless suffering — there remains only
one question: the question of the transcendent, of the Other, the
question of God. When one simply avoids or denies this question,
does one not sell humanity short, humanity's suffering no less
than its hope? Of course, we cannot prove God's existence, but
faith in God does place our existence in another light. What does
faith mean to us if we suffer? I think we might summarize this in
two points: it means that God is *present* in our suffering, and that
He takes us up into His life through the *resurrection*.

Wiesel has highlighted the significance of God's presence for
the suffering believer. All suffering must, of course, be dealt with
personally, as we have already indicated. This means that every
sick and dying person is confronted with a very particular sort of
loneliness. We may be surrounded by people who love us dearly,
but, ultimately, they are powerless to remove our loneliness in
suffering. The suffering believer realizes that he or she is always in
God's presence, whether he or she wrestles with Him or worships
Him. The believer knows that God is there and that He abandons
no one, though all may be darkness, and suffering is devoid of
anything divine. Jesus' suffering, too, was possessed of nothing
divine, and he, too, was unable to experience anything of God's
presence, only to believe in it. Faith in God's presence is not the
same as the experience of it. One of the most extreme signs of
lonely death is to be found in the inscriptions engraved in the
tombstones of military cemeteries, "Known unto God." In these
instances, humanity was not even capable of determining the
names, the identity of the dead. Is this not the most absolute
loneliness? Only faith in God can break through this utter
loneliness with the affirmation that these nameless are known to
God. Kushner insists that only faith can confirm the sense of self
worth of the afflicted person.

This brings us to the thought of resurrection. Our love for a person is suffused with the longing that his or her life might be shielded eternally, but our love is not able to effect this. Is there, then, no love powerful enough to prevent the loss of our beloved to nothingness? Jesus' resurrection says: Yes, God is powerful love. That is the faithful response to the lament of those who inquire as to the fate of the dead. Resurrection means that God offers His own life to every human being. He Himself wishes to be the future of every person. To believe in the resurrection is to believe that no one must live without meaning, that no one must live in vain, since all have the possibility of a life of their own in God. In this sense, we can say that only resurrection does not discriminate. The vast majority of humanity, especially the insignificant and the poor and those without a grave, no longer exist for our history. They are completely forgotten, they have disappeared into the abyss of forgottenness. Resurrection faith is a protest against this in its affirmation that, for God, every person is irreplaceable and of incalculable value.

Resurrection does not, however, mean facile consolation. It is not simply a soothing device, a promise of pie in the sky. That would be a justification of suffering. Neither does resurrection mean that God gives meaning to suffering. What it does mean is that God redeems humanity *in spite of* suffering. That is why resurrection faith dovetails with the demand for justice. And not simply God's justice, but ours as well. Real faith in the resurrection calls us to responsibility. We may dream of life after death only if we make life before death possible for one another (J. B. Brantschen). Whenever we dare to break through our own egotism, to stretch out the hand of peace to one another, to share our possessions with the poor, resurrection finds place in the midst of this life. To believe in the resurrection is, always and everywhere, to commit oneself on behalf of life and against death.

Let me conclude with a thought from St. Augustine: "For the man who keeps Christ in his heart does not ask, like Cain, 'Am I my brother's keeper'?" [5] *

5. *Contra Faustum*, 12,10; PL 42, 259.
* Translated from the Dutch by Terrence Merrigan.

MORAL QUESTIONING AND HUMAN SUFFERING
In Search of a Credible Response to the Meaning of Suffering

Joseph A. Selling

Why do people suffer? Why is there suffering? How can
someone believe in a God who creates, sustains, fulfills and
responds to us as persons when there is so much needless
suffering in the world? Such questions are hardly new, but it
seems that these kinds of questions have been articulated much
more explicitly and publicly in recent years. Perhaps it is a new-
found spirit of openness that has allowed these questions to
surface in the realm of public and ecclesial debate. Perhaps it is a
dissatisfaction with the "old answers" that has led more and
more people to press for a credible response. Simple statements
like "it will all work out for the best," "everything has a place in
the plan of God," or, "it is through suffering that we earn our
eternal reward," do not fall convincingly upon contemporary
ears. While some would have it that this in itself is a sign of lack
of faith by the present generation, others would suggest that this
form of questioning reveals a greater maturity of faith. Desiring
to take their faith seriously, many persons feel the need to go
beyond the simple, enigmatic phrases of the past and demand
deeper understanding, more clarity, greater consistency: *fides
quaerens intellectum.*

Most people would agree that human suffering is tragic. Examples are to be found in the images of starving children, victims of
natural disasters, agonizing sickness, and untimely death. Then
there is the suffering that results from what appears to be human
cruelty. Here one's sympathy can be directed to the victim(s) of

cruelty, whether it be a case of genocidal extermination or that of the person abandoned by one who had promised to love and to cherish. These are examples of suffering as well. They are, however, possibly more "tolerable" (with respect to theological questioning) because they seem to admit of a cause. In such cases, human agency has played at least a collaborative role; God does not have to be directly responsible for the suffering perpetrated through human sinfulness. Yet this is still suffering, and one might ask why human sin might appear more powerful than God's mercy and love. Although less directly, God can still be held accountable. Subsequently, religious faith, and the persons and institutions who represent that faith, are being called upon to respond to some serious challenges.

One of the difficulties that these challenges present to the "religious professional" — bishop, priest, theologian, catechist — is the gap that exists between the level on which such questions are often asked and the level of linguistic refinement and rational argumentation that appears to be called for to respond to the challenges and begin some movement toward comprehension. Obvious questions are relatively easy to ask. However, questions that appear obvious do not always reflect the complexity of human experience. Nor do what look like profound inquiries always strive toward an intricate and complex level of understanding. "Why am I here? Why do we do what we do? Why do two plus two equal four?" might be posing philosophical queries. They might just as well be a way of passing the time of day. It is therefore necessary first to clarify the question being asked, the level on which it is being asked, and the type of response that may or may not be expected.

The present essay presumes that the reader is interested in an analytical approach to the question of suffering that aims at shedding light upon the dynamics of the issues involved. It does not propose "practical" answers to the questions raised in relation to suffering, nor does it intend to formulate a recipe for constructing those answers. Human experience admits of multiple understandings of suffering, what it comprises, how it is borne, what is the relation and/or threat to meaning it may pose, how one even comes to call it suffering in the first place? It remains for the person dealing with the concrete instance of suffering and the issues raised by human suffering to assess what is being asked, and to respond accordingly. On the presumption that the reader already has some experience with this and related issues, whether or not they have been trained in the religious sciences, I will assume that they are more interested in attempting to articulate the relevant questions rather than finding answers for them.

Suffering and Pain

Let us begin by making a few necessary distinctions. One might legitimately ask the question, "why does God permit suffering?" Yet it would be an entirely different issue if the discussion were about pain. The experience of pain is something ambiguous. It involves the simultaneous presence of positive and negative elements. When we think about it, we might even be tempted to describe pain as something "good." For the experience of pain can function as an alarm, a warning signal that we are somehow being threatened. Were it not for the experience of pain, the threat to our well-being might go unnoticed.

The experience of pain can provoke a reflexive movement away from the source of that pain. The classic example of putting one's hand on something hot is sufficient to illustrate the point. One does not analyze the burning sensation; one spontaneously attempts to remove his or her hand from the source of extreme heat. In this case, the experience of pain functions to protect us from serious harm. In that way, we can see the experience of pain — though not pain itself — as a positive characteristic of our physical being. From the perspective of faith, we can even call it a gift from God who created human beings with this "built-in" mechanism.

Before going on, it would be helpful to expand this notion beyond the physiological paradigm. The experience of *physical* pain usually comes to mind first, but I think that it is also possible to speak of other sorts of pain. *Psychological* pain may be described as a disturbance of wholeness, order, or integration. The "automatic" mechanisms might take the form of defensiveness or compensation. *Moral* pain might be understood through the experience of guilt. Although we are all aware of the necessary distinction that must be made between guilt and guilt feelings, a genuine experience of guilt leads one to withdraw, to re-examine his or her behavior, to re-assess his or her decisions in the light of a personal sense of responsibility — even to seek some form of relief from the "burden" of guilt. *Spiritual* pain may be described as a frustration or lack with respect to meaning and fulfillment. It can lead to a search for meaning, a desire to be "saved" from a sense of emptiness.

All these examples describe the experience of pain as an ambiguous phenomenon. Certainly, pain itself may be understood as something negative. Healthy persons do not seek physical pain, no one enjoys feeling incomplete, and so forth. Nevertheless, the *experience of pain* is more complex. It admits of positive elements insofar as the experience itself serves to protect our well-being. Therefore, I would describe the experience of pain as the experience *of* something negative. The experience itself is not wholly negative, for it admits of both positive and negative elements. It would therefore be inappropriate to attempt to classify the experience of pain morally as good or bad, right or wrong. Morally speaking, the experience of pain is something ambiguous, even something "neutral"; in other words, before we can make a moral judgment we need a good deal more information.

Pain, as a human experience, is an expression of the limitedness of our human existence. Human well-being is something fragile. It can easily be threatened, and we need signals to alert us to that threat. It is curious to note how the signal itself already prompts us to take the first steps toward self-protection. We "spontaneously" respond to the experience of pain and, in some way that still needs to be analyzed and judged with respect to its appropriateness, we reflexively take the first steps to eliminate or withdraw from the source of pain.

It is therefore impossible — or at least premature — to think that we can "evaluate" the experience of pain morally. Before such an evaluation can be made, an interpretive process must take place that will bring other relevant elements to light.

The Experience of Pain

The experience of pain is the experience of something negative. The fact that such an experience may serve to alert us to immanent danger, a threat to our well-being, does not in and of itself *justify* the tolerance or perpetration of pain. For the fact that pain itself is something negative suggests quite naturally that it is something to be avoided, reduced to a minimum, even eliminated. Precisely because it is experienced as something negative, we recognize that pain is an "evil" — not yet to be classified as a moral evil, but an evil nonetheless. Because pain is an evil, we should seek to eliminate pain as much as possible.

It is here that we encounter the first steps of analysis and interpretation. The most important question we need to ask when we face the experience of pain is whether that experience is fulfilling a function that may allow us to tolerate it, at least temporarily. When the experience of pain serves to alert us to a threat to our well-being, we may tolerate its presence, even though we clearly understand that pain itself is something negative. It is not therefore appropriate to eliminate the experience of pain simply for the sake of eliminating something negative. The taking or administering of chemical substances that suppress the experience of pain could result in great harm being done to the integrity of the person. Deprived of their "alarm mechanism," human persons would suffer untold damage. This is even recognized as a medical dysfunction in the physiological order. One can immediately understand that the same conclusions would have to be drawn about substances that deprive us of the experience of psychological, moral, and spiritual pain.

On the other hand, when the experience of pain no longer fulfills the function of alerting us to danger, we are left with the experience of something negative that no longer admits of a reason for its justification (tolerance). In this case, it would appear to be incumbent upon us as persons and as fellow human beings to eliminate the evil of pain as much as possible. In fact, analyzing, dealing with, and alleviating pain has developed into a branch of medical science that studies the psycho-physiological dimensions of pain and seeks to control pain in circumstances that warrant its reduction or elimination.

In this case, we can immediately think of the care of critically and terminally ill patients. However, the spectrum of application is much broader than it first appears. Medical science is currently struggling with the phenomena of chronic and acute pain, the intensity and duration of pain, even the dysfunction of not experiencing pain, as mentioned above. Then, there are more mundane examples, such as the various techniques developed to promote "painless childbirth." There is clearly much more to be learned about the experience of physical pain. Morally speaking, it seems clear that when the presence of this not-yet-morally-classifiable experience of pain cannot be justified by the simultaneous presence of positive elements within the same experience (alert to danger), it becomes our responsibility to eliminate pain as much as possible.

Finally, it should be noted that our understanding of pain and its function has been described in relation to human well-being. A sense of well-being and/or being well provides a point of reference whereby pain itself can be identified, where the *threat* to that well-being may be located, thus providing an opportunity for a response to the threat and the restoration of well-being, integration, balance, and meaning. More needs to be said about this, especially with respect to the phenomenon of suffering.

From Pain to Suffering

If pain is the experience of something negative, suffering might be understood as a negative experience. Perhaps the most easily understood illustration can be found in the experience of chronic pain. Having alerted the person to some immanent threat or danger, the experience of pain has served its purpose. But in some cases, the pain persists even when steps have been taken to deal with the threat (if indeed that is possible). In the case of terminal illness, nothing can be done about the physiological cause of the pain. However, pain may still persist — without reason, without justification, with no apparent meaning. This is no longer an experience of something negative that may admit of justifying factors; it has now developed into a negative experience that does not seem to admit of any purpose.

There are at least two possible responses to this kind of experience. The first might consider the experience of pain that seems to be without purpose as intolerable, and prompt the person or someone responsible for the care of the person to do everything possible to eliminate the pain. A second response might hesitate to "alleviate" the pain immediately and seek first for an alternative interpretation of what is taking place. The first response is characteristic of most health care professionals. The second appears to be more common among those who deal with forms of pain that are not strictly physical in their manifestation. The psychotherapist wants to help the client to discover the reason for their feelings of non-integration; the "confessor" (formal or simply a friend) expects that the person can point to the cause of their own guilt; and the clergyman might suggest that a feeling of emptiness can be identified as a dimension of the human condition, calling one forth to recognize the reality beyond the individual self.

It is tempting to accept this simple scheme without question. Before doing so, however, we should take a closer look at the dynamics that are taking place in these different responses. The medical professional is dealing primarily with the physical dimension of pain. In the case of successful diagnosis and analysis, it might be possible to conclude that the experience of pain no longer admits of justification. Therefore, the decision is taken to eliminate the pain as superfluous. In the latter cases, the cause(s) of the pain may not yet be clear. This does not mean that the two types of responses are essentially different. It merely indicates that in the first instance some explanation has already been provided, while in the second type of response there is insufficient data to complete the picture.

What both these responses have in common is the fact that some understanding of the experience of pain is necessary before a decision can be taken about what one should do about the pain itself. That process of interpretation can lead us toward making the distinction between pain and suffering. Rather than speaking about a justification of or reason for (tolerating) pain, we can suggest that what is even more fundamental than answering the question whether we should allow pain to continue is a proper understanding of what is going on for the one who experiences pain. The first thing we usually do is look for the cause(s) of that pain. Having isolated, or at least having developed an idea about what is causing the pain, we can turn to the alleviation of the pain itself. But it is the cause that interests us — whether we are using a psycho-physiological (medical) model or attempting to deal with the person as an integral whole. What is important here is where one is looking for the causes. What then becomes crucially important is how one interprets what they may find.

If the scheme that I am suggesting here is correct, then the essential difference between pain and suffering is the presence or absence respectively of some understanding why the person is being subjected to the experience of pain. When the source of pain can be explained and the pain itself can become the object of intensive treatment, there is little need to speak of suffering — unless, of course, the attempt at treatment is a failure. In this case it would be appropriate to speak of suffering because the cause of the pain remains outside of our ability to do anything effective. The subsequent experience of pain remains without justification. It is a negative experience. (We will return to the phenomenon of non-relievable pain below.) On the other hand, when there is no success in even identifying the cause of pain, just as when there is total failure to treat the cause of pain that is known (or suspected), it appears fitting to speak of suffering in the more precise sense.

Suffering, then, is more than the experience of something negative. It is not an ambiguous phenomenon but something that is clearly, if not exclusively, negative. The reason why it is negative lies not simply in the fact that it is not or cannot be explained. The deeper reason why suffering may be called a negative experience is because we find ourselves incapable of giving any appropriate response to that experience. We cannot deal with its negativity because we do not comprehend why it is taking place.

This description may give the impression that the experience of pain admits of a number of elements that need to be understood, evaluated, and interpreted before we can formulate our moral response to what is taking place. Simultaneously, suffering appears to be a single, negative experience that is basically simple — that is, when one ignores the fact that a wide range of questions remain unanswered. My own understanding of pain and suffering would be exactly the opposite. Although pain admits of a number of elements that demand consideration, it remains a relatively straightforward, human experience that begs for an appropriate (moral) response. Suffering, however, I would understand as a complex or synthetic phenomenon, encompassing not only the experience of pain (on any and all levels) but also the disturbing fact that persons appear to be powerless to overcome its effects and to provide an adequate response. Pain demands a response, while suffering demands an interpretation.

Suffering as an "Interpreted" Experience

The observation that suffering demands interpretation does not imply that the experience of suffering does not usually receive some form of interpretation. Quite the opposite. Since there appears to be little that we can do to alleviate human suffering, we often attempt to explain why the suffering is there at all. This attempt at explanation usually takes the form of an interpretation, that is, the attempt to describe or build a "wider context" into which the (experience of) suffering will neatly fit.

Unfortunately, the most common approach to human suffering presumes that such a "wider context" already exists. The description of suffering is then expressed as the conclusion of an already carried-out interpretation. An encounter with human suffering simply calls for the articulation of an already determined meaning. I would refer to this as a *passive form* of interpretation. In this case, the experience of suffering does not lead to the demand for interpretation; it merely searches for an interpretation that is supposed to be present, but is not necessarily conscious.

The concept of suffering as an already "interpreted" experience is admittedly vague. How can an interpretation already be present when one remains unaware of what that interpretation might be? The answer to this question lies in the observation already made about looking for the cause(s) of pain: what is first important is *where* one is looking for those cause(s). If the process of interpretation is at least in part a matter of providing a "wider context," then the phenomenon of suffering as an interpreted experience becomes a case in which the context itself is responsible for the interpretation: in this case, *context creates interpreta-*

tion. It becomes the context within which suffering is interpreted that assigns meaning to the experience of suffering.

Let us take the example of the suffering one may experience in being deprived of enjoying the fruits of one's own labor. This might be expressed in the statement, "I work so hard, yet I have nothing to show for it." If the work that one performs is never identified as a personal accomplishment, the issue may never arise. When, however, one does begin to identify with the fruit of one's labor, we might experience the alienation as a form of pain: a disturbance of one's sense of wholeness and integration, a threat to one's well-being as person. Because one remains unable to identify either the cause of this pain or some justifying reason to tolerate its continuance, one may seek a context within which it can be "explained." One such possible context would be a certain vision of the structure of society itself, as is illustrated in the following quotation.

> It must be first of all recognized that the condition of things inherent in human affairs must be borne with, for it is impossible to reduce civil society to one dead level. Socialists may in that intent do their utmost, but all striving against nature is in vain. There naturally exist among mankind manifold differences of the most important kind; people differ in capacity, skill, health, strength; and unequal fortune is a necessary result of unequal condition. Such inequality is far from being disadvantageous either to individuals or to the community. Social and public life can only be maintained by means of various kinds of capacity for business and the playing of many parts; and each man, as a rule, chooses the part which suits his own particular domestic condition.[1]

If "natural differences" exist between individuals so that "un-equal fortune is a necessary result of unequal condition," one can

---

1. Leo XIII, *Rerum novarum.* The English text is from the translation found in Etienne Gilson (ed.) *The Church Speaks to the Modern World: The Social Teachings of Leo XIII* (Garden City, NY: 1954) pp. 213-214. In this translation, the text is found in number 17 of the encyclical. Various translations of this papal encyclical exist, and there is no standardization of paragraph numbering. The original Latin text, *Acta Sanctae Sedis* (Rome: Polyglot, 1890-1891) 641-670, p. 648, contains no paragraph numbers.

explain why the common worker suffers the deprivation of the fruits of his or her labor while the owner of the means of production personally benefits from the work of others. Of course, such an "explanation" would not go unchallenged in our own time. However, the point is that by situating the question within the context of some vision about natural difference and the structure of society, one automatically provides an explanation through the imposition of a context. The experience has been interpreted through the context, not through any effort to come to grips with the suffering itself.

The type of context that is frequently invoked to explain the experience of suffering (by providing an interpretative framework) can be philosophical, cultural, ideological, or even religious. It amounts to a complete set of presuppositions that serve to explain, justify and otherwise provide meaning for the suffering itself by means of a "wider context." If one is totally immersed in these presuppositions, if one never questions the context, the interpretation may be accepted as valid. If, however, one begins to question the validity of the context, the interpretation will fail.

An important aspect of every "context" that functions to create interpretation is that it is subject to evolution. Cultural and ideological — and even philosophical and religious — presuppositions change and go through development. The example cited above presupposes a very specific vision of the socio-economic structure. We can easily criticize this vision today, but it would have been more difficult to formulate that criticism one hundred years ago, when the statement was written. At that time, only a relatively few persons questioned the validity of the "wider context," thus calling the already provided interpretation into question as well. Those who did not question the interpretation were — at that time — willing to accept the justification for their lot in life as a sufficient explanation. They may have accepted their situation as "painful," but they would not necessarily have referred to it as suffering. The pain they experienced was justifiable because it was somehow necessary: without owners and managers to make decisions and insure the proper running of

things, and without workers who were willing to accept their
destiny of having to toil by the sweat of their brow, the entire
"natural structure of things" would fall apart.[2]

It may be useful to ask what caused this standard interpretation to break down? In the illustration, a certain "natural order"
was invoked in order to *explain* why the common worker experienced his lot as painful. Because the natural order was presumed to be both necessary and unchangeable, one had no choice
but to submit to its normative force. In order to follow the
natural order and to protect the function of the socio-economic
structure, it was necessary to tolerate a certain amount of pain.
That pain — the experience of something negative that may have
alerted the individual to a threat to their well-being — was
justified. The already provided interpretation (context) did not
alleviate or even respond to the pain, it merely explained it.

It was precisely the context which was used to create the
interpretation that eventually became the object of criticism. Both
the structure and the necessity of some presumed natural order
began to be questioned. Rather than passively accepting this
natural order, many persons began to ask why their own, individual sense of well-being was not more important than the integrity of a structure that was causing them pain. Furthermore, the
shared sense of well-being began to evolve. Expectations with
respect to the meaning of living well began to increase. They were
supported by a growing awareness of human equality that challenged the notion of a natural order dictating superiority and
inferiority. In other words, the interpretive context was changing.
When that context no longer served to provide an adequate
explanation, the presumed justification for the experience of pain

2. One might even suggest that the cosmic order or perhaps the plan of God
itself would be interrupted. The quotation of *Rerum novarum* provided in the text
is immediately followed with an explanation of the way things are, making
reference to Sacred Scripture: "As regards bodily labor, even had man never fallen
from the state of innocence, he would not have remained wholly idle; but that
which would then have been his free choice and his delight became afterwards
compulsory, and the painful expiation for his disobedience. 'Cursed be the earth in
thy work; in thy labor thou shalt eat of it all the days of thy life' (Gen 3:17)."

proved to be a failure. Without justification, the experience of pain was recognized as suffering — a negative experience that did not contain either purpose or meaning.

The Passive Interpretation of Suffering

Allowing context to create interpretation is fundamentally a passive response to the phenomenon of human suffering. When this passivity is allowed to function in the extreme, it may even lead to a certain fascination with suffering itself. We can hardly deny that this has been a part of our cultural and religious history. If human suffering is accepted as something necessary, it is a relatively small step to the actual seeking after some form of suffering. In this scenario, the interpretive context becomes so strong that the explanatory justification begins to function as a motive for human behavior.

Culturally, we can refer to a certain kind of "dolorism," a type of spiritual masochism that presumes that suffering is something good, something that can be beneficial or even rewarding. Religiously, this form of interpretation is not unknown in Western Christianity. The notion that suffering here on earth will somehow contribute to our eternal reward has functioned not merely as an explanatory justification for situations of human suffering against which we were powerless to act, it has also been invoked as a motive for desiring or seeking opportunities to suffer.[3] Carried to its extreme, such an ideology — initially presented in order to justify an already existing situation — evolves into a cult, something sought after for its own sake. It inspires a masochistic spirituality that not only results in the stagnation of

3. It would, of course, be more accurate here to speak of seeking opportunities to experience pain. For if the justification is already provided, the pain is considered to be "meaningful." I use the term suffering here because in the situation I am describing I would consider that justification to be spurious.

human development; it also opens the possibility of manipulation and oppression. If "suffering here on earth is good for you," then those who may be responsible for causing suffering can interpret their own behavior as performing some kind of service, or at least as fulfilling some kind of necessary function in the grand scheme of things. When such an explanation releases someone from the responsibility they bear for causing human suffering, it opens the possibility for almost inevitable abuse.

Fortunately, most persons have overcome this lopsided kind of spirituality. However, this does not excuse us from analyzing its roots more explicitly. I would suggest that one of the causes for spiritual masochism — dolorism — is an exaggerated concentration upon the suffering and death of Christ as the source of our redemption from sin. The operative term here is, of course, exaggerated. We should not ignore the historical-theological insights of the interpretation of the suffering and death of Christ as redemptive. We can, however, formulate a critical attitude that brings balance to an exaggerated emphasis. The need for a more fully integrated theological method must balance the motif of sin-redemption-salvation with the equally important perspective of creation-incarnation-eschatology. Failure to do so will inevitably lead to a one-sided understanding of the Judeo-Christian tradition.

The problem with the passive interpretation of human suffering, therefore, is not necessarily the interpretation itself. Rather, it is the tendency to invoke that interpretation immediately and exclusively. Rather than questioning, analyzing, and seeking some comprehension, an already formulated explanation is accepted. Context — the place where one looks for causes and the manner in which explanation is given — creates interpretation. The example we are using of an immediate and exclusive religious justification for human suffering superimposes an entire theological interpretation that gives meaning to suffering in place of inviting us to search for that meaning. This is a religion of answers in place of questions. It presents an image of God who may not only allow but may even inflict suffering, a God who tests, tries, and punishes human beings.

The irony of this interpretation is not only that it trivializes human suffering but also that it ultimately forces us to formulate a compensatory image of God which is equally inadequate. Human suffering is trivialized because of its relative insignificance in comparison with the so much greater, so much more intense, and so much more meaningful suffering of Christ — which takes away the sins of the world. Simultaneously, the operative image of God in this interpretation is a God who is almost exclusively transcendent, who is beyond any identification with human suffering. As compensation, one may "discover" a God who suffers. One radical image replaces another, one anthropomorphism replaces another. In the end, the image of a God who suffers along with creation is incapable of challenging the tragedy of human suffering itself. Perhaps the substitute image is even more impoverished than the image of a God who inflicts suffering as a test or a punishment. For if God *suffers* — experiencing pain without meaning or justification — then we are more alone and hopeless than our fear and anxiety could imagine.

Religion and the Interpretation of Suffering

If the only possibility open to us for dealing with suffering is to cast about desperately for some interpretation that is already provided by cultural, philosophical, or religious presuppositions, this immediate and exclusive, but passive, interpretation of suffering functions more like a rationalization, excuse, or alibi than something that might facilitate a search for meaning. We can refer to this as the project of *providing meaning* rather than searching for meaning. To many, it appears that religion as such no longer has a role to play in this project, an observation that is frequently made with some regret. I hope that it will become clear why this should not be understood as regretable, but rather as something that opens the possibility for a new understanding of the role of religion with respect to suffering.

What many would consider to be one of the traditional roles of religion in providing meaning for the phenomenon of human suffering has, at least in the developed world, been taken over by a number of other institutions in contemporary society, especially in what might be called the welfare state. There are numerous forms of "helping professions," and alongside of these one finds images projected through the various media that broadcast the message that every form of human suffering is ultimately explainable, if not relievable. Where suffering remains, that is, where no adequate explanation or remedy can be found, one finds the search for some responsible party, or at best the identification of an as yet to be overcome obstacle.

Our faith has been (re)placed into the human effort to overcome suffering. Yet, we cannot help get the feeling that what is most often being addressed here is not suffering at all but merely the experience of pain. Failing to distinguish between suffering and pain, our modern, help-giving society operates under the assumption that all human suffering is relievable. What has not yet been overcome — persistent, chronic, meaningless suffering and ultimately death itself — is only a matter of time, knowledge, and technique. Science is the savior of the human condition. So pain becomes a medical problem, guilt and anxiety are problems of psychological adjustment, and man's search for meaning becomes a never-ending tightrope walk across the chasm of absurdity. This may help to explain how a certain taboo has grown up with respect to human suffering. For if non-relievable pain cannot be provided with a meaning, it must be denied — or it must be someone's fault. Frequently, the responsible party is (some image of) God himself.

Nevertheless, the fact remains that non-relievable and meaningless suffering persists, death occurs, and no satisfactory answers can be provided for human tragedy. The question we face is whether we are willing to give up the illusion that all suffering *must* find an explanation? Is it possible to abandon the notion that meaning is going to be somehow provided for us? The inadequacy of providing an immediate and exclusive interpretation for suffering should already be evident. What we need to ask is whether there is some viable alternative and, in the context of the present investigation, whether our faith experience still has a role to play in the articulation of that alternative?

The Active Interpretation of Suffering

When context creates interpretation, the meaning or explanation that is given to human suffering is already provided. One simply determines which context will be invoked, be it some prefabricated "religious" answer or an appeal to science as salvation. Reflection upon these possibilities, however, may lead us to question the appropriateness of such a method. We may refuse to allow the choice of a context to pre-determine the interpretation that is given. The interpretation of human suffering itself is a project that demands observation, reflection, and analysis. Furthermore, it is a historical project, carried on not simply by individuals but demanding the active participation of the community of human persons as well. If we are willing to embark upon the project of interpreting human suffering, we must still be careful of the pitfalls of explanation and justification. What we seek as the product of interpretation should be "clarification" and integration into a "wider context" that is not pre-fabricated, but rather something that becomes the by-product of the interpretive process itself.

Perhaps the most fruitful place to begin the process of clarification is the historical experience of determining what human suffering is. How is it that we have come to redefine the experience of something negative (pain) as a negative experience (suffering)? How is it that something objectionable evolves into something intolerable? I have already hinted at the idea that the (at least implicit) refusal to accept a pre-fabricated interpretation of suffering has been brought about by a change in the perception and evolution of what causes suffering. The "wider context" that was formerly used to explain why the experience of something negative was necessary (because it was "natural," or necessary for the function of a socio-economic structure, or because it is the result of sin) is challenged because other presuppositions begin to change. Workers who toil by the sweat of their brow are no longer satisfied with the existing situation because they have developed new ideas about human equality, because they have begun to have greater expectations about their lot in life. An evolution has taken place in regard to the underlying concept of well-being that is essential to the definition of pain and suffering.

It was noted above that both pain and suffering originate in the experience of danger or threat to one's sense of well-being. The descriptions of physical discomfort, psychological disequilibrium, moral guilt, or spiritual vacuum are all notions relative to the underlying expectations that one holds about comfort, equilibrium, responsibility-fulfillment, and wholeness, which in turn describe our operative sense of well-being. The simple historical fact is that our individual and shared sense of well-being is evolutionary; it is in a constant state of development. This is not a case of human persons simply demanding more and more. Rather, it is part of the drive of human persons to achieve the best humanly possible.[4] When something beneficial to human persons becomes achievable, it becomes a goal of human intention. Therefore, when the removal of physical discomfort, and so forth, becomes possible, we begin to ask why that discomfort, and so forth, should not be removed (intention). It is human wisdom (prudence) that prompts us first to ask whether that discomfort serves any useful purpose (pain). If the function of that signal is found to be superfluous, then it seems humanly and

---

4. Cf. Paul Ricoeur's *"le meilleur humain possible."*

morally proper to eliminate the pain (intention translated into action).

In order to better understand the active mode of interpreting human suffering, it is necessary to distinguish between relievable and non-relievable pain so that we can identify the kind of suffering we are speaking about. We need to take into account whether the experience of something negative (pain) *can* be relieved and whether it *should* be relieved (prudence, or proportionate reason) before we deal with suffering itself. Before we do that, perhaps a few more words on the evolving sense of well-being are in order.

Another way to describe this idea is the achievement of our expectations concerning (the quality of) human life. The greater those expectations become, the higher we set our standards for the quality of life, the more difficult they become to achieve. The passive interpretation of suffering would invite us to regard those heightened expectations as unrealistic, as "utopian." The pre-determined interpretive context does not include the re-valued expectations — it merely re-presents "achievable" expectations about (the quality of) life that were presumed in a former understanding.

With an active interpretation of pain and suffering, there is no need to question the heightening of expectations for the quality of life. There does remain the important moral question about whether and to what extent we need to work for the realization of those expectations. [5] However, a theological approach that regards the creation-incarnation-eschatology perspective as equally important as the sin-redemption-salvation motif, will have little problem with the presumption that human persons should aim at the best possible human situation. In fact, from an eschatological perspective, we perceive it to be our responsibility

5. This issue is essentially a matter of proportionality. It may be possible, for example, for certain parts of a population (of the world?) to increase their standard of living. However, it is incumbent upon the persons who stand before this possibility to question whether such an improvement of living standards will not be bought at the expense of others.

to actively work for achieving the best that is humanly possible. Without this understanding, it is impossible to determine the nature of human suffering. If we cannot discern a development in our expectations of (the quality of) life, then all real suffering will have to be understood as pain — something that *must* have an explanation or justification. We would be forced back into the passive interpretation, and ultimately forced to abandon our humanity.

Suffering as a Contrast Experience

If moral reflection — as the practical extension of our faith experience — is concerned with the achievability of the best humanly possible (the contemporary state of expectations for the quality of human life, or the sense of human well-being), then it is necessary for the moral theologian as well as every member of the faith community to remain continuously open to re-defining what is meant by the best that is humanly possible. Moral reflection is, at least in part, the science of investigating and expanding the realm of human potentiality. The art or science of such reflection may not always function as the source of expanding human expectations. It must, however, always be concerned with distinguishing what can be and what cannot; what must be and what must not; what may be and what may not.

When our sense of human well-being develops, when our level of expectations becomes more demanding, we begin to detect a discontinuity between those expectations for (the quality of) life and the current experience which does not meet those expectations. It is this discontinuity that presents us with the experience of something negative, a contrast between what is recognized as possible and a situation where our expectations are not being achieved. A number of authors have already identified this as a "negative contrast experience,"[6] and I believe that this can go a long way in explaining the role of faith in general and moral theology in particular in dealing with the question of human suffering.

The first reflection that we can make, therefore, about the evolution of this sense of discontinuity (contrast) is whether it is justifiable for us to propose "heightened" expectations about (the quality of) life. It is here that moral reflection and the faith experience are intimately connected. For moral reflection without inspiration and conviction will easily degenerate into the "art of the practical," recognizing human aspiration only under the guise of that which is practically achievable (passive interpretation). When, on the other hand, moral reflection is inspired by faith, the horizon of the possible expands considerably. Faith turns its attention not to what is but to what can be. Faith proposes an understanding of being human that goes beyond the obvious (the observed) and suggests a view of being human that does not begin by taking account of, for instance, the problems of evil, selfishness, or ambiguity. Christian faith believes that "all things are possible"; it is radically founded in a real expectation for the realization of the reign of God.

In this way, we come to the paradoxical insight that moral reflection aided by faith can actually be the cause of pain, perhaps even of suffering. For it is a faith inspired understanding of the human condition that should prompt us to continuously re-evaluate our concept of human well-being. Faith addresses itself to the highest or most ultimate dimension of our existence, continuously challenging the accepted manner of interpreting that existence and rejecting complacency. When faith confirms the validity of pursuing the highest possible human expectations, it confirms the validity of the moral project. Morally speaking, we

6. The first and foremost of these authors is Eduard Schillebeeckx who first put forth the notion in "The Magisterium and the World of Politics," *Concilium* 36 (1968) 19-39, and further worked it out in "Questions on Christian Salvation of and for Man," in D. Tracy, H. Küng, & J.B. Metz (eds.) *Toward Vatican III: The Work that Needs to Be Done* (New York, 1978) 27-44.

can never be satisfied with "what is," we must always reach for what "can be." This kind of moral reflection not only deals with the failure to achieve responsibility (whether or not there is guilt), it continuously increases the demands of human responsibility, continuously creating dissatisfaction with the present state of affairs.

In summary, the description of our experience of something negative (pain) is based upon our understanding of human well-being and our expectations for (the quality of) human life. When the goals of the human project are not achieved, when we do not experience comfort, equilibrium, responsibility-fulfillment, and wholeness, we sense the negative feelings of physical discomfort, disequilibrium, guilt, and emptiness. Moral reflection that is content with what has already been achieved will tend to lower our expectations, as a form of avoiding the experience of something negative. But moral reflection which is inspired by faith will always heighten our expectations, thus increasing the possibility of experiencing something negative. Being and acting as a moral person, therefore, will not be a project aimed at the elimination of pain, it will actually increase the amount of pain (experience of something negative) by making us continuously aware that the goals of the human project are not being realized.

Nevertheless, the experience of something negative (pain), as noted in the beginning of this essay, is not yet morally classifiable. Before any moral judgment can be passed on that experience we must determine whether the pain should and can be alleviated. It is entirely possible that the experience of something negative (the non-achievement of the best humanly possible) is a signal that human persons and perhaps even humanity itself is in danger, that some threat to our well-being is present. It is likewise possible that this danger signal should not be eliminated, lest human persons become subjected to even greater harm or humanity itself is threatened with extinction. In this case, it is not only justifiable but even necessary that we allow the pain to continue. Just as our physical integrity needs the protection of some alarm mechanism, the human community needs these danger signals in order to preserve humanity itself. The negative contrast experience functions to alert us to this threat.

Relievable and Non-relievable Pain

With this understanding that the moral project itself can be the source of the experience of something negative — that it can actually cause pain — we still need to say something more about human suffering. Not all experiences of something negative are justifiable. Pain should only be tolerated when it serves a purpose in the realization of the human project (protecting physical integrity, psychological equilibrium, etc.). If the experience of something negative — which is an evil — cannot be justified, it should be eliminated as much as possible.

The same thing holds true for every sort of pain. Moral pain — guilt, or the experience of not fulfilling responsibility — is no exception. We should recognize the function of the negative contrast experience as a source for sharpening our moral sensitivity. Yet even this experience is subject to the prudential judgment of whether the experience of something negative serves a justifiable purpose. In order to judge whether the non-realization of some human aspiration should be allowed to continue as a constant source of pain, we need to consider the more complex factors of the genuine possibility for achieving these goals, reasonable probability, the definition of priorities, the articulation and transformation of values, distinguishing various levels of urgency, competing and conflicting goals, the short and long term consequences of any activity, and the presupposed, present, and future concepts of the human person. The simple observation that the achievement of a higher quality of life at the expense of the quality of life of others is unacceptable appears sufficient to establish the point.

When the experience of something negative (pain) fulfills a

human purpose, it needs to be tolerated. When it ceases to fulfill a human purpose, it should be relieved. However, what happens when we judge that the experience of pain should be eliminated but we find ourselves powerless to do anything effective? Non-justifiable, non-relievable pain is what we understand when we use the word "suffering." The question facing us here is not, what can we do about it? By definition, suffering implies a negative experience that is beyond our capabilities for effective action. The more proper question is, how do we respond to suffering?

We have already seen that the passive interpretation of human suffering is inadequate. Allowing context to create interpretation amounts to abdicating the human project. Morally speaking, we find ourselves in the realm of what might be called the trans-ethical: there is no concrete moral response to the challenge before us, but we know that it would be morally irresponsible to abandon the project of searching for meaning. Morally we are confronted with a serious choice. In the face of human powerlessness we can be tempted to redefine morality itself, reducing it to the art of the merely possible. The antithesis of moral responsibility is an ethics of power, the pragmatic reduction of human aspiration to the boundaries of what is considered "realistically" possible.

Confronted with human powerlessness, faith does not retreat to the paradigm of passive interpretation, seeking explanation and final justification through an already established meaning. Rather, it continues the process of actively interpreting the experience with the aim of redefining the context. One of the tools for accomplishing this goal is the use of narrative, the articulation of the self-understanding of the believing community. Narrative serves both to integrate the experience of suffering by partici-pating in the discovery and creation of its meaning through a process of clarification and to rescue the moral project by relativ-izing human powerlessness within the dimensions of ultimate meaning.

The use of narrative in response to the experience of human suffering allows the person(s) suffering and the community that surrounds the person(s) to review their position with respect to the experience of suffering itself. The re-telling of one's own story serves to create a context for situating and finally accepting one's suffering. As the experience becomes "one's own" (and here, by "one's own" we refer to the communitarian as well as the individual dimension), the experience is no longer evaluated as merely negative. It becomes part of the total understanding of one's integrated life and experience. Its negativity is relativized in terms of the totality of human existence and experience. Meaning is achieved through the "creation" of one's own context, one's own story.

With respect to the moral project, the faith experience serves to provide a reasonable foundation for not abandoning the process of discernment and understanding. When the dimensions of human meaning are transformed to an ultimate horizon with the knowledge that meaning is possible, even though it is not immediately detectable in purely human terms (equivalent to some configuration of the already accumulated data of observation), there is reason for courage in continuing the moral project itself. Without the faith experience, it is difficult to see what might prevent the collapse of the moral enterprise altogether.

Thus, in dealing with questions about the experience of pain and human suffering, it becomes evident that moral reflection and the experience of faith are intimately connected. The distinction between passive and active forms of interpretation is crucial for avoiding the danger of rationalization and mere justification as substitutes for the challenge to search for meaning. If we accept that only the active form of interpretation should be applied to both the moral and the religious comprehension of human suffering, such that the discernment of this phenomenon is geared to creating a context for response rather than allowing context to dictate that response, then it is clear that the role of faith in approaching human suffering is to sensitize the community of believers (and non-believers) to the fact of human suffering which often remains obscured behind a curtain of cultural, philosophical, and ideological concepts and values which are prone to accept the fact of suffering rather than to challenge the factors that make it possible. In addressing the aspirations of persons and communities, faith provides a perspective for criticizing the "accepted wisdom" with respect to the human condition in all its dimensions, including not only the transcendental but also the "earthly" dimensions of being human. This is often referred to as witness or prophecy, and forms a vital element of any truly engaged spirituality. If a faith perspective, organized and institutionalized in the form of a practiced religion, does not address this area of concern, and if it does not take a leadership role in discerning and pointing out the extent of genuine human suffering, which is often able to be thematized under the heading of injustice, then this faith or its expression through religion will lose its credibility and ultimately any claim that it may have to representing truth in a way which is humanly understandable.

The relationship between faith and suffering, therefore, especially viewed from the perspective of moral reflection, is crucial. The role of faith with respect to human suffering is not to provide answers, nor is it merely to contextualize the experience. Rather, the role of faith in regard to human suffering is to alert the human community to the dimensions of suffering which it has allowed itself to ignore or at least to tolerate unnecessarily, to participate in the process of discerning and interpreting what human suffering means, and to support human persons and humankind in their search for clarifying the meaning of suffering. When suffering is exposed as a form of relievable pain, we encounter the dynamics of the faith perspective in terms of its (radical) witness for the need to realize the best human possible: its option for the poor and the weak, its call for reconciliation, and its (eschatological) hope in transforming the possible into the real. With respect to suffering that is genuinely understood to be non-relievable, tragic, and without evident meaning, a negative experience which lies beyond the capability of moral response, the role of faith is to assist in a process of clarification that neither trivializes the moral reflection (in denying the still present role of responsibility, even on the trans-ethical level) nor reduces the meaning of the human experience of suffering through proposing a mere explanatory justification.

THE SICK AND SUFFERING PERSON

A Liturgical/Sacramental Approach

Cor Traets

In this essay we would like to consider the seriously ill, suffering person of today. How does the church community attempt to deal with these persons in a liturgical, sacramental way? Which aspects of the Christian faith should be stressed? In this regard, what image of God comes to the fore?

We will be dealing more specifically with the liturgy of the sick, hereby limiting ourselves to the anointing of the seriously ill. We will for the most part employ the *Pastoral Care of the Sick: Rites of Anointing and Viaticum.*[1] This publication is the revised official translation of the Roman Ritual of 1972[2] for the dioceses of the

1. We have made use of the following publication: *Pastoral Care of the Sick: Rites of Anointing and Viaticum* (prepared by the International Commission on English in the Liturgy), Collegeville, Minnesota, 1983. This will be abbreviated to (Revised) Ritual. In the first section of the Ritual, the anointing of the seriously ill is the subject of chapter IV (pp. 73-127) under the title "Anointing of the Sick." The anointing is also dealt with (pp. 212-215; 225) in chapter VIII (p. 199-243) in the second section of the same Ritual, entitled "Rites for Exceptional Circumstances," e.g. "when sudden illness or an accident or some other cause has placed one of the faithful in the proximate or immediate danger of death" (p. 200). In our discussion we will be focusing on the seriously ill, not on the dying. May we direct the English-speaking persons of other countries to their Ritual? An excellent presentation and discussion of the entire Revised Ritual can be found in Charles W. Gusmer, *And You Visited Me: Sacramental Ministry to the Sick and the Dying.* Studies in the Reformed Rites of the Catholic Church, VI, New York, 1984. See also *Pastoral Care of the Sick: Rites of Anointing and Viaticum. A Commentary,* Collegeville, 1983.

2. *Ordo Unctionis infirmorum eorumque pastoralis curae* (editio typica), Città del Vaticano, 1972, hereafter abbreviated to Ordo. The Revised Ritual contains excerpts from other rituals as well.

United States of America. It replaces the provisional translation
of 1973.[3] At times we will also refer to the Ritual for the Flemish
dioceses of Belgium and the Ritual for French-speaking countries.

The Anointing of the Sick as a Sacrament

How do we understand the Anointing of the Sick as a sacrament? How do we go about that task both from a contemporary
understanding of sacraments as such, and from the way in which
sickness and the sick person are approached today (and sometimes in confrontation with this approach as well)?[4]

Whenever one deals with (seriously) ill and suffering persons in
a liturgical-sacramental way, one intends, as with any other
religious ritual, to bring a faith-centered interpretation to bear on
their situation, in this case sickness and suffering. The intention is
that something should happen to them. One tries to assist them in
living through their situation: in the words of the rite, to strive
toward their salvation, that they should be raised up. Or, as in
the title of a Flemish catechetical publication of several years ago
for adults, the Anointing of the Sick is administered in the hope
that the person will be "healed to life."[5]

A Sick Person Healed

In recent decades a number of authors have indicated that

3. This provisional text was a literal translation of the Roman Ordo. See *The
Rites of the Catholic Church as Revised by Decree of the Second Vatican Ecumenical
Council and Published by Authority of Pope Paul VI* (English translation prepared
by the ICEL), New York, 1st ed., 1976, pp. 571-642.

4. The way in which the anointing of the sick is considered to function today is
also influenced by the progress made by the medical sciences in their fight against
illness; see P.-M. Gy, "Problèmes de théologie sacramentaire," *La Maison-Dieu*
110 (1972) 129-142: p. 131 and "Le nouveau rituel romain des malades," *La
Maison-Dieu* 113 (1973) 29-49: pp. 32-33.

5. The bishops of Belgium, *Geloofsboek*, (The Book of Faith), Tielt, 1987,
pp. 118-121: De ziekenzalving: tot leven genezen.

sickness affects the entire person: persons are "stricken" in the whole of their humanness. From this point of view sickness can be seen as a crisis, a disruption of communication—in connection with one's own body now experienced as an enemy, with one's environment of objects and people (from which one grows progressively isolated), with the meaning of existence with all its fragility and finiteness. The sick person not uncommonly asks the question, "Where is God now?" "Why, God?" "Where does this lead?" To a great extent it appears that the gravity of the illness and the suffering of the sick lies precisely in these multiple effects, and that the suffering itself can take many forms as well. For all these reasons, sickness is an evil.

To be healed means that bodily health is restored, to whatever extent possible. But this represents a fairly restricted view; healing means that all broken connections are repaired. Moreover, it implies more than a simple return to a previous state. True healing is essentially connected with the future: it includes arriving at a new harmony, a new integration of one's situation and a new outlook, operative at every level on which the sick person has been affected by illness. In this way, it has been observed that a person can leave the hospital "cured," even when little or no purely medical progress has been made.[6]

We will not be primarily concerned hereafter with cure or convalescence. This expression is primarily understood by the sick and those around them as physical restoration. As above, we would prefer to speak of healing (which implies the idea of wholeness, and possibly salvation), or alternately, restoration.

The intention of every sacrament is to invite people and assist them in living through a particular significant life-situation in the

6. Concerning sickness and healing in their global significance see Cl. Ortemann, *Le sacrement des malades. Histoire et signification.* Parole et tradition, Lyon, 1971, pp. 95-105; M. Alberton, *Un sacrement pour les malades. Dans le contexte actuel de la santé.* Croire et comprendre, Paris, 1978, pp. 21-35; C. W. Gusmer, *And You Visited Me*, pp. 92-94 and 139-145. See also J. Glen, "Rites of Healing. A Reflection in Pastoral Theology," in P. E. Fink (ed.), *Anointing of the Sick.* Alternative Futures for Worship, 7, Collegeville, 1987, pp. 33-63 esp. pp. 35-43, "Experience."

light of the Gospel message and in union with the living Christ. Such a situation then becomes their "salvation," their "life." The anointing of the sick aims first at the restoration of the seriously ill person,[7] a restoration in the manifold sense explained above, by the openness of the sick person in faith to the God who draws close to the person in Christ, in and through the signs performed by the church community.[8] Ultimately, we believe, it is God who heals, through human beings.

The Liturgy of the Sick as a Crystallization

God's healing presence is manifested in different ways, in and through different signs. In this way the anointing of the sick operates, as does each sacramental liturgy, against a broad human and Christian background. Specifically the liturgy of the sick functions within the whole of the multi-faceted forms of human and Christian care for the sick and suffering. In the Christian view this care already expresses God's care for humans, thus constituting a sacrament in a broader, more fundamental sense. The Ritual used in the Flemish dioceses states,

7. The reader will know that according to the understanding of the Second Vatican Council the anointing of the sick "is not a sacrament for those only who are on the point of death (*qui in extremo vitae discrimine versantur*)" but also for anyone of the faithful who "begins to be in danger of death from sickness or old age (*incipit esse in periculo mortis propter infirmitatem vel senium*)" *Constitution on the Sacred Liturgy*, no. 73. In the preparatory schema the anointing of the sick was seen more explicitly as the sacrament intended for the seriously ill: "...non est per se Sacramentum morientium, sed graviter aegrotantium" (see *Acta Synodalia Sacrosancti Concilii Oecumenici Vaticani II*, vol. II, pars II, Città del Vaticano, 1972, p. 553).

The Ordo, pp. 10 and 14-15 speaks of *periculose aegrotan(te)s* (or *aegrotant*). The Revised Ritual consciously translates the term "periculose" wherever it appears as "seriously" (e.g., p. 8, "those who are seriously ill"): see Ibid., p. 13, footnote *.

8. Our article addresses primarily the anointing of the sick as a Christian rite. For this reason we do not consider questions such as, how can sickness and suffering be dealt with outside the mediation of Jesus Christ?

The care of the sick is, in the true sense of the word, the only way that leads to the liturgy of the sick. In every form of human caring, we make the Lord himself present in the suffering and loneliness of the sick.[9]

Even the title of the Roman Ritual, *Ordo unctionis infirmorum eorumque pastoralis curae* makes it clear that the anointing of the sick must be situated in the framework of pastoral care in regard to the sick and suffering person.

The liturgy of the sick represents a crystallization of the whole process of human and Christian caregiving. It places this care explicitly in a Christian perspective, thereby turning toward God and leading to a petition for God's efficacious care for the sick. From this point of view we can call the anointing of the sick a sign, as every sacramental event is a sign, a symbolic act which both reveals and effects something.

The anointing of the sick can represent such a crystallization, and such a sign, through (a) its connection with the situation of, illness and suffering, (b) bringing insight to that situation, and (c) accomplishing something, that is, that the sick person is healed.

The Goals of the Ritual

We will use the aforementioned three aspects as a sort of structure in order to take a closer look at the Ritual. To what degree does this Ritual take account of the situation of the sick and suffering person? What sort of insight and outlook does it provide? What sort of restoration does it intend, and how does that occur? In the words of the Ritual, we pick up a number of echoes from the past. We will pose the question of how this

9. *De orde van dienst voor de ziekenliturgie* (The order of service for the liturgy of the sick), (under the direction of the I.C.L.Z., the Interdiocesan Commission for Liturgical Pastoral Care), Brussels, 1975 (hereafter abbreviated to *Orde van dienst.*) The text we cite comes from the "Pastorale Bemerkingen" (Pastoral Considerations), Ibid., pp. 19-22: no. 2. These Pastoral Considerations are unique to the above-mentioned Ritual for the Flemish dioceses.

Ritual helps us today as a celebrating community to deal with the sick in an authentically human and Christian manner. What possibilities does the Ritual offer to the sick themselves for dealing with their situation in a truly human and Christian way?[10] And always, what image of God emerges here? In this section of our discussion we will limit ourselves almost exclusively to a description of the goals of the Ritual.

The Ritual contains two types of texts. There are doctrinal texts which also include pastoral guidelines intended for those who use the Ritual. The two most important (in the order found in the Ordo) are the *Apostolic Constitution: Sacrament of the Anointing of the Sick*, of Pope Paul VI (pp. 5-9), and a *General Introduction* (pp. 10-22). The latter is a translation of the *Praenotanda* (pp. 13-22) of the Roman Ordo. We have already noted that the Ritual for the Flemish dioceses adds several pages of "Pastoral Considerations" which are well worth reading. On the other hand, the Ritual for French-speaking areas[11] has greatly revised, rearranged and expanded the Roman Ritual with pastoral notations, resulting in a Ritual which successfully speaks a more contemporary language. This inspired the Revised Ritual in, among other things, its general structure. More importantly for us, the Revised Ritual follows the French Ritual in adding a pastoral Introduction (pp. 24-27) in its first section, and the expansion of the pastoral and rubrical introductions for the separate chapters of the Ordo (e.g. concerning chapter IV, Anointing of the Sick, pp. 74-79.)

10. See D. N. Power, "Let the Sick Man Call," *The Heythrop Journal* 19 (1978) 256-270. In connection with the interpretation of earlier texts, this author cites Paul Ricoeur on page 258: "What is to be interpreted in a text is a proposed world, a world that I might inhabit and wherein I might project my ownmost possibilities." See P. Ricoeur, "The Hermeneutical Function of Distantiation," *Philosophy Today* 17 (1973) 129-141: p. 140. Is that not valid, *mutatis mutandis*, for our treatment of the present Ritual as well? Cf. also the short but sensitive article by A. Hollaardt, "Ziekenzalving en christelijke spiritualiteit" (Anointing of the sick and Christian spirituality), *Tijdschrift voor Liturgie* 64 (1980) 317-319.
11. *Sacrements pour les malades: pastorale et célébrations* (Commission internationale de traduction pour les pays francophones), Paris, 1977.

Secondly, there are the liturgical texts with which the sick persons themselves come in contact. The Revised Ritual as well as the Flemish Ritual have partially revised these from the Roman Ordo, and here and there added newly composed alternate texts. This is even more the case for the Ritual for the French-speaking areas.[12]

Liturgical texts have their own peculiar character. By necessity their manner of expression is general. Their content, language and style are fairly traditional.[13] They are prayer texts. They function in the context of a community celebration. They express a Christian and ecclesial view of the situation.[14] What is striking is that the Ritual offers a supple text. In the General Introduction no. 40 we read,

> The minister should take into account the particular circumstances, needs and desires of the sick and of other members of the faithful, and should willingly use the various opportunities that the rites provide.[15]

At almost every point in the celebration, one may choose from a number of texts.[16] And further:

12. Hereafter we will refer to the following texts by these abbreviations: AC (= Apostolic Constitution); G. Intro. (= General Introduction); Intro. (= Introduction to a separate section or to a chapter of the Ritual); LT (= liturgical text(s)). With the exception of the AC where a page number will be given, each abbreviation will be followed by the number of the indicated text in the Ritual. Where necessary, a page number may also be indicated.

13. It would be worthwhile to explore further to what degree the LT of our Ritual are dependent upon earlier liturgical and theological texts, among other things for what is involved in the central formula used in the actual anointing (concerning this formulation, see P.-M. Gy, "Le nouveau rituel," pp. 41-42).

14. Concerning the special characteristics of a liturgical ritual, see A.H.M. Scheer, "Kanttekeningen bij ziekenliturgie. Vanuit institutie-theoretisch en pastoraalliturgisch gezichtspunt," (Comments on the liturgy of the sick: from an institutional-theoretical and pastoral point of view), Praktische Theologie 14 (1987) 395-413, p. 395.

15. See also Introduction, 100.

16. In this regard a large choice of biblical texts can be found in Part III of the Ritual (pp. 245-328) entitled Readings, Responses and Verses from Sacred Scripture. Some of these texts are intended to be used (as well) for a different occasion than an anointing of the sick, e.g., during a visit to the sick or when giving communion to the sick (addressed in chapters I-III of the Ritual), or else for the commendation of the dying (chapter VI of the Ritual.)

The priest should follow the structure of the rite in the celebration, while accommodating it to the place and the people involved. (G. Intro., 41)

Connection with the Situation of the Sick and Suffering Person

The General Introduction begins by indicating the reality of sickness and suffering:

> Suffering and illness have always been among the greatest problems that trouble the human spirit. Christians feel and experience (*sentiunt et experiuntur*) pain as do all other people(....) (no. 1)

Concerning the liturgy itself[17] we should expect that when the minister greets all those present (LT 115) and speaks to them by way of introduction (in the "Instruction" LT 117), the sick and those who surround them should feel that they are addressed directly in their actual situation. The "Pastoral Considerations" of the Flemish Ritual already indicated stipulate, with good reason,

> In this Ritual it is not possible to provide a ready made introduction (that is, by the minister) because the circumstances always vary. (Ibid. no. 5)

Is this not the case for many other texts as well? Indeed during the whole celebration one may not pass over what people in fact are experiencing. To this end the liturgical text strives to create an atmosphere in which the sick and all those present can express, or can hear expressed, their pain, anxiety and questions, their hopelessness, despair and anger, as well as their hope and expectations. They can reach out to God: "Where are you? What is your

---

17. Outline of the Rite of Anointing (outside Mass): *Introductory Rites*: Greeting, Sprinkling with Holy Water, Instruction, Penitential Rite; *Liturgy of the Word*: Reading, Response; *Liturgy of Anointing*: Litany, Laying On of Hands, Prayer over the Oil, Anointing, Prayer after Anointing, the Lord's Prayer; (*Liturgy of Holy Communion*: Communion, Silent Prayer, Prayer after Communion); *Concluding Rite*: Blessing.

purpose in all of this?" To this end the Ritual offers a number of appropriate alternate texts. [18]

Perceptions of Sickness and Suffering

The Ritual offers a Christian and ecclesial vision of illness and suffering from the starting point of the scriptural message about God and humans. In the crisis situation of illness and suffering, the Ritual tries to assure the sick person that God remains compassionate. The first subsection of the General Introduction is entitled, "Human Sickness and its Meaning in the Mystery of Salvation." This is not to say that suffering in and of itself has meaning. Yet, where people are consciously taken up into the mystery of salvation, they become capable of living through or bearing their suffering in a meaningful way. The General Introduction clearly states,

> Although closely linked with the human condition, [19] sickness cannot as a general rule be regarded as a punishment inflicted on each individual for personal sins (see John 9:3). (G. Intro., 2)

Nonetheless the Ritual does not examine further the connection between sickness and sin.

1) As concerns the particular message on sickness and suffering, we turn our attention first to the doctrinal texts. What is most remarkable here is the rather paradoxical manner in which they regularly speak of sickness and suffering. The sick will know that they are sheltered in God's healing love and care, yet the sickness must in any case be combatted. At the same time the sick

18. See in part III of the Ritual, three of the four Scripture readings from the book of Job: 3:1-3, 11-17, 20-23 (p. 247); 7:1-4, 6-11 (p. 248); 7:12-21 (p. 249). It is somewhat surprising that Psalm 22 is absent from these biblical texts where portions from several psalms of lament can be found.

19. In the original Latin version, "Infirmitas, etsi arcte cum hominis *peccatoris* condicione conexa (...)" (*Praenotanda*, no. 2; our emphasis).

person is asked to deal with the illness in an active way, as a Christian. We want to illustrate this in regard to what is said concerning God, Jesus Christ, and the Church.

In his providence God undertakes the struggle against sickness as well: through the sick persons themselves, but also through the doctors and all those involved in the care of the patient.[20] On the other hand,

> ... we should always be prepared to fill up what is lacking in Christ's sufferings (*passionum*) for the salvation of the world as we look forward to all creation's being set free in the glory of the children of God. (G. Intro., 3)

The reference is to Col 1:24, as well as to Rom 8:19-21. But was the writer of Col 1:24 thinking of sickness?[21] What is more, the sick, according to General Introduction no. 3, fulfill a witnessing task in the Church.

God has made all of this clear in an extraordinary and decisive manner in and through Jesus Christ. The sick should realize how deeply they are loved by this Christ, who "during his life often visited and healed the sick" (G. Intro., 1) as a sign that in him, the Messiah, the Reign of God has definitively begun. But at the same time Christ has come to share in human suffering, and suffers deeply in all his members even now, in order to accompany humans on the way to eternal life.[22] Those who are sick learn from him that "sickness has meaning and value for their own salvation and for the salvation of the world" (G. Intro., 1).

Where the Ritual addresses the church community which gives

---

20. See G. Intro., 3 and 4.

21. See *La Bible. Traduction oecuménique* (T.O.B.), Paris, 1988, p. 2855, note (a) concerning the interpretation of Col 1:24. The afflictions (*thlipseis*) of Christ that the apostle fills in, are connected with the preaching of the Gospel. Beginning at a later time (TOB. mentions Augustine here) and up to the present some have understood this verse as an exhortation for each Christian to bear suffering in union with the Lord, for the sake of the church community. See also R.P. Martin, *Colossians and Philemon*. The New Century Bible Commentary, London, 1974, pp. 69-70. One would do well to take care in using certain Scripture readings in the liturgy.

22. Cf. G. Intro., 2.

visible form to Jesus' attention and care for the sick in its liturgical and sacramental acts[23] we see the same paradoxical attitude toward sickness and suffering. This comes to the fore more specifically where the doctrinal texts refer three times to the passage on the Anointing of the Sick from the *Dogmatic Constitution on the Church* (no. 11): once in full in the *Apostolic Constitution*, and twice in the *General Introduction*. The conciliar text explains (and we cite from the Revised Ritual):

> By the sacred anointing of the sick and the prayer of its presbyters, the whole Church commends the sick to the suffering and glorified Lord, so that he may raise them up and save them (see James 5:14-16)"

Subsequently the council fathers bring a second aspect to the fore:

> The Church exhorts them, moreover, to contribute to the welfare of the whole people of God by associating themselves willingly with the passion and death of Christ (*sese Christi passioni et morti libere sociantes.*)[24]

By contrast the Ritual for the French-speaking regions refers only once (no. 54, 2) explicitly to *Lumen Gentium* in its revision of the *Praenotanda*, and then only to the first part of the conciliar text.

---

23. See G. Intro., 5 and Intro., 43.

24. This paragraph in the *Dogmatic Constitution on the Church* is also cited in G. Intro., 5 and 34. Both the Roman *Praenotandum* 34 and its translation in G. Intro., 34 mistakenly refer in footnote 23 to no. 21 of the Constitution, instead of no. 11.

The Latin Ordo uses in the AC (p. 7 and 9) the term *alleviare*, following the majority of versions of the old Vulgate translation of Jas 5:15; we find the same term in the Dogmatic Constitution on the Church, no. 11, in its original Latin version. Elsewhere in the Ordo we find the term *allevare*, possibly according to the Neo-Vulgate edition of 1970: this is found in *Praenotanda* 5 and 8, and in LT 70 and 76. In the first English language edition these verb forms were translated respectively by: restore his health; lighten their suffering; raise them up; raise them up; restore his health; raise you up (see *The Rites of the Catholic Church*, 1976, AC, pp. 578 and 580, and the above mentioned sections.) The 1983 edition has consistently used the verb "raise up" (thus rendering the Latin *allevare*, and a better translation of the Greek *egeirein*), even where *Lumen Gentium*, no. 11 is cited in translation.

We meet the second aspect of the conciliar text in revised form in no. 55. We will come back to this in the last section of our essay.

2) The particular liturgical texts make clear to the sick and those around them that God takes care of them, and that the living Christ draws near to them in a supportive way as well.

These texts speak of Christ who was and who remains compassionate to the sick. They consistently present the Christ of the Passover, the one who through suffering and dying has attained full and everlasting life, for our sake. The attention centers on this Christ and on our union with him from the beginning of the celebration. When the sick person and those present are sprinkled with holy water, one of the following may be used: "Let this water call to mind our baptism into Christ, who by his death and resurrection has redeemed us" (LT 116; in the Ordo, LT 69). To him, who "by his paschal mystery has won for us salvation, and renews among us now the wonders of his passion," the Lord, Have Mercy of the Penitential Rite is addressed (cf. LT 118, p. 87.) The Scripture readings announce the message of Christ's Passover as well. Other readings present the Jesus who helped and healed the sick during his public ministry.

In addition, the liturgical texts speak of how the sick share in the suffering of Christ, for example in the alternate text after the anointing:

> Give him/her the firm confidence that his/her sickness is not meaningless but salutary, through your passion in which you give him/her a share.[25]

What is emphasized here is that through this sharing, the situation of being sick can become a situation of healing. Or more accurately, because the sick person is in union with Christ who by his death opens the way to life, that person can experience illness in a salvific way.

---

25. According to the rather free translation in the Flemish Ritual (p. 57) of a portion of the prayer from the Ordo, no. 77 (p. 36). See Latin text and English translation in our footnote 50.

Christ's Passover evokes an eschatological aspect. Since Vatican Council II emphasis has been placed on the idea that the anointing of the sick is no longer (or no longer primarily) the sacrament of the dying, but of the seriously ill. Does this imply that death is passed over in silence, or that we ignore the seriousness of the situation? The Ritual, or at least the way in which some have celebrated the sacrament, has been criticized on this account.[26] But does not every serious illness make us conscious of the death that, sooner or later, we must undergo? Certainly the whole Ritual, and the anointing of the sick as well, directs our attention to our final destination. This eschatological perspective comes to the fore, among other places, in a number of Scripture readings and in the words of the anointing itself.[27]

Throughout the entire liturgical event, those surrounding the sick gain a clearer perspective on the situation, and on their own calling in regard to the sick.

What is Effected by the Anointing of the Sick?

A restoration should occur—that already appears in the words of the sacrament at the double anointing:

> Through this holy anointing may the Lord in his love and mercy help you with the grace of the Holy Spirit. May the Lord who frees you from sin save you and raise you up.[28] (LT 124)

26. Cf. among others H. Denis, "Quand meurt l'extrême-onction. Essai sur le renouveau de l'onction des malades," *Lumière et Vie* 138 (1978) 67-79, esp. pp. 71-73, where the author writes: "... il faudrait peut-être se méfier d'un christianisme qui approcherait la mort avec 'des ministres rassurants'" (p. 72); F. Isambert, *Rite et efficacité symbolique*. Rites et symboles, 8, Paris, 1979, ch. IV: "Un rite discuté, l'onction des malades," on p. 115, "... le passage de l'*Extrême-Onction* à l'*Onction des Malades* traduit sans aucun doute... un désir d'occultation, au moins relative, de la mort."

27. Some of these Scripture readings, in part III: Rom 8:14-17 (p. 261); Rom 8:18-27 (p. 262); 2 Cor 16-18 (p. 269); 1 Pet 1:3-9 (p. 276); 1 John 3:1-2 (p. 277); Rev 21:1-7 (p. 278); Luke 12:35-44 (p. 309). See also the end of the concluding blessing (LT 130, C): "May God fill your heart with peace and lead you to eternal life." In some prayers after communion in the Flemish Ritual the ultimate completion is explicitly brought to the fore, in contrast to the English Ritual.

28. After each of the two anointings the sick person answers "Amen." The text in the Latin Ordo says: "Per istam sanctam Unctionem et suam piissimam

We will examine first the nature of the latter two terms, "save" and "raise up." These are what one might call "open" terms, and as such they aid in understanding the comprehensive meaning of this restoration. It concerns the restoration of the whole person, the person's healing and being raised up, both now and in the future, even beyond death.[29] Thus the anointing of the sick leads up to a pre-celebration of resurrection together with the Lord.

We find this very broad meaning expressed in a varied vocabulary. We read about saving and raising up, but also about life and healing. The person's own wholeness, "body, soul and spirit"[30] is the focus.[31] Thus we pray for strength and power, (in the struggle against evil as well), relief, comfort, courage and patience, hope and trust, and liberation from all evils. God is repeatedly petitioned for healing.[32] Depending on the state of the sick person, each of these terms takes on its own shades of

misericordiam adiuvet te Dominus gratia Spiritus Sancti; ut a peccatis liberatum te salvet atque propitius allevet" (no. 76).

29. Concerning the particular range of meaning of *sôzein* (save, make well) and of *egeirein* (to raise up) in Jas 5:15, the opinions of authors differ. See A. Verheul, "Le caractère pascal du Sacrement des malades. L'exégèse de Jacques 5,14-15 et le nouveau Rituel du Sacrement des malades," in A.M. Triacca and A. Pistoia (ed.), *La maladie et la mort du chrétien dans la liturgie. Conférences Saint-Serge, 1974.* Bibl. "Ephemerides Liturgicae" "Subsidia," 1, Rome, 1975, pp. 361-379, esp. pp. 369-372.

30. Cf. LT 123, p. 93.

31. See also in connection with the following lexicon the cited terms and indications (with reference to the Roman Ordo) in A.M. Triacca, "Gli 'effetti' dell'unzione degli infermi," *Salesianum* 38 (1976) 3-41: pp. 35-38.

32. It occurs to us that in the Revised Ritual the terms "to heal, healing, health" (in Latin including *mederi, sanare, sanitatem,* sometimes *salus* as well) mostly if not exclusively indicate a physical and spiritual restoration in this life. See, e.g., G. Intro., 6: "A return to *physical* health may follow the reception of this sacrament if it will be beneficial to the sick person's salvation" (our emphasis: the original Latin text speaks only about "sanitatem, si saluti eius spirituali expedierit, consequatur"). In the concluding blessing according to the Ordo, no. 79, the minister says "sanet te Dei Filius," which is translated in the Ritual as "May God the Son heal you" (LT 130, B). Following the rubrical indications of the Ordo the same blessing can be used as well for the liturgy for a dying person (Ordo nos. 99; 114; 133). Here the Revised Ritual has in fact changed "heal" to "comfort" (LT 194, B; 210, B). Apparently the Ritual does not foresee a final "healing" through death.

meaning. For this reason the minister is permitted to choose the prayers and the words corresponding to the actual situation and the concrete possibilities of the sick person. The anointing itself is followed by a choice of prayers (LT 125), which should be suited to the particular condition of the person anointed: someone who might reasonably expect a physical healing or improvement; an incurably ill person; and now according to indications in the Ritual itself, in extreme or terminal illness, in advanced age, before surgery, for a child, for a young person.

Indeed our prayer is that the sick be saved and raised up, by God the Father through Jesus Christ: *per istam sanctam Unctionem (...) adiuvet te Dominus* in the Latin version of the main sentence, on which *te salvet et propitius allevet* is grammatically dependent. God accomplishes this through the grace- and life-giving power of the Spirit: "May the Lord (...) help you with the grace of the Holy Spirit (*gratia Spiritus Sancti*)."[33] This salvation and raising up does not occur outside the faith of the sick person, of the minister and of all those surrounding the sick person. The Ritual places great emphasis upon this faith. Reference is made to the "prayer of faith,"[34] sometimes explicitly in the context of Jas 5:14-15, that is, the prayer that arises from faith and is its expression. This faith, in the words of the Ritual, looks back (*respicit*) to the death and resurrection of Christ, and looks ahead (*prospicit*) to the Reign yet to come (in its fullness).[35]

33. The Holy Spirit has been called by A. Verheul "le don par excellence du Christ ressuscité à son Eglise": Idem., "Le caractère pascal du Sacrement des malades," (see our footnote 29) p. 377. This efficacious Spirit, given to us as a gift, is cited more than once, sometimes in a Trinitarian context, in the LT: 115, C (at the greeting); 123 (at the thanksgiving over the blessed oil, and at the blessing of the oil where used); 124 (the anointing); 130, B and D (some of the prayers after the anointing; 130 (the concluding blessing, especially B where it is said, "May God the Holy Spirit enlighten you." See E.J. Lengeling, "'Per istam sanctam unctionem...adiuvet te Dominus gratia Spiritus Sancti.' Der Heilige Geist und die Krankensalbung," in G.J. Békés and G. Farnedi (ed.), *Lex orandi, lex credendi.* Studia Anselmiana, 79—Sacramentum, 6, Rome, 1980, pp. 235-294.

34. See e.g., AC, p. 5; G. Intro., 7; Intro., 52; LT 117; 121; 123 (p. 93); 140 (p. 110).

35. "...infirmum enim salvabit fides eius et Ecclesiae, quae Christi mortem et resurrectionem respicit unde suam efficacitatem sacramentum haurit (cf. Iac 5,15),

Because of this prayerful faith the liturgical/sacramental words and acts become the signs whereby God's help comes near to the sick. The primary ritual acts are the laying on of hands (LT 122) and the double anointing (LT 124). The laying on of hands, a sign of blessing and invocation[36] expresses both human contact, and a means of bestowing life and health.[37] The anointing is a sign of the healing, strengthening and comfort of Christ who infuses the sick person with the grace and power of the Spirit.[38] The fundamental sign of God's healing presence is in fact the community which surrounds the sick person with prayer and active caring. In one of the alternate prayers following the anointing in the Flemish Ritual we read, "Lord Jesus...let him/ her recognize your love in our care and encouragement."[39] The words which are spoken and the gestures performed within the sign of an authentic community will come across as credible and

et futurum prospicit regnum, cuius pignus in sacramentis praebetur" (*Praenotanda*, no. 7). "Quae" is more likely connected to "fides" than to "Ecclesiae" (see A. Verheul, "Le caractère pascal du Sacrement des malades," p. 374).

36. See Intro., 106.

37. Thus at the end of the litany that precedes this rite: "Give life and health (*vitam et salutem*) to our brother/sister N., on whom we lay our hands in your name" (LT 121). Let us not forget that the laying on of hands has from ancient times often served as a symbol of the imparting of God's Spirit.

38. Cf. Intro., 107. We can see how the Spirit is explicitly introduced into the first part of the anointing itself. Furthermore, in the first alternate prayer for the blessing of the oil, it is said: "(...) Graciously listen to our prayer of faith: send the Holy Spirit, the Consoler, into this precious oil (...)" (LT 123, p. 93).

39. See, among others, Intro., 98: "The sacrament of anointing effectively expresses the share that each one has in the suffering of others" (see also Intro., 43; and the welcome by the priest, when the anointing takes place within a eucharistic celebration: LT 135.)

For that matter the whole surrounding community is involved during the celebration in most of the prayers. Is it possible that this occurs so often that the sick themselves feel somewhat like the "object" of the event? This seems to be the opinion of, among others, J. Glen, "Rites of Healing" (our footnote 6), p. 52, as well as of Ottmar Fuchs (in his study cited in footnote 43.) Certainly the celebration must unfold such that the sick feel supported—in whatever way, even without words—in connecting themselves with the prayer. And in Intro., 100 we read: "The *sick person* and others may help to plan the celebration, for example, by choosing the readings and prayers. It will be especially helpful if the *sick person*, the priest, and the family become accustomed to praying together" (our emphasis).

sincere. At the same time the many forms of non-sacramental care undertaken by the community are confirmed, and draw the community into a closer unity. The anointing of the sick should thus affect all those involved with the sick.

What does wholeness, healing, being raised up, consist of for the sick? That varies among different individuals. But the wholeness to which the anointing of the sick is directed is broader than a purely physical relief, broader even than a sort of spiritual encouragement. In faith the sick rediscover a deeper communion with God: they know themselves to be sheltered in God's love. They recover at the same time a deeper sense of human community. They rediscover themselves as well at the deepest level of their being as a person and as a Christian (even if they should remain physically or psychically ill.) The sick see the future open up, even beyond death. They become conscious that they have a vocation as sick and suffering persons, an invitation to follow Christ in their own special way. The two aspects that we noted above as paradoxical are not opposed to each other. Each of them is directed to wholeness, the restoration of the sick.   In this way the faith of the sick is deepened and their hope awakened: they are reborn to love. Does all of this not give to the sick the relief, the comfort and rest, the strength and power of which the liturgical texts speak? Much of this concerns the community as well, specifically the family and all those affected by what happens to the sick person they love: "(The) message of hope and comfort is also needed by those who care for the sick, especially those who are closely bound in love to them."[40] Do they not need healing as well?

What one might call sacramental grace consists precisely, in our opinion, in this restoration of shattered connections, in the recovery of communion with God and with others, the recovery of one's own identity, the discovery of a new future, a new

40. Intro., 98. In this regard J. Glen, "Rites of Healing," rightly uses the term "co-sufferers" several times (e.g., on p. 42-43). See in the same collection of P.E. Fink (ed.), *Anointing of the Sick*, pp. 103-122: M.F. Duffy, "Rituals of Healing for Families of the Terminally Ill."

vocation and claiming it as one's own. This indeed is grace, a gift of God.

We do not, however, find this notion of restoration and sacramental grace expressed as such in our text. What is notable is that paragraph 6 of the General Introduction, in which the effects of the anointing of the sick are summarized, begins thus:

> This sacrament gives the grace of the Holy Spirit to those who are sick: by this grace the *whole* person is helped and saved.[41]

The anointing of the sick is unmistakeably directed to the recovery of communion with God and with others. These texts mark out clearly the dimensions and constituent elements involved.

An Evaluation

In our third and final section we will evaluate the intentions of the Ritual and the possibilities it offers. "Positive" and "negative" will for the most part coincide. Attention is primarily directed to the nature of Christian faith and on the image of God that emerge from these texts.

The Doctrinal Texts

The texts approach illness and suffering, the salvation God wills and the meaning of the anointing of the sick in a fairly consistent manner. This doctrine (certainly that of the General Introduction) seems to us in fact to be a bit too abstract and traditional in language for those who have to use the Ritual.

We pointed out previously that paragraph 2 of the General Introduction indicates a certain relationship between sin and sickness (emphasizing that the latter generally is not the result of

---

41. "(...) qua *totus* homo ad salutem adiuvatur" (*Ordo*, no. 6; our emphasis). Subsequently in the same no. 6 we find what this grace of the Holy Spirit further consists of (or may consist of.)

one's own sins.) How in fact is this relation perceived? Does this suggest "original sin" whereby sickness and suffering come into the world?[42] But what exactly is "original sin," and is it not the case that sickness and death are inherent in the human condition as such? Or are the authors primarily trying to say that we humans frequently encounter difficulty in dealing with our sickness in a meaningful human and Christian way due to our "wounded nature?" Or is it the intention to focus attention on the idea that through sin (including structural sin) of others, a great deal of evil, among which sickness and suffering arises? The latter idea does not seem to be expressly intended by the Ritual.

The liturgy of the anointing of the sick also does not seem to us to be exaggeratedly penitential in intent. But in fact God's forgiveness of sin is justifiably implored and expected.

The Liturgical Texts

Some authors point out that suffering in its extreme form sets itself against every philosophical or theological system. But does that not apply, more or less, to every sort of suffering? Therefore rather than continuing to speak of suffering and the suffering person, one is better served by speaking to the person, and with the person to God. The liturgical texts of the Ritual attempt to do just that. Even in their unavoidably objective and general vocabulary and phraseology they appear to actually address the sick person as human and Christian, as well as those nearby. They are directed toward making the anointing of the sick a prayer event. In their "performative" character they promote union with God and among humans. This marks genuine progress compared with the earlier ritual of the sick.

Usually there will be an undeniable distance between a liturgi-

42. The bishops of Belgium, *Livre de la foi*, Tournai, 1987, p. 128: "Dieu n'a pas créé le mal et il ne veut pas la souffrance. Celle-ci est entrée dans le monde par le 'péché des origines.' Lutter contre la maladie c'est donc combattre le mal dont elle est le signe et la conséquence."

cal text that expresses a Christian, ecclesial view, and the insight
of the ordinary Christian (and the minister as well?). But is it not
one of the goals of a liturgical celebration to "elevate" the vision
of the participants and bring them closer to the richness of the
Gospel message? By saying this we do not mean to deny that a
genuine problem exists in connection with the liturgical language
actually used. A great deal is expected in this regard from the
minister and all those involved in planning the liturgy. They must
use a language which truly and honestly addresses the sick.

The Question of God

In its liturgy the Ritual does not let the question of God
disappear. But does it allow enough space for the question?
Doesn't it come up with the answer too quickly? On the other
hand one must not remain too long with an "exploratory"
liturgy, since the sick expect, in one way or another, some form of
confirmation. Do, however, the sick have the opportunity to
express how abandoned they feel, both by their fellow humans
and by God? We know that the severity of illness lies to a great
extent in the feeling of isolation. Are not the questions and
complaints, the possible anger and rebellion on the part of the
sick or their relatives not much too quickly blunted and repressed?

Ottmar Fuchs discusses this and related elements in connection
with the German Ritual.[43] Along with him we are of the opinion
that it would be advisable in some circumstances first to let the
sick person speak (or others capable of speaking instead), so that
they might discover a God who even in distress does not abandon

43. See O. Fuchs, "Klage, Eine vergessene Gebetsform," in H. Becker et al.
(ed.), *Im Angesicht des Todes: Liturgie als Sterbe- und Trauerhilfe. Ein interdiszi-
plinäres Kompendium*, 2, St. Ottilien, 1987, pp. 939-1024, esp. pp. 1008-1011: "Die
Feier der Krankensakramente." Several years ago the same author published an
extensive study on Psalm 22, *Die Klage als Gebet. Eine theologische Besinnung am
Beispiel des Psalms 22*, Munich, 1982.

people. A great deal depends on the situation of the person in question. With some, one may need to follow the same path as the petitioner in Psalm 22: from complaints and accusations of "Why?" to an expression of trust and surrender.[44] For other individuals one might find instead that

> With the elements left to choice in the Ritual, it would be possible to construct a complete rite which would have as its main theme the paschal mystery.[45]

The Image of God

The image of God in the Ritual is reassuring. The texts reveal a caring God who watches over people, who is compassionate toward them, one from whom they may expect help and strength. With God one feels secure. The Flemish Ritual in this regard gives an alternate Opening Prayer including the phrase, "Strengthen us in the faith that we are held secure in your love."[46] Yet the intention is not to persuade the person to become resigned, since at the same time the Ritual speaks of a God who wants humans to combat illness, and invites the sick to align themselves with the suffering and dying of Christ.

We have already noted that this paradoxical element marked Christ's own lifetime in the first place: he healed the sick, yet he himself came to share in our existence right up to the darkness of

44. Cf. O. Fuchs, "Klage. Eine vergessene Gebetsform," p. 1010. Indeed it does not seem impossible that the sick person would move from rebellion to acceptance during the celebration itself. It can also happen—and it does not seem at all artificial to us—that during the celebration the sick person summarizes (or can hear summarized) the journey that he or she experienced before coming to the sacrament.

45. "Avec les éléments laissés au choix dans le Rituel, il serait possible de composer tout un rite ayant comme leitmotiv le mystère pascal." A. Verheul, "Le caractère pascal du Sacrement des malades," p. 376.

46. Orde van dienst, p. 48. In this connection see also a study on the anointing of the sick published several years ago, J. Lamberts, Geborgen in Zijn Liefde. Het sacrament van de ziekenzalving (Sheltered in His Love: the Sacrament of the Anointing of the Sick). Woord en Beleving, 14, Tielt, 1987.

suffering and death. In this way he broke through our "spontaneous" notions of God. At the same time he opened for us the way to eternal life. Thus in a sacramental way he draws near to the sick, in the power of his Spirit: so that they might find healing and relief in him, and be united to him in his Passover.[47]

We do not wish to bring the latter into question—it belongs essentially to the vocation of the Christian. But we do need to avoid using a language that is too "heavy," not the least when we are dealing with the sick themselves and those around them. We must take into account each individual's concrete situation and possibilities. According to the General Introduction to the Ritual, the sick should be urged "to associate themselves willingly with the passion and death of Christ" (nos. 5 and 34), and "to fill up what is lacking in Christ's sufferings for the salvation of the world" (no. 3). How can we make the ordinary Christian sensitive to this?

On this point the French-language Ritual is generally more discreet. The authors do not want to speak excessively about something which asks too much of the sick and quickly appears unrealistic. These authors indicate as well that the sick should be assisted in actively dealing with their situation, to struggle for health, to give witness.[48] But they have attempted to paraphrase the Latin texts in such a way as to focus attention on the attitude of love and surrender to which the sick are invited. The sick deal with their situation by following Jesus and being together with him, not so much by aligning themselves in an "objective" way with the suffering and death of the Lord. Referring to Col 1:24:

47. P.-M. Gy, «Le nouveau rituel», writes, "Mais les chrétiens ne peuvent pour autant négliger les aspects apparemment opposés de souffrance offerte en communion avec la Passion, de témoignage rendu aux valeurs spirituelles, et en même temps de lutte énergique du malade et des médecins contre le mal physique, lutte qui elle aussi répond à un vouloir du Christ. On retrouve dans l'onction des malades ces deux faces de l'attitude chrétienne envers la maladie, qui correspondent aux deux faces du mystère pascal" (p. 8).

48. See *Sacrements pour les malades* (note 11), no. 5.

In continuing *to love*, even in the heart of the trial, he (the ill Christian) remains in the footsteps of Jesus Christ and participates with him in the salvation of the world.[49]

In the same doctrinal and pastoral notes the sese *Christi passioni et morti libere sociantes* from *Lumen Gentium*, 11 is not explicitly cited. We read once, in line with the conciliar text, that the terminally ill need the grace

to conquer the anxiety of death and live the hope of the resurrection in associating themselves with the *loving attitude* of Jesus Christ in his passion and death.[50]

In order to avoid an excessively heavy and activistic language some pastors have been inclined to focus the sights of the sick especially on God as the foundation of all trust and source of all hope. Or they speak primarily of Jesus Christ who came forward to meet the sick in a helping and healing way, and in one way or another is still present to the sick today. Yet one cannot at the same time keep silent about the Christ of the Passover. This "pass-over" is the consequence of the whole liberating, caring and healing ministry of the earthly Jesus. Besides, the living Christ is close to every person beginning at baptism, even before one actively opens oneself to him. He is present and suffers in

49. "En continuant *à aimer*, au coeur de l'epreuve, il (le chrétien malade) se maintiendra sur les traces de Jésus Christ et participera avec lui au salut du monde." (Ibid.).

50. *Sacrements pour les malades*, no. 55: "pour vaincre l'angoisse de la mort et vivre l'espérance de la resurrection en s'associant à *l'attitude aimante* de Jésus Christ dans sa passion et dans sa mort." Our emphasis in both French texts cited.

In this perspective it is interesting to compare the English and French "translations" of a passage from the Latin Ordo:-*Ordo*, no. 77: "et de suorum concedas efficacia sperare dolorum, quem tuae voluisti Passionis esse participem." -*Ritual*, LT 125, C (p. 96): "Since you have given him/her a share in your own passion, help him/her to find hope in suffering."-*Sacrements*, no. 134: "Donne-lui de conserver l'amour dans son épreuve comme tu l'as fait toi-même dans ta Passion."

Cf. however *Sacrements*, no. 6, where it is stated concerning the seriously ill and suffering person, "...il saura s'unir à Jésus Christ dans sa passion." This, however, is corrected by, "Pour le Christ, les souffrances n'étaient pas une fin en soi. Il en fit le chemin qui mène à la vie, grâce à son amour pour nous et pour son Père (cf. Eph 5,2; Jn 13,1)."

everyone who is afflicted. [51] He wants to accompany each person on the way to eternal life. Therefore the sick person him or herself is in a very real sense a sacrament of Christ.

The sick are invited to open their eyes and heart to the already present Lord, and to place their confidence in him by means of the faith community. In this connection we consider the *Pastoral Considerations*, no. 7, of the Flemish Ritual particularly worthwhile. Translated, the text reads:

> Whoever has been committed to Christ beginning in baptism, and destined for eternal life, is recommitted to him upon entering this special phase of life. The person is anointed for Christ, in other words participates in Jesus' Easter mystery in this concrete situation of illness, in which suffering becomes the passageway to glory. [52]

Here all activist language is avoided. The sick and all around them are invited to surrender themselves with all their pain, despair, and powerlessness to him who has come to share in this powerlessness. He found life, not because he suffered, but because he held fast to the Father throughout his suffering and dying, and his heart remained open for humans. At the end of the celebration this Christ is invoked:

> May he go before you to guide you and stand behind you to give you strength. [53]

In this way the sick themselves become a source of grace for others.

> Continue to believe that your old age, your illness, your suffering has value for the church, and contributes to the building up of the community; that your suffering, like that of the Lord can be a source of power and comfort for the sick and the healthy. [54]

51. See G. Intro., 2.

52. *Orde van dienst*, p. 22.

53. This provisional text of 1973 is a literal translation of a portion of the concluding blessing according to the Ordo, no. 237: "(Dominus Iesus Christus) ante te sit ut te deducat, post te sit ut te muniat." The Revised Ritual has: "May (the Lord) guide you and give you strength." (LT 130, A).

54. *Orde van dienst*, p. 66 (from an alternative greeting in the anointing of several sick persons). Cf. from LT 125 D (p. 96): "Keep him/her firm in faith and serene in hope, so that he/she may give us all an example of patience and joyfully

Suffering in and of itself is worthless. But when the sick can share in the life attitude of Jesus Christ, who grew in faith and trust despite anxiety and pain, and in the patience and the human courage which goes together with it, can they not themselves become a means of power and comfort for other sick persons, for the healthy around them, and for the wider world?

So that the liturgy does not speak in too facile a manner about a God who in Jesus Christ is present to the sick to help and heal them, it is vital that all those who are associated with the sick person outside of the liturgy should make God's presence perceptible and credible in their human and Christian caregiving. A Flemish hospital chaplain has rightly written,

> The anointing of the sick is the religious translation, into a ritual of words and deeds, of God's care for humans, of God's "looking after" humans. But without the caregiving goodness of humans the anointing becomes inauthentic and empty. ... If the anointing of the sick can become a religious celebration of previous care which is then nourished and deepened in the celebration, then the sick will experience wholeness again. [55]

To Be Healed

Our final consideration concerns the restoration, the healing intended by the anointing of the sick. This restoration is founded in the fact that the sick discover (or rediscover) a sense of community with God and with other persons, [56] and at the same time accept themselves in their concrete vocation as human and Christian, which essentially involves an ultimate future. In this

witness to the power of your love" (Prayer after anointing for those whose health is seriously impaired by advanced age.)

55. Translation from the text published in Dutch: R. Van Landschoot, "Pastoraat en ziekenzalving," in J. De Broek (publ.), *Pastorale gids voor verzorgingsinstellingen*, Brussels, 1980, p. 6.

56. "(...) l'onction vient en aide au malade pour qu'il surmonte la crise de la communication avec le monde et Dieu." (Cl. Ortemann, "La pastorale des sacrements auprès des malades," *La Maison-Dieu* 113 [1973] 115-132: p. 126.)

regard we support a number of findings in the area of ritual effectivity, more specifically concerning restoration and healing. These cultural- anthropological conclusions ought to be set in a christological and ecclesial context.[57] Are we doing right, however, by the expectations of the sick? Do they not expect in the first place a physical healing, or at least relief, by means of anointing?

The anointing of the sick has for some time now been more authentically understood in its sacramental significance because it is no longer primarily considered as a means of physical healing, even less so as an exclusive means of preparing oneself for the hereafter.[58] David Power comments:

> (...) the accent is not on healing, nor on forgiving, nor on preparing for death. It is on the sick person, who through this experience, discovers God in a particular way and reveals this to the community. All the other factors enter in, but they are related to this as organizing centre.

And a bit further:

> It is not by coming out of sickness that the crisis is resolved, but by some word that indicates its meaning and reshapes the sick man's relation to the earth and to human community.[59]

Undoubtably the rediscovery of relationships, of one's personal, human and Christian identity and vocation, and of an authentic future will influence in one way or another the physical and

57. See L.-M. Chauvet, *Symbole et sacrement. Une relecture sacramentelle de l'existence chrétienne.* Cogitatio Fidei, 144, Paris, 1987, esp. pp. 142-147; 329-385.

58. About the history of the anointing of the sick and of the understanding of its effects: B. Poschmann, *Penance and the Anointing of the Sick.* The Herder History of Dogma, New York, 1964, pp. 233-257; R. Béraudy, "Le sacrement des malades. Etude historique et théologique," *NRT* 96 (1974) 600-634; H. Vorgrimler, *Busse und Krankensalbung.* Handbuch der Dogmengeschichte, IV, 3, Freiburg im B., 1978, pp. 215-234; J.L. Empereur, *Prophetic Anointing. God's Call to the Sick, the Elderly and the Dying.* Message of the Sacraments, 7, Wilmington, 1982, ch. I (pp. 15-78): "The History of the Sacrament of Anointing"; see also W.H. Cuenin, "History of Anointing and Healing in the Church," in P.E. Fink (ed.), *Anointing of the Sick,* pp. 65-81.

59. D.N. Power, "Let the Sick Man Call," (see note 10), pp. 262-263.

psychic condition of the sick person. Why should one not be permitted to pray to God in certain situations for physical health and healing? This does not mean that the the anointing of the sick will take over from medical care. The intention is to place this care in a Christian faith-centered perspective.

The sick person must be introduced to an authentic understanding of the meaning of the anointing of the sick. We quote one last time from the *Pastoral Considerations* of the Flemish Ritual:

> The anointing of the sick can really only take place at the moment that the sick person is ready to accept this sickness as a Christian and to pass through it. (no. 7)

Just as is every sacrament, the anointing of the sick is intended for Christians. Sacraments have to do with their "being in Christ." The form that this readiness takes can vary from individual to individual. [60] Above all, is it not true that many of the sick, in their own way, expect from the anointing of the sick just what they, considering their concrete situation, might expect? Most likely hospital chaplains can tell us a good deal about this. This does not take away the fact that even other forms of religious ritual guidance of sick and suffering persons must be sought out, which can possibly lead into the anointing of the sick. The Ritual offers in any case a number of real initiatives in this regard. [61]

Finally, no one may in the name of God or of Jesus Christ trivialize human suffering. We may not explain away or idolize suffering. We must above all help the sick to discover the One of whom the Ritual so often speaks: Jesus Christ. He shared in

---

60. The fact that along with this "acceptance" questions and complaints may exist or precede acceptance, can be clearly seen in what we have written above. But the questions and the complaints are directed toward God. In this way the isolation is already broken through, and a beginning made toward salvation and healing.

61. See chapters I-III of the Ritual.

human powerlessness, in suffering and dying. As a living presence he bears witness that nothing and no one can prevent God from being and remaining our God. In this way the anointing of the sick becomes essentially the sacrament of the hope that is given to us by this God.*

* Translated from the Dutch by Susan Roll.

"YOU HAVE STRIVEN WITH GOD" (Gen 32:28)
A Pastoral-Theological Reflection
on the Image of God and Suffering

Kristiaan Depoortere

Specification of the Subject

Pastoral theology reflects on pastoral care. Pastoral care has as its purpose to encourage the faithful in their attempts to adopt the life-style of Jesus. Pastoral care is what Jesus charges Peter with: "Strengthen your brethren"(Luke 22:32), that is, "Assume the service of encouragement."[1]

With regard to suffering, pastoral theology neither reflects on suffering in general nor does it check the theological accuracy of the different systems of religious attribution of meaning. It considers concrete experiences, which arise, exist and evolve in pastoral relationships. In other words, pastoral theology looks at the function of the faith-strengthening or the faith-encouragment of believers who are suffering.

To delineate our subject, we have to specify the term "believers who are suffering." Our principal focus is personal, innocent, unavoidable suffering, more precisely, being gravely ill. So we do not intend to treat the whole gamut of human suffering, neither of individuals nor of the human race itself.

A second specification must be mentioned. In this essay we shall consider a particular segment of the pastoral relationship,

---

1. R.Zerfass, *Menschliche Seelsorge. Für eine Spiritualität von Priestern und Laien im Gemeindedienst*, Freiburg, 1985, p.85.

namely, where the question of God arises. Although the idea of God's being introduced is broader than the notion of God's being specifically mentioned, it implies a serious abstraction, since the religious segment is only a part of pastoral guidance and cannot be separated from the rest of it. Nevertheless we hope this limited approach can function as an example and offer some insights into suffering itself and into the pastoral relationship as well.

After these limitations, we have to broaden our subject.

By "pastors," we mean professional pastoral ministers (ordained or lay persons[2]) in the first place, but we also include professional pastoral ministry in function of volunteer pastoral care, that is, service for the purpose of faith-strengthening in the church, the service of those who want to assist sick people and help them to face their life-situation with the help of the gospel. It is a major task of the professional pastorate "to help the faithful help each other."[3]

Secondly, the service of faith-encouraging cannot be narrowed to the individual guidance of sick persons. We must also think of common guidance in reflection and contemplation groups, in prayer and in liturgy.[4]

The particular focus of this essay is therefore a reflection on the function of the ministry of faith-encouragment, when gravely sick men and women ask the "why" of God.

2. In Flanders about forty lay people - mostly women - are engaged on a full-time basis and officially appointed to pastoral care in health services, such as in hospitals or homes for the elderly. The greater part of them have obtained a master's degree in religious sciences and followed a fifth year of specialized training "pastoral care in health services".

3. R.Caplan, *Helping the Helpers to Help. The Development and Evaluation of Mental Health Consultation to Aid Clergymen in Pastoral Work*, New York, 1972.

4. The specifically liturgical aspect of this problem is treated explicitly in the essay by Cor Traets.

The Sick and the Pastor:
Global Description of the Situation

The Sick

The sick-in-general do not exist. "Being a patient" admits of as many varieties as does "being a human." The following characteristics cannot, therefore, be any more than mere generalities.

Many authors think that people suffer and die longer and more intensively than formerly. Longer, because medical science contributes to the prolongation of life and not rarely to a prolongation of suffering.[5] Some people are chronically sick. Among them aged demented patients form a special problem. It is not surprising that questions of euthanasia arise more frequently than they did in the past. Do patients suffer more intensively than in the past? There is probably less physical pain, because of selective painmitigating techniques.[6] But... by mitigating physical pain without anesthetizing or removing consciousness, other kinds of suffering become more acute.[7] Suffering is more than pain. There is psychic and moral suffering, suffering from loneliness and from the conscious experience of decay. Along with this suffering and all sorts of other pain, there is the question of meaning, the struggle with senselessness.[8] By day patients ask "I have headaches, can I have a pill?", but by night "I have headaches, what did I do to earn this?"[9] The night's questions ask why.

5. P.Verspieren, *Face à celui qui meurt. Euthanasie, Acharnement thérapeutique, Accompagnement* (Temps et Contretemps), Paris, 1984, p.13: „Quand l'effort médical n'aboutit qu'à prolonger la souffrance..."

6. B.Beth, *L'accompagnement du mourant en milieu hospitalier*, Paris, 1985, pp.69-138, gives a detailed survey of the present-day selective pain-treatment, which works analgesically but is hardly anesthetizing. See also P.Verspieren, *op.cit.*, pp.81-134.

7. J.Vimort, *Ensemble face à la mort. Accompagnement spirituel*, Paris, 1987, pp.17-34; P.Verspieren, *Face à celui qui meurt*, pp.165-199.

8. For instance: H.Vetter, *Der Schmerz und die Würde des Persons*, Frankfurt, 1980.

9. M.Pijnenburg, "Levensbeschouwing en verpleegkundige zorg," *Metamedica* 64 (1985) 272-273.

To be ill is to be lonely. A network of previous relationships is brusquely broken: professional relationships, friendships and soon, even family relationships. In a culture where competition in the production-process is highly valued, the unproductive life is marginalized. In a culture where the development of the individual ego is highly valued, illness and death are tragic.

For most people, being gravely ill means an unexpected confrontation with a totally new situation. Healthy people control their life. Most pain can be avoided. If they know about untreatable suffering, they brush it aside: "Before my time comes, something will be found to prevent cancer." Personal, unavoidable pain comes to people who are totally unprepared. And we are not even citing social apathy,[10] the ban on sorrow and anxiety and the taboo on death, which have never been promulgated but are operative everywhere. Uncontrollable things are masked in our society. Unexpected serious illness comes face to face with that reality.

In this sense, religion confronts contemporary humanism. Every religion brings a message of dependence and trust-despite-losing-control. Every religion relativizes the domination of life. Every religion relativizes the individual ego. Some forms of contemporary humanism are virtually impermeable to religious values. Thus, it is not surprising that faith in personal survival after death is eroding. If there is one gesture of uncontrolled abandon and trust, it is the belief in resurrection.

10. D.Sölle, *Leiden*, Stuttgart, 1973, worries about a society, where pain is avoided at any cost, where marriage is broken off at the first problem, where periods of mourning are very short, where the dead disappear quickly from memory. Such a blindness is only possible, she says, in a society of banal optimism. Proportionally to this situation without suffering, the curve of life levels off, so that even happiness and joy fade away from experience. There is a glasswall between the subject and the reality. We see dying children on television, but they vanish when we change the program. Real suffering however does not disappear by turning off a button. Our society creates an illusion of a quarantine. It is dangerous to smuggle away illness and death as it alters transitoriness of existence in a veiled and therefore dangerous threat, which can unexpectedly pounce upon us at any moment. We do not live in the reality that urges itself upon us as nameless fear because of its negation.

To face uncontrollable suffering is to fall into a vacuum, where pre-religious feelings arise (vengeance, fate, violation of taboos, etc.) or scraps of childish faith reappear. The question of meaning breaks into life, overwhelms and overruns it.

Pastors

The pastor-in-general exists as little as does the patient-in-general. Pastoral ministry is in the plural. The plural is also limited, however, since there aren't enough pastors. They cannot offer the opportunity of personal guidance sick persons need, neither in parishes nor in hospitals.[11] The pastoral ministry is under-manned. Because of this a dilemma arises: should one forgo the systematic visitation of patients and work "on request" or should one become a pastoral centipede, who pays visits at lightning speed.

Pastors are in the plural in a second sense. They differ from each other as regards their formation, sensibility and approach. Younger pastors have been trained in a different way from older pastors. Lay pastoral workers often are under pressure from factors not experienced by their ordained colleagues. One pastor favors staying with a dying person, even if this takes a lot of time. Another cannot cope with the experience. Many priests are hesitant because of the renewed theology of the sacrament of sick. From their training they know that sacraments are concentrated moments in a relationship of personal guidance. The pastoral encounter with a sick person is often compared with a celebration of the Word, introducing the sacramental sign. Professors speak about the ecclesiological dimension of anointing. Yet, under the

11. In Belgium, the standard staffing for pastoral workers in health services is at least one full-time person for 200 hospital beds (Official Statute - League of Belgian Catholic Health Services, 1975). With shortened stays in the hospital, the impossibility of personal contact is obvious. Suppose that the pastoral worker spends all his/her time on personal contact, a simple calculation, based on a 40-hour workweek, gives but 10 minutes for each patient.

pressure of the family and their own conscience, priests go on "administrating the last rites." The same theological trends insist on the value of personal encounter in sacramental practice. This leads to the following question: is not the one who supports the sick — be he or she ordained or lay — the preferable person to do the anointing as a seal on the whole ministerial experience? It is said that "The sacrament of the sick does not function as a death notice." So one pastor organizes something like a "feast of the fourth age" and another anoints almost clandestinely.

Pastoral care is evolving — for pastors as well as for believers who are sick. Among ministers and believers there is a different sensitivity. Even changes in the religious meaning of suffering complicate the pastoral relationship. It looks as if there are different choices today: God Almighty? God Allgood? Or do you prefer Kushner? One image of God requires a different approach from another, including another style of prayer or hymn. A family demands a "papal blessing *in articulo mortis*," but the priest has never heard of that. Some people seem to ask for the bare minimum, while ministers find their new offering so much richer.[12] Pastors are trained in verbal communication, but can they handle symbols? I recently heard about the disturbing case of a younger woman, who opened her hand at the very moment of death and dropped a purse, containing a few photos and a relic of St. Rita, the patroness of the incurably ill (and the family did not know that she was aware of her desperate situation!).

There are many other problems we have not mentioned. For example, the fact that every pastor represents a church. For one patient this immediately opens possibilities of contact; for another it immediately recalls disappointments from early childhood.

In short, pastoral care in the health services is not very easy. It's a matter of fostering processes of personal integration in a totally new situation and relating to the gospel and to the

---

12. P.Pruyser, *The Minister as Diagnostician. Personal Problems in Pastoral Perspective*, Philadelphia, 1976.

community of believers... Among all these various issues we will
focus on one element. What kind of religious meaning do people
ascribe to their suffering? What does this attribution of meaning
imply in the context of pastoral care?

The Religious Meaning(s) of Suffering

The attribution of religious meaning to suffering can be ana-
lysed according to different models. Elisabeth Kübler-Ross' description of approaching death is one workable method. Other
authors have mapped out different experiences of terminally ill
patients, not infrequently with important nuances somewhat
different from those of Kübler-Ross.[13] With some adjustment,
these studies can be extended to the entire problem of dealing
with suffering. In any case, these studies treat the religious
meanings of suffering only indirectly.

There is also Dorothee Sölle with her phases in the handling
the pain: of speechlessness, through complaints, to rational and
active language.[14] Because of the role she assigns to language in
adopting an active attitude towards suffering and her specific
social approach to the problem, it is hardly possible to omit her
contribution in any discussion about dealing with pain on a
pastoral level.

A third model has been developed by Johannes van der Ven.[15]
He analyses different kinds of attribution of religious meaning to

13. Cf. B.G.Glaser & A.L.Strauss, *Awareness of Death*, 1965; E.Lau, *Tod im
Krankenhaus. Soziologische Aspekte des Sterbens in Institutionen*, Cologne, 1975;
J.Hinton, "Approaching Death," in *Modern Trends in Psychosomatic Medicine*,
London, 1976, pp. 471-490; R.Kastenbaum, "Psychological Perspectives on
Death," *Annual Review of Psychology* 28 (1977) 225-249; P.Sporken, *Heb jij
aanvaard dat ik sterven moet. Stervenden en hun helpers*, Baarn, 1981.
    14. D.Sölle, *Leiden*, Stuttgart, 1973.
    15. J.A.van der Ven, „Zin en onzin van het lijden: proeve van een ontwikke-
lingsmodel," in *Rond godsdienst en psychoanalyse. Essays voor Dr. A. Uleyn*,
Kampen, 1986, pp.188-207.

suffering (direct causality, indirect causality and a post-causal model) and the behavior associated with it. The correlation between the patient's image of God and his or her attitude towards suffering will form an integral part of our approach.

For our pastoral-theological point of view, however, Adolphe Gesché offers the most appropriate framework.[16] He discerns five moments in the process of integrating suffering, which he designates with classical terms: *contra Deum*, *pro Deo*, *in Deo*, *ad Deum*, and *cum Deo*. We will use the main elements of his approach, placing them in a new order and complementing them with corresponding patterns of a behavioral nature and some pastoral suggestions.

Nevertheless, it is important not to reduce this framework to a chronological sequence. A sequence of succeeding phases is not in keeping with reality. Therefore we will avoid such terms as "stadia" or "phases", using by preference "feelings" or "experiences," which can arise together with other feelings, in a different order or simply without order. The relationship between the sick person and God is very variable; it cannot be circumscribed within one specific category.

A Plea on Behalf of God

Unlike Gesché we consider the *pro Deo*-moment to be in the forefront. A plea on God's behalf is the most obvious approach to suffering by the faithful. A person who believes tries to involve God in his or her real life. Faced with the negative aspects of life, a believer does not attack God directly. On the contrary — and this is typical for the *pro Deo*-moment — he or she defends, exonerates or acquits God. *Pro Deo*: despite suffering, the believer pleads on God's behalf.

There are at least two varieties within this approach. In the first, people exonerate God because He is a fair Judge. Although

16. A.Gesché, "Topiques de la question du mal," *RTL* 17 (1986) 393-418.

the suffering person is "innocent," there is a search for guilt in one's own life. In the second variety, people remark that personal guilt does not offer a sufficient explanation of suffering. At the same time there must be some link between God the Creator and suffering, but this link exists without any bad intentions on God's part. So they acquit God as the supreme Educator, who intends something good in the pain and suffering that is being experienced.

1) The First Plea on Behalf of God: God is a Fair Judge

This vision is the existential version of a certain kind of negative theodicy: God is not responsible for suffering and calamity; human beings are. Nevertheless God is concerned with suffering. He is a fair Judge, who punishes evil — or in a milder version — allows evil to be punished. The world view behind this position is often very matter-of-fact. The relationship between God and humans is characterized by terms such as insult-appeasement, guilt-expiation, crime-punishment. The principle of the world-order is retribution or repayment. God is the guardian and the guarantor of this system of justice. The friends of Job make just such a plea in favor of God. They argue that God is just and that Job is guilty, even if Job does not remember why he is guilty. Job may be secretly guilty, but in the end "he that mischief hatches, mischief catches." We find the negative image of this under-standing of retribution in such expressions as: "Why did I deserve this?" or, in regard to others, "They lived the life of Riley..." or "She had an accident, when she came from Mass" or "God will find them!" Some prayers asking saints to stop God's punitive hand are related to this idea.[17]

Such a vision does justice neither to God nor to humans. It is unfair to God, since it reduces Him to a merely moralistic God, who tries to set the world right by means of punishment and

---

17. This vision is critically assessed in *Salvifici Doloris* by Pope John-Paul II, 1984, no.10.

reward.[18] That is not the image of God we find in the gospel nor in Job, who challenges God to prove that He is not "a watcher of men" (7:20) but their "Redeemer."[19] After his purification oath (31:35-37), Job is proved right by God (42:7-8).

Attaching this meaning to suffering is also unfair to humans, since it supports the idea of suffering without the involvement of the human will and abandon without resistance. It does not make a sufficient distinction between suffering that can (and thus must) be fought and suffering that lies beyond all human possibilities of control. Such an explanation of suffering often leads to self-torturing attitudes. In a vicious circle, transgression leads to guilt and guilt expects the punishment to be paid. If punishment does not come or if the guilt is not expiated by suffering, a person looks for more severe penalties in order to be redeemed of guilt. Yet when "punishment" comes, it is not accepted without revolt.[20]

This abandon-without-protest is not infrequently related to Elisabeth Kübler-Ross' description of the depressive phase in the experience of approaching death. The patient feels let down by everyone. At the same time the patient is hardened in his own isolation.

With regard to pastoral care, two elements seem to be very important: the sick person thinks that a believer must "protect" his God. This is one reason, among others, why he takes the guilt upon himself. Regarding this element, there would be a significant progress, if the patient were to avoid protecting the pastoral worker as well. Then the patient's pain could come out and a primary relationship could be built up. The *pro Deo*-element is in

18. Cf. H.Zahrnt, *Wie kann Gott das zulassen?/Hiob - Der Mensch im Leid*, Munich, 1985.
19. Job 19:25-27: „For I know my Redeemer lives, and at least He will stand upon the earth; and after my skin has been thus destroyed, then from my flesh I shall see God, whom I shall see on my side, and my eyes shall behold, and not another. My heart faints within me!"
20. A.Knockaert, "Catéchèse de la souffrance: présupposés pédagogiques," *Lumen Vitae* 37 (1982). P.310 refers to S.Lebovici, *Les sentiments de culpabilité chez l'enfant et chez l'adulte*, Paris, 1971, pp.59-65.

the third person: the patient speaks "about" God, he pleads "for" God rather than speaking "with" or "to" Him. Every time this third person-relationship is replaced by one in the second person, an I-thou-relationship is created with an immediate positive effect on the problem of guilt, deeply interwoven as it is with the image of God as Judge. So pastors should treat questions of guilt prudently and allow the patient to express a guilty conscience instead of brushing it aside with, "You certainly had good intentions" or giving absolution too quickly. If the sick person can say something and nonetheless feel accepted by the pastor, mitigating circumstances will eventually be discovered. Through this experience of being accepted-in-spite-of, an "other" God can appear — perhaps the God of the workers of the eleventh hour.

Although the image of retribution does not stand the test of reality, it can be stuck deep in a patient's feelings. Retribution as a link between guilt and suffering offers an orderly system, which gives those in despair a certain control over uncontrollable reality. Furthermore, there is certainly enough sin in everyone's life to "legitimize" punishment. Finally, some currents of Christian spirituality solidly support this image.[21]

2) The Second Plea on Behalf of God: God is Supreme Educator

In a second version of the *pro Deo*-element there is also a link between God and suffering. In this version, divine causality is probably more direct than it is in the other version, since God positively intends something with suffering: He tests or chastens. This interpretation of suffering is the existential version of a more affirmative theodicy: "God tests his best friends" or "If we have to endure this on earth, our reward will be greater in heaven." The idea of "discipline for our good" is not absent from the

21. C. Ortemann, "Quelle parole chrétienne sur la souffrance?," *Lumen Vitae* 37 (1982) 296-300.

Bible: See, in this regard, the framing-story in Job,[22] Wisdom
3:4-6 and Hebrews 12:6-8.

Other expressions such as "God intends the best for people" or
"I'm not a good patient, because I can't accept God's will" bring
us closer to the classic cosmological theodicy of Leibniz, where
everything has its place in the best possible world, although some
secondary developments seem unavoidable.[23] So we are not far
from a metaphysical theodicy, which, based on *ens et bonum
convertuntur*, denies the existence of evil simply and in principle.

As does the first explanation, this second interpretation of
suffering has served to comfort and encourage many of the
faithful throughout the ages. It does not necessarily lead to
resignation or to a denial of the reality of suffering. On the
contrary, as Paul Ricoeur[24] suggests, its inner dynamism can lead
to hope. Some people can learn from suffering; they later admit it
was a stimulus to growth.[25] Resistance may incite creativity. In
some cases suffering can function as an alarm. It gives a warning
before a greater calamity happens, just as dizziness can prevent a
fall by giving an illusion of a fall before a real fall takes place. It
is also possible that suffering can break open an egotistically
closed life.

Despite these occasional educational results, this vision of
suffering, for the most part, does justice neither to God nor to
humans. First of all, this interpretation of suffering does not
stand the test of reality. Perhaps some may grow by suffering —
or grow through suffering — but the risk of not growing at all is
greater. Some people are chastened by suffering, but still more

22. Job 1-2 and 42. Although it is Satan who tests Job, this does not occur
without the knowledge of God. Eliphaz, one of Job's friend argues in the same
way: 5:17-18.
23. G.W.Leibniz, *Essais de Théodicée sur la bonté de Dieu, la liberté de l'homme
et l'origine du mal*, 1710. The idea of "secondary developments" can be found in
P.Teilhard de Chardin, *Le phénomène humain*, Paris, 1948.
24. P.Ricoeur, *Philosophie de la Volonté. Finitude et Culpabilité. Tome II: La
Symbolique du Mal*, Paris, 1960, pp.47-50.
25. J.B.Brantschen, *Warum lässt der gute Gott uns leiden?*, Freiburg im Breisgau, 1986; G.Greshake, *Der Preis der Liebe. Besinnung über das Leid*, Freiburg im
Breisgau, 1979.

become broken or embittered. Moreover, there is no honorable proportion: there is an excess of suffering, which cannot be justified by any educational result. Do you pay for the deepening of your life by the death of your child?[26] The risk of passive resignation is as great as the chance that somebody will courageously put his or her trust in God. And God has to cover up this lack of logic? Furthermore such an idea has too frequently supported the abuse of power by the mighty of the world.

In pastoral care, attempts to improve this image have sometimes been made by adding a questionable theological interpretation of expiation, as if God had to be appeased by the death of his Son and by the suffering of human beings. Some prayers and hymns are simply abuses of the marvellous "In my flesh I complete what is lacking in Christ's afflictions" (Col 1:24).[27]

If pastoral workers adopt such a view, they place themselves above God and their fellow humans who are suffering. Their pastoral care is at best reduced to a kind of abstract pity. At the same time sick people are not allowed to express their feelings, because everything has an ultimate meaning, which is absolutely beyond understanding (at least the understanding of the sick!).

For more adequate guidance in this situation the remarks of Elisabeth Kübler-Ross on denying death are revelant. She suggests that denial, to which the aforementioned vision is existentially related, must be seen as a rest period in the processing of suffering. She advises counsellors to grant the sick person this break. Apropos religious integration, it may happen that the whole problem of the relationship between God and suffering becomes too heavy. The patient brushes away questions, saying: "God knows better. He does not intend bad things." If, with that kind of language, the sick person indicates that he does not want to speak now and cannot cope with further confrontations at the

26. H.Kushner, *When Bad Things Happen to Good People*, New York, 1981.

27. C.Ortemann, "Quelle parole," pp.299 and 306; A.Knockaert, "Catéchèse," pp.315-316; a more fundamental approach of the problem in M.Bellet, *Le Dieu Pervers* (Connivence), Paris, 1979, pp.15-49.

moment, a period of rest should be allowed. This pastoral attitude, however, neither implies that ministers have to foster this behavior nor that they attack it frontally. They should pay sufficient attention to the patient so that they can see when the patient wants to go on with his integration process.

Complaint against God

A second movement in the process of giving meaning to suffering can be called *contra Deum*: against God.

Contra Deum is the opposite of *pro Deo*, but here, too, extremities touch each other. Blaming oneself easily turns into blaming God. Accusing God gives the faithful feelings of guilt. Self-torture and aggression differ from one another only in direction. Both *pro* and *contra* relate suffering to God, but the manner is different. In the *contra Deum*-movement God is not defended, excused or justified; He is accused or eliminated.

Contra Deum is most clearly characterized in its radical atheistic version, *Malum, ergo non est Deus:* because evil exists, God does not exist. If this atheistic vision were merely a rational argument, it could easily be invalidated by a demonstration of its internal logical contradictions.[28] The atheistic position is, however, much more than mere argumentation. It is a cry, addressed as solidly against suffering as it is against God. Often it is a cry against a certain idea of God more than it is a cry against God per se. Believers can also recognize it: the *contra Deum* is not exclusively atheistic. It would indeed be easier to believe if there were no suffering. When someone asks: "Why did I deserve that?," the *pro Deo* is not far from a *contra Deum*.

This kind of explicit or implicit atheism, unleashed by the reality of human suffering, not infrequently finds its origin in very

28. Without supporting this easy reduction of atheism, A.Gesché, "Topiques," pp. 394-395, gives some examples: "Does not a decision in favor of the non-existence of God, based on the existence of evil, somehow presuppose his existence?" or "Does not an unbeliever reproach God with his non-existence?".

lofty — and all too human — expectations about God. Disappointed expectations. Both belief and unbelief can proceed from disappointed hopes. Gesché rightly asks whether some of God's opponents might not have a higher opinion of God than many of his defenders, who hardly feel up to a real confrontation with Him.[29]

In regard to this attitude, Elisabeth Kübler-Ross has described a phase in the process of dying which can be related to our point of view: aggression and revolt. She notes that the aggression of the sick person is often directed to the closest person, the one of whose love he or she is most sure.

When this contra-attitude develops into a pure revolt against God and everyone else — for both are on the firing line — the patient runs the risk of becoming completely isolated. People get angry with a God of punishment and retribution. Yet they know they ought not to be angry with Him, because this is really culpable. So they hate both God and themselves, and are left all alone.

This situation is a difficult challenge in pastoral care. Discussions are not useful and neither is the attempt to persuade the patient that the image of God is wrong. The problem of the sick person is evident: a disappointment with a certain view of almighty God. But this image is so mixed with childish phantasies and affective atavisms that it is absolutely resistant to intellectual argumentation.

Counselling manuals generally recommend that feelings of aggression be permitted. Yet most ministers are oriented towards the positive: they want to pass over the dark sides of life and to help immediately and effectively. Nevertheless, the tolerance of shadows can initiate a process in which light can be rediscovered. The pastor then functions as an intermediary. By means of this non-condemnatory closeness, the patient experiences security and dares to face the entire situation step by step. So the pastoral worker figures as a living example of a new relationship to God.

29. A. Gesché, "Topiques," p.396.

Some ministers think that they have to defend God. Then conversation with the sick person turns into a contest of aggression and contra-aggression. Attention is paid to the arguments and not to the situation of the patient. God does not need this defence and the patient is certainly not helped by it. Contra-aggression confirms aggression. Confirmation is necessary, but at a deeper level. The patient is not the aggression. The patient knows that. The patient knows that he is unreasonable. Yet it is too much and too difficult for him or her at the moment.

If a patient experiences anger and knows that he or she is nevertheless accepted as a person, there is some likelihood that he or she might move on to another level of reaction, namely that of direct contact with God. The patient resolutely begins to use direct address. This, however, is a radically different experience of suffering.

An Appeal to God

A third way of attributing religious meaning to suffering can be entitled *ad Deum*.[30] The question of suffering is directly address-ed to God himself.

Pro Deo as well as *contra Deum* focus on the "why" of pain. In a certain sense they keep both suffering and God at a distance.

Ad Deum starts when someone has "the courage to be afraid."[31] The person no longer closes the eyes to suffering; he or she allows it really to enter into life. This is a fundamental "pathic" moment, when the patient approaches both God and suffering as an intangible mystery.[32] The sick person completely abandons any is dominant attitude.

At once another God emerges, the living God, who is in direct

30. Before this Gesché places an *in Deo*-moment ("Topiques," pp. 399-403), where the problem of suffering is taken so seriously that it becomes a question of God. And he uses an image from electricity: Place the problem of suffering in God himself, let suffering traverse the word God as a resistor (p.401).

31. See M.D.Molinié, *Le courage d'avoir peur*, Paris, 1975.

32. J.van der Ven, "Zin en onzin," p.196.

confrontation with the patient. The preceding attempts to make sense of suffering "spared" God. They intended — even the *contra Deum* — to reconcile God and misery.[33] However, they tried to resolve the opposition by eliminating one of the terms. They lifted God beyond suffering or kept Him outside, even when He was called "cause." This cause never became a real You; He was never a living opponent. The *ad Deum*-movement sees the development of a real relationship between God and the sick person. This is a daring relationship which no longer attributes mitigating circumstances to God.[34]

With regards to attitudes, the patient moves from discourse "about" to talking "with". His or her speech encompasses all possible states: questioning (why, God?), challenging (where are You, God?), accepting (Thy will be done, Lord), imploring (deliver me, God). *Ad Deum* is a faithful *contra Deum*. *Ad Deum* does not swallow the question nor formulate it in the third person. *Ad Deum* changes a problem into direct address and a cry for help. A vocative is never a blasphemy.[35] When people speak with God, they save their own dignity and — whichever terms they use — their respect for God. To speak is to set oneself in front of an unpleasant situation. To address someone is to believe in his presence, to call for him, to call upon him.

Dorothee Sölle draws a sketch of how one can evolve from being a speechless victim to lamenting and then to complaining and "psalmpraying." She adds that such a move never occurs without involving one's fellow humans, who dare to begin a relationship with the victim. They make God visible in a certain

---

33. Cf. U.Hedinger, *Wider die Versöhnung Gottes mit dem Elend. Eine Kritik des christlichen Theismus und A-theismus*, Zurich, 1972.

34. A. Gesché, "Topiques", p. 401, cites G. Bernanos, *Journal d'un curé de campagne*, Paris, 1936, p.115: "The last imprudence is prudence, when it softly prepares us to have no longer use for God" and (p.398) also V.Jankelevitch, *Le Pardon*, Paris, 1967, pp.100-106.

35. Gesché has an untranslatable play on words: "*sans mot dire*" is really "*maudire;*" to remain silent is blasphemy, it is to no longer talk to God ("Topiques," p.403).

sense. In a very deep sense they are "sacraments of an encounter with God."

Being with God

If the sick person and the bystanders really do permit this cry to God, a new moment of meaning may appear: *cum Deo*, with God.[36]

Gesché says that the *cum Deo*-dimension consists of an experience of solidarity: God raises the problem of suffering himself and He does so vitally in Jesus Christ, his Son, who suffered and died on earth.

Afterwards the meaning expands. God has not only shared the passion of Christ, he also empathizes with the suffering of every human being and bears misery together with human beings (this is the first sense of the verb *tollere*). Harold Kushner can be situated at this level of attribution of meaning: God is in solidarity with and stands by his suffering people. His involvement means a real *supplément d'âme*. Kushner, however, plays God's solidarity off against his omnipotence and thinks that he has to abandon the Almighty in order to save his goodness. As if there was not an omnipotence of love in Him! In this way the sense of *tollere* tends toward helpless resignation.[37] Some authors formulate a similar caution with regard to Kübler-Ross' "acceptance" as the ultimate stage in the process of dying. Her notion of acceptance seems too passive to them. Therefore it can hardly serve as a basis for specific pastoral guidance.[38]

At this point Gesché wants to go further, to a third dimension. God does more than suffer-with. His solidarity is not merely

36. A.Gesché, "Topiques," p.407-413.
37. For the image of a powerless God see, e.g., the epilogue of H.Kushner, *When Bad Things Happen to Good People.*
38. K.D.van Kampen, *Aanvaarding van de dood? E.Kübler-Ross en de pastorale stervensbegeleiding*, Den Haag, 1986.

affective. It is effective. He intervenes. He strives with men and women against evil and suffering. This means a formal break with previous images of God. There is no longer a coalition between God and suffering. God does not use suffering for anything, not even for the well-being of humans. God is not only indignant and offended because of suffering; He is the adversary of evil, pain and suffering: *cum Deo contra malum*. "Evil is not an objection against God; God is the objection against evil."[39] God's solidarity, first discovered as com-passion, turns into a more effective assistance: He acts together with us against suffering.

There is another sense of the verb *tollere*: to take away or to overcome. God has adopted a first name: Jesus Christ. *Cum Deo* becomes *cum Christo*. The victory over suffering and death is Easter. It happened in Christ's life: death no longer has the last word (Phil 2:6-11). It is promised to everyone who relies on Him. Christ has striven with God, together with God, against death. Throughout his life Jesus showed how powerful is God's opposition to suffering. God is not indifferent to suffering. On the contrary, pain affects and hurts Christ.[40] He cured the sick. He never considered recovery as a kind of reward for a virtuous life. Repeatedly He denied the alliance between sin and suffering.[41] When Jesus Christ entered upon his passion, the highest sense of the verb *tollere* appears: the mystery of divine compassion is greater and more powerful than the mystery of iniquity.[42]

Cum Deo inspires an attitude of resistance and trust. Resistance and trust do not exclude one other. They can protect each other. Resistance can save trust from passive resignation — something that is important even from a psycho-somatic point of view. Trust can keep resistance within the limits of reality. The expres-

39. A.Gesché, "Topiques," p.410.
40. F.Varillon, *La souffrance de Dieu*, Paris, 1975, e.g., pp.35-38 on the word *esplagknistê* (Luke 7:13 and 15:20) "which evokes a motion of the intestines"(p.35). In the same context: Matt 9:36; 14:14; 15:32; John 11:31-32:36.
41. E.g., John 9:3; Luke 13:2,4.
42. Cf the title of the article of E.Schillebeeckx, "Mysterie van ongerechtigheid en mysterie van erbarmen. Vragen rond het menselijk lijden," *Tijdschrift voor Theologie* 15 (1975) 3-25.

sion "You have striven with God" (Gen 32:39) translates, in its ambiguity, this interaction of resistance and trust. Furthermore it suggests that *cum Deo* is never a definitively acquired state. In a touching conversation with a terminal patient, Paul Sporken calls this attitude an "acceptance with protest."[43]

The idea of a suffering God — with all the dimensions we have touched upon — offers opportunities for a pastoral ministry to sick people. The vision insists on God's participation in the world of the sick. God appears as an ally, who calls forth a liberating resistance and a liberating trust. The vision highlights the fact that the Will of God intends — without any ambiguity — the well-being of human beings. In such a context people can faithfully say "Thy will be done," because God's Will is salvation. Finally, *cum Deo* implies God's ultimate power: suffering will not have the last word. The last word will be reserved for the Power which appears in the apparent weakness of Love (2 Cor 12:9).

This presupposes, however, that the reality of resurrection is forthrightly introduced into pastoral care. It also means that such terms as God's power and his supremacy are part of the Christian message and preaching, provided, however, that they are resolutely re-thought in the sense of the (defenseless) power of love[44] and are never isolated from the human fight against suffering. Otherwise God runs the risk of being merely a fellow-sufferer instead of an ally against suffering. If He is in solidarity only in undergoing suffering, the suffering human loses a partner and opponent. He or she may no longer express aggression or complaint, lest he or she cause God even more "pain".

43. P.Sporken, *Heb jij aanvaard dat ik sterven moet*, pp.106-108.
44. The term "defenceless supremacy of love" is used by G.Greshake and H.Zahrnt.

Some Pastoral Suggestions

The pastoral care of those who suffer can profit from a two-fold effort: the exoneration of suffering and the exoneration of God.[45] First, the exoneration of suffering. Most suffering does not have a responsible cause. A too facile connection of suffering, guilt and punishment leads to self-torture and aggression against oneself or against others. Undeserved guilt breaks off relationships of human closeness which a sick person needs so much. Secondly, the exoneration of God. By linking suffering with God in a broadly generalized scenario of crime and punishment, one's relationship with God is distorted. Every time that there is created an impression of a coalition between God and suffering, God runs the risk of being reduced to a capricious power. Such a God is not the God of the gospel. There is only one power in God: the power of love. Johannes van der Ven's plea for a post-causal model in the interpretation of suffering seems to evoke this double exoneration.[46]

In order that this model of interpretation become a model of experience, a community of believers is required. Nobody can be freed from the self-incriminating experience of suffering without the support of a believing community. This is the constitutively ecclesiological dimension of faith.

A faithful community organizes the care of the sick with professional and voluntary workers, with a service whereby the sick can be identified, provided with systematic counselling, and so forth, right up until the prayers of intercession during the worship service. Such intercession names the suffering found in the community or elsewhere and so makes it somewhat manageable. This prayer evokes solidarity and introduces the sick into a network of relationships with other believers who together appeal to God.

45. A.Knockaert, "Catéchèse," pp.309-314.
46. J.van der Ven, "Zin en onzin," pp.195-199.

Gathering a community around the sick also includes an opportunity for personal counselling. A dialogue can be initiated which offers the sick person an occasion to speak about what he or she feels. A conversation that answers theological questions is not wrong, except when it serves to circumvent existential problems. A patient is not merely an affective being. Some patients search for a clarification of their faith. Unfolding the *cum Deo*-dimension can be really freeing for them. Pastors should be sufficiently well prepared for this task.

Still more important is the conversation of the sick persons themselves. Initially, patients are almost the direct object of suffering, but, step by step, through their complaints and the expression of their feelings, they become capable of making suffering itself an object — first, the object of emotions, then of reflection, and finally of prayer.

Helping sick people to pray is an essential part of pastoral counselling. One can pray spontaneously or by using well-known prayers along with visitors. Praying includes both verbal and non-verbal elements. Most ministers, however, are not sufficiently skilled in non-verbal elements and symbols. The sacrament of the sick occupies a central place in the spiritual care of sick persons. Other "healing services" can also be organized. They are different from the sacrament of the sick. Sincerity requires that the difference between them not be covered over. Other rituals, still to be developed, can introduce the anointing and enhance it. Perhaps they run a slight risk of being understood as the harbingers of death. In any event, lay pastoral workers or the family can lead these various prayers.

Do ministers have the right to intervene in the process of making sense of suffering? Respect for the patient's image of God is the basic principle to be followed. Unprejudiced listening may discover the liberating presence of God beneath outmoded words (but also on the contrary: an oppressive idea of God behind modern words). If pastoral workers discover a religious experience different from their own, it may be good to talk this over. This may be necessary if the different visions come between spouses or create tensions in a sick room. Real intervention and correction seem wise only when a given interpretation of suffering really prevents sick persons from expressing their feelings or when it terrifies them. Even then the pastor will be attentive lest he confuse his personal problem with the patient's.

Pastors must critically evaluate their own contribution. The images of God which appear in some prayers or hymns do not always contribute to a beneficial processing of suffering.[47] Pastoral workers should help each other to formulate prayers[48] in which the idea of a God who "disposes" of people is replaced by a more evangelical God. People who reject the image of the disposing God can experience difficulties in praying for the easing of suffering. This, however, does not mean that the prayer of complaint is no longer possible. On the contrary, when all demands for "automatic" intercession are lost, one can ask for the Holy Spirit. That request never goes unanswered, says the gospel.

In brief, the religious counselling of suffering people stands to profit if it seeks to remain close to the gospel.[49] Reference can be made to Christ's passion, but no comparison should be made between his suffering and ours. The passion of Jesus is the obverse side of his singular vocation. It is messianic suffering, the consequence of his option to be a prophet.

Reference to Jesus can really help people, especially when it shows God's commitment in human suffering or when it shows how Jesus deals with sick people. It can help someone to change dismay into attention for others. Jesus stopped loving neither during his life nor in his passion. In the passion He reveals the Father, the one who loves unconditionally. Such a vision cannot

47. K.-F.Daiber, *Leiden als Thema der Predigt. Berichte über eine Predigtreihe*, Munich, 1978; H.Arens, *Die Predigt vom Menschfreundlichen Gott*, Munich, 1980, pp.99-172: J.L.Gonzalez, *Liberation Preaching. The Pulpit and the Oppressed*, Nashville, 1980.

48. A similar statement can be made apropos the prayers printed on mourning cards.

49. C.Ortemann, "Quelle parole," p.306.

be reconciled with the image of a Father who asks for the sacrifice of his Son in order to forgive human beings. Suffering does not "serve" anything; it certainly does not serve to appease God. Why should a person have to suffer in order to become a saint? Such a notion falls under the criticism of the gospel itself. No particular life-situation is, in itself, more or less advantageous to faith: no national, racial, social or religious condition, neither poverty nor illness. If illness was particularly beneficial, Jesus would not have healed the sick. What is essential both for the sick and for the healthy, for the poor as well as for the rich, is the response of the heart. Pastoral care intends to provide for the suffering a situation in which, despite their circumstances, they can grow in receptivity and hope. That situation also prevents isolation. Suffering often isolates people from God and from others. If a community of believers reaches out, it testifies to the promise that nothing and nobody has to separate people from the love of God (Rom 8:35-39). When this happens to the sick and suffering, salvation is at work, healing.

SELECTED BIBLIOGRAPHY

Johan Vanhoutte

For the benefit of those who want to gain a deeper insight into the ongoing exploration of the topic "God, suffering and evil" a number of important publications have been listed here in alphabetical order. Most of the publications have been written in English or have been translated into English. Some general themes are treated by several authors:

* A handful of contributions can be grouped under the rubric of the "Free Will Defence," including Ahern, Davis, Plantinga, Reichenbach, Swinburne.

* For some examples of process theodicy, see Cobb, Cooper, Ford, Frankenberry, Griffin, Hartshorne, O'Donnell, Suchocki, Van der Veken and Lippens, Vanhoutte, Vitali, Williams.

* Approaches from the perspective of political and liberation theologies are taken by Boff, Chopp, Cone, Cooper, Cox, De Schrijver, Dussel, Guttierrez, Hedinger, Janssen, Metz, Moltmann, O'Donnell, Schillebeeckx, Sobrino, Sölle, Surin.

* For different reactions of religious thinkers to the Holocaust we can cite Batstone, Baum, Berenbaum, Bourel, Brown, Estess, Garrison, Greenberg, Jonas, Katz, Levinas, Metz, Rosenfeld, Rubenstein and Roth, Schüssler Fiorenza and Tracy, Seeskin, Wiesel.

* Recent concentration on the suffering of God is reflected in the works of Barth, Bonhoeffer, Creel, Fiddes, Fiorenza, Fretheim, Galot, Geffré, Gesché, Hall, Heschel, Jüngel, Kitamori, Kamp, Kushner, Kuyper, Lee, McWilliams, Moltmann, Oelmüller, Surin, Vanhoutte, Varillon, Welker, Woollcombe, Zahnrt.

Ahern, B.M., *The Problem of Evil*, New York, Schocken, 1971.

Barth, H.-M., "Angesichts des Leiden von Gott reden," *Pastoral-Theologie* 75 (1986) 116-131.

Batstone, D.B., "The Transformation of the Messianic Idea in Judaism and Christianity in Light of the Holocaust: Reflections on the Writings of Elie Wiesel," *JES* 23 (1986) 587-600.

Baum, G., "Theology after Auschwitz: A Conference Report," *The Ecumenist* 12 (1974) 65-80.

Becker, E., *The Structure of Evil: An Essay on the Unification of the Science of Man*, New York/London, Free Press, 1976.

Beker, J.C., *Suffering and Hope: The Biblical Vision and the Human Predicament*, Philadelphia, Fortress, 1987.

Berenbaum, M., "The Uniqueness and Universality of the Holocaust," *American Journal of Theology and Philosophy* 2 (1981) 85-96.

Boff, L., *Passion of Christ, Passion of the World: The Facts, Their Interpretation, and Their Meaning Yesterday and Today*, New York, Orbis, 1987.

Bonhoeffer, D., *Letters and Papers from Prison*, enlarged edition edited by E. Betghe, New York, Macmillan, 1972.

Bourel, D., "'Bien qu'il tarde'... Théodicée dans le judaïsme contemporain?" *Archivio di Filosofia* 56, 1-3 (1988) 139-146.

Brantschen, J.B., *Warum lässt der gute Gott uns leiden?*, Freiburg im Breisgau, Herder, 1986.

Bro, B., *Le pouvoir du mal*, Paris, Cerf, 1976.

Brown, R.M., *Elie Wiesel: Messenger to All Humanity*, Notre Dame/London, University of Notre Dame Press, 1983.

Burkle, H.R., *God, Suffering, & Belief*, Nashville, Abingdon, 1977.

Caretto, C., *Pourquoi, Seigneur? L'énigme de la souffrance*, Paris/Montréal, Médiaspaul/Editions Paulines, 1986.

Chopp, R.S., *The Praxis of Suffering: An Interpretation of Liberation and Political Theologies*, Maryknoll, NY, Orbis, 1986.

Cobb, J.B., Jr., *God and the World*, Philadelphia, Westminster, 1969, especially II.4, "Evil and the Power of God," pp. 87-102.

Cone, J.H., *God of the Oppressed*, New York, Seabury, 1975.

Cooper, B., "How Does God Act in Our Time? An Invitation to a Dialogue between Process and Liberation Theologies," *USQR* 32 (1976) 25-35.

Cowburn, J., *Shadows and the Dark: The Problems of Suffering and Evil*, London, SCM, 1979.

Cox, H., "Complaining to God: Theodicy and the Critique of Modernity in the Resurgence of Traditional Religion. The Example of Latin American Liberation Theology," *Archivio di Filosofia* 56, 1-3 (1988) 311-325.

Creel, R.E., *Divine Impassibility: An Essay in Philosophical Theology*, Cambridge, Cambridge University Press, 1986.

Davis, S.T., ed., *Encountering Evil: Live Options in Theodicy*, Atlanta, GA, John Knox, 1981.

de Halleux, A., "'Dieu le Père tout-puissant,'" *RTL* 8 (1977) 401-422.

De Schrijver, G., "Theodicy, Justification, and Justice: A Critique of Leibniz from the Perspective of Latin American Liberation Theology," *Archivio di Filosofia* 56, 1-3 (1988) 291-310.

Dougherty, F., ed., *The Meaning of Human Suffering*, New York, Human Sciences, 1982.

Duquoc, C., "The Folly of the Cross and 'The Human,'" *Concilium* 155, 5 (1982) 65-73.

Duquoc, C. and Floristan, C., eds., "Job and the Silence of God," *Concilium* 169, 9 (1983).

Dussel, E., "The People of El Salvador: the Communal Sufferings of Job," *Concilium* 169, 9 (1983) 61-68.

Elphinstone, A., *Freedom, Suffering and Love*, London, SCM, 1976.

Estess, T.L., "Elie Wiesel and the Drama of Interrogation," *JR* 56 (1976) 18-35.

Fiddes, P.S., *The Creative Suffering of God*, Oxford, Clarendon, 1988.

Fiorenza, F.P., "Joy and Pain as Paradigmatic for Language about God," *Concilium* 10, 5 (1974) 67-80.

Ford, L.S., "Divine Persuasion and the Triumph of Good," in D. Brown, R.E. James, Jr. and G. Reeves, eds., *Process Philosophy and Christian Thought*, Indianapolis/New York, Bobbs-Merrill, 1971, pp. 287-304.

Frankenberry, N., "Some Problems in Process Theodicy," *Religious Studies* 17 (1981) 179-197.

Fretheim, T.E., *The Suffering of God: An Old Testament Perspective*. Overtures to Biblical Theology, 14, Philadelphia, Fortress, 1984.

Galot, J., *Dieu souffre-t-il?*, Paris, Lethielleux, 1976.

Galligan, M., *God and Evil*, New York/Paramus, Paulist, 1976.

Garrison, J., *The Darkness of God: From Hiroshima to Harrisburg*, Grand Rapids, MI, Eerdmans, 1983.

Geach, P.T., *Providence and Evil*, New York/Cambridge, Cambridge University Press, 1977.

Geffre, C., *The Risk of Interpretation: On Being Faithful to the Christian Tradition in a Non-Christian Age*, New York/Mahwah, Paulist, 1987, especially VII, "From the God of Theism to the Crucified God," pp. 111-128.

Gerstenberger, E.S. and Schrage, W., *Suffering*, Nashville, Abingdon, 1977.

Gesché, A., "Topiques de la question du mal," *RTL* 17 (1986) 393-418.

Id., "Odyssée de la théodicée. Dieu dans l'objection," *Archivio di Filosofia* 56, 1-3 (1988) 453-468.

Greenberg, I., "Cloud of Smoke, Pillar of Fire: Judaism, Christianity, and Modernity after the Holocaust", in E. Fleischner, ed., *Auschwitz — Beginning of a New Era?*, New York, KTAV, 1977, pp. 7-55.

Griffin, D., *God, Power, and Evil: A Process Theodicy*, Philadelphia, Westminster, 1976.

Gutierrez, G., *On Job: God-Talk and the Suffering of the Innocent*, Maryknoll, NY, Orbis, 1987.

Hall, D.J., *God and Human Suffering: An Exercise in the Theology of the Cross*, Minneapolis, Augsburg, 1986.

Hartshorne, C., "Whitehead and Berdyaev: Is There Tragedy in God?" *JR* 37 (1957) 71-84.

Id., "A New Look at the Problem of Evil," in F.C. Dommeyer ed., *Current Philosophical Issues: Essays in Honor of Curt John Ducasse*, Springfield, IL, Charles C. Thomas, 1966, pp. 201-212.

Id., *Omnipotence and Other Theological Mistakes*, Albany, NY, State University of New York Press, 1984.

Hauerwas, S., *Suffering Presence: Theological Reflections on Medicine, the Mentally Handicapped, and the Church*, Edinburgh, T. & T. Clark, 1988.

Hebblethwaite, B., *Evil, Suffering and Religion*. Issues in Religious Studies, London, Sheldon, 1976.

Hedinger, U., *Wider die Versöhnung Gottes mit dem Elend. Eine Kritik des christlichen Theismus und A-Theismus*. Basler Studien zur historischen und systematischen Theologie, 60, Zurich, Theologischer Verlag, 1972.

Heschel, A.J., *The Prophets. Part I and II*, New York/London, Harper and Row, 1962.

Hick, J., *Evil and the God of Love*, London, Macmillan, 2nd. ed., 1977.

Janssen, H.G., *Das Theodizee-Problem der Neuzeit. Ein Beitrag zur historisch-systematischen Grundlegung politischer Theologie*. Europäische Hochschulschriften: Reihe 23, Theologie, 198), Frankfurt am Main, P. Lang, 1982.

John Paul II, "Apostolic Letter Salvifici Doloris: The Christian Meaning of Human Suffering," *Origins* 13 (1984) 609-624.

Jonas, H., "The Concept of God after Auschwitz: A Jewish Voice," *JR* 67 (1987) 1-13.

Jossua, J.P., *Discours chrétiens et scandale du mal*, Paris, Chalet, 1979.

Jüngel, E., *God as the Mystery of the World: On the Foundation of the Theology of the Crucified One in the Dispute Between Theism and Atheism*, Grand Rapids, MI, Eerdmans, 1983.

Kitamori, K., *Theology of the Pain of God*, London, SCM, 1966.

Kamp, J., *Souffrance de Dieu, vie du monde*, Tournai, Casterman, 1971.

Katz, S.T., *Post-Holocaust Dialogues: Critical Studies in Modern Jewish Thought*, New York/London, New York University Press, 1983.

Küng, H., *Gott und das Leid*, Einsiedeln, Benziger, 1971.

Kushner, H.S., *When Bad Things Happen to Good People*, New York, Schocken, 1981.

Kuyper, L.J., "The Suffering and the Repentance of God," *Scottish Journal of Theology* 22 (1969) 257-277.

Lee, J.Y., *God Suffers for Us: A Systematic Inquiry into a Concept of Divine Passibility*, The Hague, Martinus Nijhoff, 1974.

Levinas, E., "La souffrance inutile," *Giornale di Metafisica* 4 (1982) 13-25.

Madden, E.H. and Hare, P.H., *Evil and the Concept of God*, Springfield, IL, Charles C. Thomas, 1968.

McCloskey, H.J., *God and Evil*, The Hague, Martinus Nijhoff, 1974.

McGill, A.C., *Suffering: A Test of Theological Method*, Philadelphia, Westminster, 2nd. ed., 1982.

McWilliams, W., *The Passion of God: Divine Suffering in Contemporary Protestant Theology*, Macon, GA, Mercer University Press, 1985.

Metz, J.B., "The Future in the Memory of Suffering," *Concilium* 8, 6 (1972) 9-25.

Id., *The Emergent Church: The Future of Christianity in a Postbourgeois World*, New York, Crossroad, 1981, especially 2 "Christians and Jews after Auschwitz. Being a Meditation also on the End of Bourgeois Religion," pp. 17-33.

Id., "Facing the Jews: Christian Theology after Auschwitz", *Concilium* 175, 5 (1984) 26-33.

Moltmann, J., *The Crucified God: The Cross of Christ as the Foundation and Criticism of Christian Theology*, London, SCM, 1974.

Id., *The Trinity and the Kingdom of God: The Doctrine of God*, London, SCM, 1981 especially II, "The Passion of God," pp. 21-60).

Id., "The Motherly Father: Is Trinitarian Patripassianism Replacing Theological Patriarchalism?," *Concilium* 143, 3 (1981) 51-56.

Nemo, P., *Job et l'excès du mal*. Paris, Grasset, 1978.

O'Connell, T., *What a Modern Catholic Believes About Suffering and Evil*, Chicago, Thomas More, 1972.

O'Donnell, J.J., *Trinity and Temporality: The Christian Doctrine of God in the Light of Process Theology and the Theology of Hope*, Oxford, University Press, 1983.

Oelmüller, W., ed., *Leiden*. Kolloquium Religion und Philosophie, 3, Paderborn, Ferdinand Schöningh, 1986.

Peterson, M.L., "Recent Work on the Problem of Evil," *American Philosophical Quarterly* 20 (1983) 321-339.

Phillips, D.Z., "On Not Understanding God," *Archivio di Filosofia* 56, 1-3 (1988) 597-612.

Pike, N., ed., *God and Evil: Readings on the Theological Problem of Evil*, Englewood Cliffs, NJ, Prentice-Hall, 1964.

Plantinga, A., *God, Freedom, and Evil*, London, George Allen & Unwin, 1975.

Id., "Epistemic Probability and Evil," *Archivio di Filosofia* 56, 1-3 (1988) 557-584.

Rahner, K., "Why Does God Allow Us to Suffer?", Theological Investigations, 19, New York, Crossroad, 1983, 194-208.

Reichenbach, B.R., *Evil and a Good God*, New York, Fordham University Press, 1982.

Ricoeur, P., *The Symbolism of Evil*, Boston, Beacon, 1969.

Id., "Evil: A Challenge to Philosophy and Theology", in H. Deuser, G.M. Martin, K. Stock and M. Welker, eds., *Gottes Zukunft — Zukunft der Welt. Festschrift für Jürgen Moltmann zum 60. Geburtstag*, Munich, Kaiser, 1986, pp. 345-361.

Rosenfeld, A.H., *A Double Dying: Reflections on Holocaust Literature*, Bloomington, IN, Indiana University Press, 1980.

Rubenstein, R.L. and Roth, J.K., *Approaches to Auschwitz: The Legacy of the Holocaust*, London, SCM, 1987.

Schiffers, N., "Suffering in History," *Concilium* 8, 6 (1972) 38-47.

Schillebeeckx, E., *Christ: The Christian Experience in the Modern World*, London, SCM, 1977, especially pp. 670-730.

Schlette, H.R., *Skeptische Religionsphilosophie. Zur Kritik der Pietät*, Freiburg, Rombach, 1972.

Schüssler Fiorenza, E. and Tracy, D., eds., "The Holocaust as Interruption," *Concilium* 175, 5 (1984).

Seeskin, K.S., "The Reality of Radical Evil," *Judaism* 29 (1980) 440-453.

Sobrino, J., *Christology at the Crossroads: A Latin American Approach*, New York, Orbis, 5th. ed., 1982.

Id., "A Crucified People's Faith in the Son of God," *Concilium* 153, 3 (1982) 23-28.

Sölle, D., *Suffering*, London, Darton, Longman & Todd, 1975.

Sparn, W., *Leiden — Erfahrung und Denken. Materialien zum Theodizeeproblem*. Theologische Bücherei, 67, Munich, Kaiser, 1980.

Stivers, R., *Evil in Modern Myth and Ritual*, Athens, GA, The University of Georgia Press, 1982.

Suchocki, M., *The End of Evil: Process Eschatology in Historical Context*, Albany, NY, State University of New York Press, 1988.

Surin, K., "Theodicy?" *HTR* 76 (1983) 225-247.

Id., *Theology and the Problem of Evil*, Oxford, Basil Blackwell, 1986.

Swinburne, R., "The Free Will Defence," *Archivio di Filosofia* 56, 1-3 (1988) 585-596.

Taylor, M.J., ed., *The Mystery of Suffering and Death*, Staten Island, NY, Alba House, 1973.

"Theodicy and Religious Education," *Religious Education* 84 (1989) 5-76.

Van der Ven, J.A., "Towards an Empirical Theodicy," *Archivio di Filosofia* 56, 1-3 (1988) 359-380.

Van der Veken, J. and Lippens, E., eds., *God and Change: Process Thought and the Christian Doctrine of God*, Leuven, Center for Metaphysics and Philosophy of God, 1987.

Vanhoutte, J., "God as Companion and Fellow-sufferer: An Image Emerging from Process Thought," *Archivio di Filosofia* 56, 1-3 (1988) 191-225.

Varillon, F., *La souffrance de Dieu*, Paris, Le Centurion, 1975.

Vetter, H., *Der Schmerz und die Würde der Person*, Frankfurt am Main, Knecht, 1980.

Vitali, T., "Organicism, Evil and Divine Redemption," *Archivio di Filosofia*, 56, 1-3 (1988) 227-244.

Welker, M., ed., *Diskussion über Jürgen Moltmanns Buch 'Der gekreuzigte Gott'*, Munich, Kaiser, 1979.

Wiesel, E., *Night*, London, Fontana/Collins, 1972.

Id., "Art and Culture after the Holocaust", in E. Fleischner, ed., *Auschwitz — Beginning of a New Era?*, New York, KTAV, 1977, pp. 403-416.

Wiles, M., *God's Action in the World*, London, SCM, 1986.

Williams, D.D., *The Spirit and the Forms of Love*, New York, Harper & Row, 1968.

Woollcombe, K.J., "The Pain of God," *Scottish Journal of Theology* 20 (1967) 129-148.

Zahrnt, H., *Wie kann Gott das zulassen? Hiob — Der Mensch im Leid*, Munich, Piper, 1985.

INDEX OF NAMES